MW01169685

BOTTOM LINE ISSUES IN RETAILING

Bottom Line Issues in Retailing

The Touche Ross Guide to Retail Management

RANDY L. ALLEN

CHILTON BOOK COMPANY
RADNOR, PENNSYLVANIA

Library of Congress Cataloging in Publication Data
Allen, Randy L.
  Bottom line issues in retailing.
  (Chilton's better business series)
  Includes index.
  1. Retail trade—Management. I. Touche Ross & Co.
II. Title. III. Series.
HF5429.A565 1984   658.8'7   83-45388
ISBN 0-8019-7409-7
ISBN 0-8019-7410-0 (pbk.)

Chilton's Better Business Series

1 2 3 4 5 6 7 8 9 0   3 2 1 0 9 8 7 6 5 4

Contents

PART TWO: TECHNOLOGY AND RETAILING 77

PART FIVE: RETAILING IS PEOPLE   241

Acknowledgments

The ideas in this book represent a cross section of the efforts of many of my colleagues at Touche Ross & Co. and Garr Industries. I therefore wish to express my appreciation to them for their contagious enthusiasm, thoughtful insights, patience, perseverance, and consideration for the projects we have worked on together and in the development of this book. For providing information and material, and for reading and critiquing the manuscript, I am indebted to: Robert Baker, Robert Bartlett, Harvey Braun, Irwin Cohen, Evan Fenton, Joseph Fleckinger, Terry Foran, Richard Furash, Paul Gallagher, Edward Goldberg, Nicholas Lamberti, Joseph Martin, Michael Mayo, Daniel McCarthy, Neil Levy, Alan Phelps, Josh Polan, Thomas Rauh, Arthur Rawl, Stewart Rog, Edwin Ruzinsky, Marc Schwarz, Theodore Shapiro, William Smith, Brian Sobelman, Eric Thebner, and Joy Warren.

In particular, I would like to thank Cosmo Ferrara for his help in coordinating, assimilating, and reworking into a single volume the thinking of so many people drawn from so many sources. My special thanks, too, go to Sandra Lentoski and Jane Batt for typing and proofreading the many drafts of my manuscript.

I would be remiss if I did not mention my gratitude to *Discount Store News*, *Chain Store Age*, and *National Home Center News*, in which some of this book's material first appeared. I thank their publisher, Lebhar-Friedman, as well as *Progressive Grocer*, which also has published some of this material in a different form.

Lastly, I thank my associates in the retail industry. Their willingness to let Touche Ross help them find a better way has been the driving force behind our practice and the inspiration for this book.

Introduction

Bottom Line Issues in Retailing is not a primer in retail basics. Nor is it a compendium of everything anyone would ever want to know about managing in the retail environment. Instead, this book addresses a number of key issues facing retailers today. Each of the issues—merchandise management, information processing, retail accounting, business planning, store operations, and management skills—has a direct impact on a company's profitability.

The approach to many of these issues is quantitative. The text discusses ways in which the retailer can take the quesswork out of decision making and rely instead upon a thorough understanding of quantified data. What that data is, how it can best be captured, and how it can be converted into actions that increase productivity and profitability are considered and analyzed.

Part one, Merchandise Management, for example, presents formulas for planning merchandise purchases. The formulas use the hard facts of past performance and reasonable expectations based on objective assessments of the future. How much to buy, in what assortments, when, and according to what terms are questions answered not by individual instinct but by mathematical calculation.

Part Two, Technology and Retailing, details the latest methods of gathering critical data and converting it into the useful information on which merchandise and other business planning is done. The role and future of the point-of-sale terminal, of electronic communication with vendors, and the fundamental issue of "who needs what information" receive extensive treatment.

Part Three, Retail Managerial Accounting, shows that this function is indeed more than keeping the books. The accounting role is shown to be a vital force in alerting management to actual performance in a volatile economy.

Part Four, Planning for Success, presents techniques for staying ahead of the economy, the competition, and one's own growth through practical research and careful planning. Case studies reveal what can happen to a retail company that does not keep one eye on its own operation and one on trends in the industry. The physical aspects of store location and merchandise display are also presented. This section shows how research such as demographics and "drive time models" enter into the selection of a site for a store. It also shows how analysis of GMROI by item determines merchandise display in a planogram. Guidelines for an efficient distribution center make conservation a profitable reality.

Part Five, Retailing Is People, focuses on the "people skills" a retail manager needs. Techniques for effective communication, interviewing, and use of time and staff are detailed.

An Epilogue on the Technological Evolution as it affects retailing discusses not only technological developments that are still in the future but also those that are being experimented with today.

The issues and techniques addressed in this book should be of interest to three groups of readers. Decision-making executives can use the information in this book as a standard against which to measure their own companies in these critical areas. Retailers on the way up, who often see only one company's way of doing things, can discover in these pages a more global, and perhaps more sophisticated, approach to retail management. Last, but not least, students of retailing, both in schools and in company training programs, can use this book to supplement and broaden their education.

Part One

MERCHANDISE MANAGEMENT

1

Merchandise Planning

OVERVIEW: This chapter details the nucleus of all merchandise planning—the six-month merchandise plan. This plan is developed from an analysis of historical data and an assessment of trends and expectations. The plan enables buyers to decide, with a reasonable degree of accuracy, how much to buy and when, in order to achieve the sales plan and the gross margin needed to make the company profitable. The six-month merchandise plan is prepared on the basis of classifications or groupings of similar merchandise within the department. The assortment and buying plans, which guide the buyer in selecting merchandise and vendors on a profitability basis, are developed from the merchandise plan.

In the large retail store, customers can find almost everything they need to equip and decorate their homes, repair their cars, and clothe, entertain, and beautify themselves and their families. A seemingly endless array of merchandise is available in a wide variety of styles, colors, sizes, and prices to suit a wide range of shoppers. The merchandise is displayed in an organized and attractive manner to make shopping as convenient and pleasant as possible.

Harmoniously orchestrating the multitude of people and activities we find in the large retail store requires superior organizational and management skills. It requires successful coordination of a number of divisions— merchandising, finance, operations, and personnel. Merchandising, because of the nature of the business, takes top priority.

Regardless of how smoothly other functions are run, if merchandising is not done well, the company cannot succeed.

Successful merchandising requires both an instinctive reading of what people will want to buy and an analytical appraisal of sales performance and trends. The instinctive feel for the right merchandise is something a person learns by listening to customers, by handling the goods, and by working with experienced merchants and vendors. It is the analytical side of retailing, however—the side that deals with evaluating and predicting the numbers—that is the focus of this chapter on merchandise planning.

The Need for Planning

Most of us have experienced the occasional difficulty of choosing gifts for our families or friends. Answering questions such as "Who gets what?", "What do they already have?" and "What should I spend on each person?" can be a headache. The retail buyer has an even more frustrating job. He or she must predict the customer demands for an entire season and plan all inventory purchases accordingly. Many stores in different geographic locations with different customer characteristics might be involved. Customer preferences by store, size and color considerations, the fashion look for the season, local climate, and acceptable price lines are just some of the factors that the buyer must integrate into planning.

If this were not a formidable enough task in itself, buyers must also deal with the facts of today's economy. Rising inventory costs, increased store operating expenses, inflation, potential shortages, and increased central office expenses are some of the factors that have contributed to tight operating budgets.

The retailer's objective is to maximize profit and return on investment. The buying staff can support this objective by providing increased gross margins, minimizing unnecessary markdowns, reducing costs and expenses, and efficiently managing the inventory investment. One of the main tools for sound inventory management is a sound merchandise plan. By following a formal merchandise planning process, the merchant can successfully manage inventory and help meet company sales and profit objectives.

Approaches to Planning

Traditionally, merchandise planning has been structured around either a top-down or bottom-up approach. As the name implies, the top-down approach starts with upper management identifying a gross dollar value for departmental sales. The buyer takes this dollar figure and allocates it among the merchandise classifications by store. (A classification is a homogeneous grouping of merchandise with the same end use, *e.g.*, dress shirts or food processors.)

The bottom-up approach starts with the buyer's estimate of unit sales at the classification level (i.e., the number of dress shirts or food processors that will be sold). The buyer then looks at price-line history and translates unit sales into dollar sales for each classification. The total departmental sales figure is the sum of dollar sales of all classifications. This method is possible only if past-season unit control records are available.

A third approach to planning, the interactive approach, combines the top-down and bottom-up methods. In the interactive approach, top management provides broad guidelines based upon economic trends, store expansion possibilities, and other economic factors. The buying staff then follows the bottom-up approach. Reviews and modifications by management ensure that the overall guidelines have been followed. The potential sales of each merchandise classification are analyzed before the dollar plan is completed. When revisions are necessary, the total dollar figures for each classification generally do not change. What does change, however, is the distribution of those dollars within each merchandise class. The interactive approach results in the most accurate merchandise plan.

Interactive merchandise planning is composed of several distinct elements:

- Company merchandise policy (goals and objectives)
- Past sales information
- Qualitative merchandise plan
- Six-month merchandise plan (unit and dollar classification plan)
- Six-month department plan
- Assortment plan
- Buying plan

Each of these elements will be examined in the following pages.

Company Merchandise Policy

In order to coordinate the buying plans of each department with the overall philosophy of management, each buyer should review the company's current merchandise policy. This will provide insight into the current and potential customer base, fashion image, merchandise quality level, price lines and price ranges, marketing approach, customer service level, and desired profit margins. Adhering to the company merchandise policy not only sets store standards but also creates consistency throughout the various departments.

Past Sales Information

After determining and reviewing the company's overall merchandise policy, the next step is to review all past sales information. This information includes unit control records; the previous year's six-month merchandise plan; monthly departmental contribution reports; trade, market, and vendor information; and input from store operations. The unit control records are especially important. They provide key statistics on sales, merchandise on hand, receipts, transfers, returns to vendors, markdowns, etc. at the style level. Understanding these performance statistics is indispensable in the planning process.

Qualitative Merchandise Plan

Once the buyer has reviewed management's overall objectives and the pertinent background information, he or she is ready to prepare the qualitative merchandise plan for the upcoming season. This plan addresses the qualitative or subjective aspects of the customer, the merchandise, and the merchandising techniques.

The qualitative merchandise plan should address the following subjects:

- Customer definition (today and tomorrow)
- Departmental sales makeup (staple, seasonal, or promotional)
- Key department merchandise trends
- Major vendors
- Programmed vendor development
- Classification performance comparison
- Import plans
- Advertising review
- Monthly action plan
- Specific problems in attaining goals

The qualitative merchandise plan (Figure 1-1) should be a written document, prepared by the buyer, and reviewed with the merchandise manager as supporting documentation for the six-month merchandise plan. It should be consistent with the total store image and related standards of price and quality. It must also be consistent with the dollar guidelines defined by the six-month merchandise plan and with the unit plans that support the dollar plans. The qualitative merchandise plan need not be completed before beginning to plan purchases. What is important is that the historical data be understood before mapping out this season's strategy.

The qualitative merchandise plan covers the following items:

1. This year's gross plan vs. last year's actual: This year's planned sales and inventory figures are very preliminary goals identified by the retailer. Last year's figures are from the final season departmental reports of last year.

2. Department profile: Using available customer profile studies, define the department's current customer and identify the new department target customer, if policy changes so dictate.

3. Department sales makeup: This section reports total sales by classification. It is obtained from classification sales analysis and includes information from the final season departmental reports of last year.

4. Key department merchandise trends: Unit control reports and department sales reports reveal the trend of growth or decline of certain types of merchandise. It is important that management anticipate product life cycles and attempt to forecast trends in products, styles, and colors. Another important consideration is vendor information regarding new products.

5. Major vendor analysis: Information on the performance of different vendors and their products is critical in preparing the assortment and buying plans. Accurately evaluating vendor performance and formulating this year's gross plan depends upon the following information:

- How successful the vendor's merchandise is in the market.
- What the sell-through percentages are at different points in the season.
- Percentage of merchandise (based on units) sold at original retail versus markdown price.
- Total percentage of merchandise sold at a markdown price.
- Profitability of each vendor.

6. Programmed vendor development: Vendor programs should be developed for key vendors whenever possible. These programs allow the buyer to schedule purchases of basic merchandise well in advance when demand is highly predictable. The quantity and early commitment to more staple merchandise usually results in favorable trade discounts. However, the buyer must plan seasonal promotions before committing to any seasonal vendor programs. When developing vendor programs, the buyer must also keep upcoming delivery schedules in mind.

7. Classification comparison: It is important to compare this year's planned performance with last year's actual performance. Any large variances should be justified for reasons such as changes in merchandise policy, new items carried in a classification, items dropped from a classification, changes in promotional effort, or the preliminary nature of the plan data.

8. Import review: This part of the plan is important when there is a large volume of foreign purchases. Some considerations are delivery schedules, control of merchandise quality, return of merchandise, freight charges, and currency fluctuations.

Figure 1-1. QUALITATIVE MERCHANDISE PLAN

Season: _____

Buyer: _____ Date: _____

      Department Number: _____

      Department Name: _____

1. This Year Gross Plan _____ % Change _____
   Last Year Actual _____

2. Department Profile
   A. Customer Definition (Today):

   _____

   _____

   B. Customer Definition (Future):

   _____

   _____

3. Departmental Sales Makeup

	Seasonal Merchandise	Staple Merchandise	Promotional Merchandise
Last year actual $ and %			
This year gross plan $ and %			

4. Key Department Merchandise Trends:

   _____

   _____

5. Major Vendors (List in order of importance and designate major vendors with an "M"):

Vendor	Dept. No.	Last Year Actual	Gross Plan

6. Programmed Vendor Development (List and discuss plans to build the business with one or two vendors, covering planned volume increase, advertising, special arrangements, etc.):

_____

_____

7. Classification Comparison (Explain how to achieve the plan in each major class):

_____

_____

8. Import Review (Give last year's purchases and this year's plan):

_____

_____

9. Advertising Review (Compare this year's promotional calendar to last year's):

_____

_____

10. Monthly Action Plan (Describe the specific way in which goals will be achieved by month for the season):

_____

_____

Figure 1-1. (*Continued*)

11. Discuss Specific Problems That Will Be Encountered in Attaining Your Goals and How to Overcome These Problems

_____

_____

_____

_____

12. Merchandise Presentation:
    A. New Stores:

    _____

    _____

    _____

    _____

    B. Major Presentations:

    _____

    _____

    _____

    _____

9. Advertising review: Review last year's promotional calendar and adjust as necessary. Work from this to prepare a calendar for the upcoming year. Promotions must be planned and coordinated before orders are placed, especially for special vendor promotions that will affect the buyers' planned purchases for the season.

10. Monthly action plan: This is the detailed monthly workplan describing what actions will be taken, and when they will be taken, to achieve all goals.

11. Specific problems: Management should try to foresee possible problems and plan alternative courses of action or corrective measures.

12. Merchandise presentation: The merchant should provide overall guidelines for the display of merchandise. This can include suggestions on types of fixtures, layouts, etc.

Six-Month Merchandise Plan

The qualitative merchandise plan includes a good deal of subjective judgment. Nevertheless, it provides the basis for the six-month merchandise plan, which is the critical quantified document in the merchandise planning process (see Figure 1-2). (The six-month merchandise plan is sometimes referred to as a unit and dollar classification plan.)

As a department grows, the buyer usually has more difficulty in pinpointing its strengths and weaknesses and in planning purchases. So, to more accurately identify customer demands and plan purchases, departments have been broken down into merchandise classifications. For example, in the men's department, merchandise may be broken down into classifications such as suits, accessories, shirts, sport coats, outerwear, and so on. By grouping merchandise into classifications and using the qualitative merchandise plan, the buyer can see potential growth areas. Classification planning prevents duplication of merchandise in certain price lines and helps the buyer analyze the timing of the sales cycle (beginning, peak, and end) of each class of merchandise.

Most retailers do all their planning at the classification rather than at the individual unit level. However, it is necessary to consider unit information and price line analysis in formulating the classification plans.

The primary objective of merchandise planning is profit improvement. As the buyers review each classification and outline their expectations for the new season, management can develop a comprehensive picture of projected profitability at the class level, department level, and company-wide level. During management's review of the plans, investment dollars can be redistributed among classifications to fine-tune the plan toward achievement of overall company goals and objectives.

In preparing a six-month merchandise plan, we generally build up classification plans to the department level. For every classification, the buyer must first consider

Figure 1-2. SIX-MONTH MERCHANDISE PLAN

Department: _____
Classification: _____
Season: _____

Original Plan _____
Date _____

PLANNING PARAMETERS		BEGINNING OF SEASON Units	BEGINNING OF SEASON Dollars	Month 1 Units	Month 1 Dollars	Month 2 Units	Month 2 Dollars	Month 3 Units	Month 3 Dollars	Month 4 Units	Month 4 Dollars	Month 5 Units	Month 5 Dollars	Month 6 Units	Month 6 Dollars	SEASON TOTALS Units	SEASON TOTALS Dollars
RETAIL RECEIPTS & ADDITIONAL MARKUPS	LAST YEAR	4785	$74,300	5844	$61,100	3199	$59,400	6782	$56,200	1815	$27,600	350	$7,800	1120	$16,600	23,895	$285,000
	PLAN	6070	72,400	4690	58,000	4890	52,900	4120	44,800	870	7,900	870	11,700	860	10,900	27,290	258,200
	% PLAN TO LAST YEAR																
	REVISED PLAN																
	ACTUAL																
SALES	LAST YEAR			2946	$38,300	4447	$49,700	3609	$39,700	4400	$39,600	3310	$33,100	2270	$22,700	20,962	$223,100
	PLAN			3700	44,000	4500	52,000	4000	42,800	4000	41,600	3720	35,200	2600	24,000	22,520	239,600
	% PLAN TO LAST YEAR																
	REVISED PLAN																
	ACTUAL																
MARK DOWNS	LAST YEAR				$5,300		$3,700		$2,400		$2,800		$3,900		$3,600		$19,700
	PLAN				5,800		3,200		3,000		3,000		3,700		2,800		21,500
	% PLAN TO LAST YEAR																
	REVISED PLAN																
	ACTUAL																
REDUCTIONS — EMPLOYEE DISCOUNT	LAST YEAR				$400		$500		$1,200		$200		$400		$1,700		$4,400
	PLAN				500		700		400		400		500		400		2,300
	% PLAN TO LAST YEAR																
	REVISED PLAN																
	ACTUAL																
REDUCTIONS — SHORTAGES	LAST YEAR			85	$1,100	196	1,500	109	1,200	133	1,200	100	1,000	70	700	633	$6,700
	PLAN			110	1,500	140	1,600	120	1,300	120	1,200	120	1,100	80	700	800	7,200
	% PLAN TO LAST YEAR																
	REVISED PLAN																
	ACTUAL																
B.O.M. STOCK	LAST YEAR	1700**	$20,000**	6465	$84,300	9300	$102,300	7936	$87,300	11,000	$99,000	8230	$87,800	5220	$52,200	7000	$40,100
	PLAN	1700**	20,000**	7770	92,400	8650	98,800	8800	94,200	8800	91,200	5550	52,800	2600	24,000	800	7,000
	% PLAN TO LAST YEAR																
	REVISED PLAN																
	ACTUAL																
STOCK TO SALES RATIO	LAST YEAR				2.2		2.1		2.2		2.5		2.5		2.3		
	PLAN				2.1		1.9		2.2		2.2		1.5		1.0		
	% PLAN TO LAST YEAR																
	REVISED PLAN																
	ACTUAL																
CUMULATIVE MARKUP PERCENT	LAST YEAR				41%		40%		40%		39%		39%		38%		38%
	PLAN				40%		40%		40%		40%		40%		40%		40%
	REVISED PLAN																
	ACTUAL																
CUMULATIVE GROSS MARGIN PERCENT	LAST YEAR				33.6%		32.8%		32.8%		31.9%		31.4%		29.4%		29.4%
	PLAN				29.6%		31.8%		32.5%		32.6%		32.2%		32.1%		32.1%
	REVISED PLAN																
	ACTUAL																

*Retail receipts = purchases planned to be brought into inventory
**Carry Over Stock

SEASONAL STATISTICS

	MARKDOWN % SALES	EMPL. DISCOUNT % SALES	SHORTAGE % SALES	AVG. B.O.M. STOCK	INVENTORY TURNS
LAST YEAR	8.9%	2.0%	3.0%	78,300	2.84 TIMES
PLAN	9.0%	1.2%	3.0%	65,800	3.64
% PLAN TO LAST YEAR					
REVISED PLAN					

planned sales and planned reductions. Planned end-of-the-month (EOM) stock can be derived from the sales plan based on established inventory investment objectives. Using these planned figures, planned purchases or an initial open-to-buy (OTB) can be calculated. The OTB is a running balance of sales, purchases, on-orders, receipts, and reductions that permits the buyer to monitor and revise his budget. Finally, target initial mark-ups can be projected and used to develop overall class and department gross margins.

Let's look at these steps in depth.

Planned Sales

Sales planning is the most difficult part of the merchandise planning process. No one has yet developed a crystal ball to predict sales. However, there are many techniques for developing a good sales plan.

Generally, the buyer begins with an overall forecast of total sales for the department. This can first be developed quantitatively using statistical forecasting methods and then modified qualitatively by examining general market trends and economic conditions. This overall projection must reflect seasonal variations, planned store openings or closings, and expected changes in competition, as well as general economic conditions.

There are many other factors that influence sales, however, and only by developing the plan at the classification level can the buyer begin to understand and shape the sales forecast. In reviewing each classification, the buyer should consider the following:

- How much merchandise in the classification is staple or basic and how will this be changing?
- How much of the merchandise was promotional last year? Will the promotional mix change much this year?
- Is the classification growing faster or slower than the overall department?
- What new products or categories should be added this year and which ones are likely to be dropped?
- How is my customer changing? Has the company expanded into new markets that represent either opportunities or threats to this classification?
- Has there been a shift in price line acceptance by my customers?
- How will inflation impact prices?

By answering these questions and reviewing last year's sales history in detail, the buyer can develop an informed sales plan. For basic merchandise, this might be done by estimating unit sales and extending out at the new retail price. For seasonal or promotional merchandise, estimates can be developed by projecting unit sales for each price line and adjusting for inflation. Then, after each classification is built up to the department level, refinements can be made to bring the overall department projection in line with management's objectives.

The following example illustrates the bottom-up sales planning procedure in a hardgoods area. Consider a lawn mower department with three classifications: walking lawn mower, riding lawn mower, and tractor lawn mower. Assume all stores can be categorized into types A, B, C, D, E or F, according to total dollar sales or lines of merchandise carried. Furthermore, there are five subclassifications or models for the riding lawn mower class:

Model	Price/Unit
25″ 5HP Equipped	$300
25″ 7HP Deluxe	340
25″ 7HP Super Deluxe	400
30″ 7HP Equipped	360
30″ 7HP Deluxe	430

With the above information, plus the information from unit control records, the buyer can develop planned unit sales by store category, using a form like that shown in Figure 1-3. The first step is to estimate the unit sales by store type and extend to retail. For example, in an A store in the month of April the following unit sales are estimated and extended to retail:

		A Store	
Subclass	Price/Unit	Units	Dollars
25″ 5HP Equipped	$300	3	$ 900
25″ 7HP Deluxe	340	3	1,020
25″ 7HP Super Deluxe	400	2	800
30″ 7HP Equipped	360	3	1,080
30″ 8HP Deluxe	430	1	430
			$4,230

The procedure is repeated for all categories of stores.

Assuming the number of stores of each type is as shown in column 2 below, then the planned sales for the riding lawn mower classification are:

Store Type	Number	×	Sales/Store	=	Store Total
A	3		$4,230		$12,690
B	6		3,530		21,180
C	8		2,730		21,840
D	10		2,390		23,900
E	7		1,660		11,620
F	4		960		3,840
Total	**38**				**$95,070**

Figure 1-3. SALES ANALYSIS BY STORE TYPE

Department: Lawn Mowers
Classification: Riding
Month: April

Subclassification (Assortment)	Price/Unit	A Store Units/Dollars	B Store Units/Dollars	C Store Units/Dollars	D Store Units/Dollars	E Store Units/Dollars	F Store Units/Dollars
25″ 5 HP Equipped	$300	3/$900					
25″ 7 HP Deluxe	$340	3/$1,020					
25″ 7 HP SuperDeluxe	$400	2/$800					
30″ 7 HP Equipped	$360	3/$1,080					
30″ 8 HP Deluxe	$430	1/$430					
Store Type Total		12/$4,230					

This procedure is repeated for all three classifications of the lawn mower department. The sum of the sales forecasts for the three classifications gives the department sales forecast. If this sales forecast does not match management's plan for the department, the forecast and plan must be refined so they are consistent with each other.

In the softgoods area, the buyer develops estimates by projecting unit sales for each price line, adjusted for inflation. Then, as each classification is built up to the department level, refinements can be made to bring the overall projection in line with management objectives. Based on a price line analysis, the planned sales in units within each price point of a classification in month 1 is determined and extended to dollars by the average price:

| | Month 1 | | |
Price Line	Average Price	Planned Sales in Units	Planned Sales in Dollars
$9–11	$10	700	$ 7,000
11–13	12	2,500	30,000
13–15	14	500	7,000
		3,700	**$44,000**

The above analysis is repeated for all six months in the season. Then the season's sales forecast for the classification can be figured as follows:

Month	Planned Sales in Units	Planned Sales in Dollars	Average Price per Unit
1	3,700	$ 44,000	$11.89
2	4,500	52,000	11.55
3	4,000	42,800	10.70
4	4,000	41,600	10.40
5	3,700	35,200	9.51
6	2,600	24,000	9.23
Season Total	**22,500**	**$239,600**	**$10.65**

As is typical in a softgoods plan, the average price drops during the season as markdowns are taken to clear out merchandise. These projected sales figures are then inserted in the six-month merchandise plan (Figure 1-2).

Planned Reductions
Reductions consist of *employee discounts, markdowns,* and *stock shortage.* There are two reasons for including these components in the six-month merchandise

plan. First, since they directly affect the gross margin, reduction estimates are necessary to properly project department and classification profitability. Second, since they represent reductions to inventory, they should be factored into the planned purchases to ensure that adequate merchandise is on hand to meet sales targets.

Employee discounts remain fairly constant from year to year when expressed as a percentage of sales, unless, of course, company policy regarding discounts changes dramatically. Therefore, when planning employee discounts, it is generally safe to use last year's percentage of sales as a guide for each department or classification.

Employee discounts in dollars are calculated by multiplying the discount percentage by the planned sales for the month. For example, assuming the employee discount percentage for February is 1.2% and planned sales for the month are $44,000, the employee discount in dollars is .012 x $44,000 = $528.

Stock shortage can be factored into the plan in much the same way. Unless the company is making substantial changes to its shortage control program, historic trends for the department or classification can be used in estimating shrinkage as a percentage of sales.

Like employee discounts, the dollar amount of stock shortage is found by multiplying the estimated stock shortage percentage by the planned sales for the month. For example, if the stock shortage percentage for month 1 is 3% and planned sales are $44,000, the planned stock shortage in dollars is .03 x $44,000 = $1,320.

Planning *markdowns* is a difficult task for some retailers to face. When discussing markdowns, very often the buyer will respond, "Look, I don't control the weather" or "How can I predict what the competition will do to attract my customers?" True, but there are also factors contributing to markdowns that *can* be controlled. These factors include overlapping merchandise across departments; merchandise quality; vendor performance; size, color, and material selection; and assortment breadth.

In projecting markdowns for the six-month merchandise plan, the buyer should review last year's results very closely. In addition to the considerations listed above, the buyer should ask the following questions:

- What were my markdowns (as a percentage of sales) last year for each month in the season?

- How aggressive were pricing policies last year? Will they change this year?

- What was the timing of major promotions and clearances last year? How will they be altered this year?

- How deep were our first markdowns last year? Will we be more aggressive this year?

- Were there problems last year with the timing of incoming merchandise either at the beginning of the season or with reorders? How did this affect the markdowns taken last year?

After evaluating the answers to these questions, the buyer is in a position to estimate monthly markdowns as a percentage of planned sales. In addition, the company will be in a better position to control markdowns in the future.

Planned markdowns are derived in the following manner:

1. Determine the total planned markdowns as a percentage of total sales for the six-month period. Sources of information include past experience, anticipation of carryover merchandise from previous season, industry figures, and management-directed policy changes. A percentage factor for any revisions to price lines should be included in the percentage.

Figure 1-4. MONTHLY MARKDOWN DOLLARS

Month	Planned Distribution of Markdowns	×	Total Markdown Dollars	=	Monthly Markdown Dollars
1	.27		$21,564		$ 5,822
2	.15		21,564		3,235
3	.14		21,564		3,019
4	.14		21,564		3,019
5	.17		21,564		3,666
6	.13		21,564		2,803
TOTAL	**1.00**	**×**	**$21,564**	**=**	**$21,564**

Figure 1-5. MONTHLY MARKDOWNS AS PERCENTAGE OF MONTHLY SALES

Month	Monthly Markdown Dollars	÷	Planned Sales	× 100 =	Markdowns as Percent of Planned Sales	Considerations
1	$ 5,822		$44,000		13.23%	Carryover merchandise from fall and holiday lines.
2	3,235		52,000		6.22	Small markdowns on slow-moving merchandise.
3	3,019		42,800		7.05	Same as Month 1.
4	3,019		41,600		7.26	Special promotion.
5	3,666		35,200		10.41	Begin clearances.
6	2,803		24,000		11.68	Season clearances.
	$21,564	÷	$239,600	× 100 =	9.0%	

Figure 1-6. MONTHLY PLANNED REDUCTIONS

Month	Planned Sales Dollars	Markdowns %	Markdowns Dollars	Employee Discount %*	Employee Discount Dollars	Stock Shortage %*	Stock Shortage Dollars	Total Monthly Reduction Dollars
1	$ 44,000	13.23	$ 5,822	1.2	$ 528	3.0	$1,320	$ 7,670
2	52,000	6.22	3,235	1.3	676	3.0	1,560	5,471
3	42,800	7.05	3,019	1.0	428	3.0	1,284	4,731
4	41,600	7.26	3,019	1.0	416	3.0	1,248	4,683
5	35,200	10.41	3,666	1.5	528	3.0	1,056	5,250
6	24,000	11.68	2,803	1.8	432	3.0	720	3,955
TOTAL	$239,600	9.0%*	$21,564	1.26%	$3,008	3.0%	$7,188	$31,760

2. Determine the total dollar value of the markdowns planned for the season. The dollar value of planned markdowns equals the markdown percent expressed as a decimal times the planned sales in dollars. For example, if planned markdowns are 9% of total planned sales, and planned sales are $239,600, the total dollar value of planned markdowns is .09 x $239,600 = $21,564.

3. Determine the distribution of the total percentage of markdowns planned by month and compute the dollar value by month. Note that each month's markdowns will not be the same. Instead, markdowns should be planned around store promotions, special events, and clearances. Carryover merchandise from the previous season might increase markdowns planned for the first month of the new season. These calculations are illustrated in Figure 1-4.

Monthly markdowns can be further considered as a percentage of planned monthly sales, as shown in Figure 1-5.

Using the methods described above, each reduction can be planned using the projected sales figures developed on page 19. The resulting monthly reductions are shown in Figure 1-6. These reductions are rounded to the nearest hundred and entered in the six-month merchandise plan (Figure 1-2).

Planned Stock

Projected stock levels are another important element of the six-month merchandise plan. The retailer's primary investment is in his inventory, and careful planning is required to ensure an adequate return on investment. Keeping inventory levels at a minimum without sacrificing sales has several positive effects on the overall profitability of the company:

- Lower inventories mean lower carrying costs in terms of interest expense, warehousing costs, insurance, handling costs, and shrinkage.

- Lower inventories mean higher gross margins by reducing the need for markdowns due to overstock conditions.
- Lower inventories mean lower average investments in inventory and therefore a better return on investment for the company.

In planning monthly stock levels, several different techniques can be used depending on the characteristics of the merchandise within the classifications and the availability of historical information. The three techniques are the *stock-to-sales method*, the *weeks-of-supply method*, and the *stock turnover method*.

The *stock-to-sales method* is generally used to plan monthly stock levels for highly seasonal merchandise because it allows stock levels to vary according to the needs of the business. However, it can also be successfully applied to staple stock merchandise. Stock-to-sales (S/S) is a ratio of the amount of inventory on hand at a particular date to the sales for a defined period of time (*e.g.*, a month). The ratio is calculated as follows:

$$\text{S/S ratio} = \frac{\text{Retail stock on hand at specific date (in dollars)}}{\text{Sales for a period of time (in dollars)}}$$

Either beginning-of-month (BOM) or end-of-month (EOM) stock can be used in calculating the ratio.

In using the S/S method for planning stock levels, the buyer selects target S/S ratios by classification for each month in the season. Desired S/S ratios can be developed by referring to historic performance within the classification and published trade association statistics. The target S/S ratios are simply multiplied by the planned sales for the month to generate a planned stock level for each month. For example:

Month	Planned Dollar Sales	×	Planned Dollar BOM S/S Ratio	=	Planned Dollar BOM Stock
1	$ 44,000		2.1		$92,400
2	52,000		1.9		98,800
3	42,800		2.2		94,200
4	41,600		2.2		91,500
5	35,200		1.5		52,800
6	24,000		1.0		24,000
Total	**$239,600**				

The *weeks-of-supply method* is a good approach to planning stock levels for staple merchandise. It assumes a relatively constant level of demand and supply over a longer period of time than does the S/S method. In the weeks-of-supply method, the buyer establishes for each classification the weeks of supply of inventory needed at the end of each month throughout the season. This figure is based on estimated rates of sale, lead times, and safety stock levels. The buyer may use a constant weeks-of-supply figure throughout the season or varying figures depending on his knowledge of the marketplace.

Once the target weeks-of-supply figures have been established, monthly EOM stock levels can be calculated. *The planned EOM stock level for any particular month should equal the amount of sales planned for the next weeks-of-supply period.* For example, if at the end of February the buyer specifies that six weeks of supply should be on hand, then the planned EOM stock level for February is calculated by adding planned sales for March (four weeks) and one-half of planned sales for April (two weeks).

Consider an example in the men's tie department. Normally four weeks of supply is necessary to sustain sales. However, it is very difficult to get shipments from the vendors in the month of July. In order to sustain the regular sales activities in both July and August, the buyer wants to have eight weeks of supply in inventory by the beginning

Figure 1-7. COMPARISON OF STOCK PLANNING METHODS

	Stock-to-Sales Ratio	Weeks of Supply/Stock Turnover Method
Definitions	The ratio of the dollar amount of planned stock at a point in time to the dollar amount of planned sales for a period of time	The amount of stock required to begin a period based on the number of weeks of supply of merchandise
Method is based on	Dollars Actual figure for a period (usually a month)	Units or dollars Average figure for a period Rate of stock turnover
Formulas	S/S = $\dfrac{\text{Retail stock at specific date}}{\text{Sales for a period}}$	Weeks of supply needed = Number of weeks in planning season ÷ Stock turnover
		Planned stock = Sum of sales for the number of weeks of supply from the beginning of the month
Uses	Planning In classifications with widely varying sales on a monthly basis	Planning In classifications with stable sales

of July. Therefore, the planned weeks of supply for June to August BOM inventory would be as follows:

Beginning of Month	Weeks of Supply
6	4
7	8
8	4

Once the target weeks-of-supply figures have been established, monthly BOM stock levels can be calculated. These calculations are illustrated below, using a constant weeks-of-supply objective of five.

Month	Planned Sales	No. of Weeks in Month
1	$15,000	5
2	12,000	4
3	10,000	4
4	10,000	5
5	8,000	4
6	8,000	4
7	10,000	5

$$\text{Month 1 BOM} = \text{Sales for month 1 (5 weeks)}$$
$$= \$15,000$$

$$\text{Month 2 BOM} = \text{Sales for month 2 (4 weeks)} + \text{1 week sales for month 3}$$
$$= \$12,000 + \frac{\$10,000}{4}$$
$$= \$14,500$$

$$\text{Month 3 BOM} = \text{Sales for month 3 (4 weeks)} + \text{1 week sales for month 4}$$
$$= \$10,000 + \frac{\$10,000}{5}$$
$$= \$12,000$$

$$\text{Month 4 BOM} = \text{Sales for month 4 (5 weeks)}$$
$$= \$10,000$$

Month 5 BOM = Sales for month 5 (4 weeks) + 1 week sales for month 6

$$= \$8,000 + \frac{\$8,000}{4}$$

$$= \$10,000$$

Month 6 BOM = Sales for month 6 (4 weeks) + 1 week sales for month 7

$$= \$8,000 + \frac{\$10,000}{5}$$

$$= \$10,000$$

The stock turnover method of developing inventory plans is preferred by some buyers and managers. Stock turnover measures the rate at which inventory is acquired through purchases and then removed from stock through sales. The higher the rate or turnover generated, the more profit the buyer brings to the company. Turnover is calculated by dividing total sales achieved within the season by the average inventory for the season.

For example, using last year's BOM stock, end-of-season stock, and season total sales figures from Figure 1-2, last year's stock turnover rate would be calculated as follows:

Season total sales = $222,100

$$\text{Season average inventory} = \frac{\text{Sum of BOM stock and end-of-season stock}}{\text{Months in Season} + 1}$$

$$= \frac{\begin{array}{c}\$84,300 + 102,300 + 87,300 + \\ 99,000 + 82,800 + 52,200 + 40,100\end{array}}{6 + 1}$$

$$= \frac{\$548,000}{7}$$

$$= \$78,286$$

$$\text{Stock turnover rate} = \frac{\text{Season total sales}}{\text{Season average inventory}}$$

$$= \frac{\$222,100}{\$78,286}$$

$$= 2.84 \text{ times}$$

To use the stock turnover method to plan inventories, first a reasonable turnover objective is selected based on published industry data and/or historical performance (as in the above example). The turnover objective is then converted into a weeks-of-supply figure using this formula:

$$\text{Weeks of supply} = \frac{\text{Number of weeks in the season}}{\text{Stock turnover objective}}$$

Once the weeks-of-supply has been established, inventory levels are planned using the standard weeks-of-supply method described previously. For example, if the planned stock turnover is 2.81 for a classification within a department, the average number of weeks of supply of stock that should be on hand at any one time during a six-month (26-week) season is:

$$\text{Average number of weeks of supply} = \frac{\text{Number of weeks in a planning season}}{\text{Stock turnover rate}}$$

$$= \frac{26}{2.81}$$

$$= 9.3$$

No matter which method is used to plan inventory levels, it is important to evaluate the results before submitting the final plan to management. If there are market constraints that will not permit achieving the calculated plan, adjustments should be made to the planned figures to reflect this information. The buyer should not submit the plans to management simply because the numbers work out well. The plan should be workable and achievable based on the buyer's current knowledge of the market.

Planned Purchases

Once the buyer has completed the job of planning sales, reductions, and stock levels, a monthly planned purchases figure can be calculated. This figure tells the buyer how much merchandise to buy to raise the available stock up to the level required for the period.

The dollar value of planned purchases must be accurate. Too few purchases can result in out-of-stock situations; too many purchases can result in oversupply, which ties up cash and incurs unnecessary interest charges.

Reliable planned purchases can be determined using the following formula:

$$\substack{\text{Planned} \\ \text{purchases}} = \substack{\text{Planned} \\ \text{sales}} + \substack{\text{Planned} \\ \text{reductions}} + \substack{\text{Planned EOM stock} \\ \text{(current month)}} - \substack{\text{Planned EOM stock} \\ \text{(previous month)}}$$

For example, given a planned sales for the month of $40,000, planned reductions of $4,800, planned EOM stock of $80,000, and the previous month's planned EOM stock of $84,000, the planned purchases would be $40,000 + $4,800 + $80,000 - $84,800 = $40,000. Monthly planned purchases based on previously developed sales, reductions, and stock figures are shown in Figure 1-8.

Once the merchandise plans have been reviewed and accepted by management,

Figure 1-8. MONTHLY PLANNED PURCHASES

Month	Planned Sales	+	Planned Reductions	+	Planned EOM Stock	−	Planned BOM Stock	=	Planned Purchases
1	$ 44,000		$ 7,600		$ 98,800		$ 92,400		$ 58,000
2	52,000		5,500		94,200		98,800		52,900
3	42,800		4,700		91,500		94,200		44,800
4	41,600		4,600		52,800		91,500		7,500
5	35,200		5,300		24,000		52,800		11,700
6	24,000		3,900		7,000		24,000		10,900
	$239,600		$31,600		$368,300		$453,700		$185,800

the buyer's initial open-to-buy is set up based on the planned purchases for the season as indicated on the plan.

Planned purchases are listed in the six-month merchandise plan as Retail Receipts. This designation indicates that purchases are planned to be received into inventory in the month specified.

Planned Markups

After determining how much inventory to purchase, the retailer must next determine the markup. To generate a gross profit, merchandise must be sold at a price that more than covers the cost of merchandise and backroom costs. Markup is the difference between selling price and cost.

For example, if the retail selling price of a hand tool is $16.00 and its cost to the retailer is $12.00, the markup is $4.00.

Markup can be expressed either in dollars, as in the above example, or as a percentage. Using the markup percentage enables the buyer to make comparisons among various items, departments, or stores. The markup percentage is calculated by dividing the markup in dollars by the retail price. Using the hand tool example to illustrate, the formula is as follows:

$$\text{Markup percentage} = \frac{\text{Markup dollars}}{\text{Retail price}} = \frac{\$4.00}{\$16.00} = .25 \text{ or } 25\%$$

Buyers must be aware of different types of markups. The *purchase markup* is the markup obtained on total purchases excluding freight and cash discounts. *Individual markup* is that which is obtained on an individual basis. The *cumulative markup* is obtained on total year-to-date purchases plus beginning inventory. And because merchandise does not always sell at an original markup figure, the *maintained markup* is the difference between the final sales price and the initial purchase price inclusive of freight and cash discounts.

Let us illustrate markup calculations with some examples.

1. Find the percent markup when the retail price is $50.00 and the cost is $25.75.

$$\text{Markup dollars} = \text{Retail price} - \text{Cost}$$
$$= \$50.00 - \$25.75 = \$24.25$$
$$\text{Markup percent} = \frac{\text{Markup dollars}}{\text{Retail dollars}}$$
$$= \frac{\$24.25}{50.00} = .485 \text{ or } 48.5\%$$

2. Find the cost to the retailer when the retail price is $150 and the planned markup is 40%. To calculate this, we use the *cost percent*, which is 100% (representing the total retail price) minus the markup percent.

$$\text{Cost percent} = 100 \text{ percent} - \text{Markup percent}$$
$$\text{Cost to the retailer} = \text{Retail dollars} \times \text{Cost percent}$$
$$= \$150 \times (100\% - 40\%)$$
$$= \$150 \times 60\%$$
$$= \$150 \times .6$$
$$= \$90$$

3. Find the retail price given when the cost and markup percentage are $600 and 40% respectively:

$$\text{Cost percent} = 100 \text{ percent} - \text{Markup percent}$$
$$\text{Retail price} = \frac{\text{Cost}}{\text{Cost percent}}$$
$$= \frac{\$600}{100\% - 40\%}$$
$$= \frac{\$600}{60\%}$$
$$= \frac{\$600}{.6}$$
$$= \$1,000$$

4. Find the cumulative markup percent if:

		Cost	Retail
Beginning of year stock	=	$ 50,000	$ 80,000
Purchases	=	60,000	91,000
Total		**$110,000**	**$171,000**

Markup dollars = Retail price − Cost = $171,000 − $110,000 = $61,000

$$\text{Markup percent} = \frac{\text{Markup dollars}}{\text{Retail dollars}} = \frac{\$61,000}{\$171,000} = .36 \text{ or } 36\%$$

Retailers prosper when they are price-sensitive to their customer base and at the same time meet expense and profit needs. Merchandise costs, reductions, backroom costs, operating expenses, and desired profits must all be considered in setting markups. Actual performance must also be reviewed to see if the markups satisfy expense and profit needs. If they do not, the retailer must determine if the markup was insufficient or if another factor was out of line.

Markups must cover costs and provide a profit, but they must be realistic in terms of what the customer is willing to pay. Finding this delicate balance requires experienced judgment. The six-month merchandise plan provides a planning and review vehicle to test and hone that judgment.

Planned Gross Margin

Reliable markups are necessary to ensure that the retail price will cover costs and provide a reasonable profit. The profit generated on merchandise is called *gross margin*. It is the difference between net sales and the total cost of merchandise. The planned gross margin (cumulative gross margin percent) is the last item in the body of the six-month merchandise plan. Gross margin, obviously, will be affected by the planned initial markup, as well as by sales, inventory, and purchases.

The profit, or gross margin, can be calculated by using the following formula:

Gross margin = Net sales − Total cost of sales

Total cost of sales includes the cost of the merchandise sold plus backroom costs.

In computing the anticipated gross margin percentage as part of the six-month merchandise plan, then, all components detailed thus far are considered. The formula looks like this:

$$\text{Gross margin percent} = \frac{\left[\left(\text{Season sales} - \text{BOS inventory} + \text{Season purchases} - \text{EOS stock}\right)\left(1 - \text{Cumulative purchase markup percent}\right)\right]}{\text{Season sales}}$$

In performing the computation, first complete the operations within each set of parentheses and multiply the results together. Note that the cumulative purchase markup percent must be expressed as a decimal (*e.g.*, .40 instead of 40%) because it is being subtracted from 1 instead of from 100%. Next, subtract the result from the sales for the season and divide that number by the sales for the season. Do not make the mistake of canceling out the sales for the season in the numerator and denominator of the equation. Substituting numbers for words, the calculation would look like this:

$$GM\% = \frac{[(\$38,300 - \$84,300 + \$61,100 - \$102,300)(1 - .41)]}{38,300}$$

$$= \frac{38,300 - (43,100 \times .59)}{38,300}$$

$$= \frac{38,300 - 25,429}{38,300}$$

$$= .336 \text{ or } 33.6\%$$

In the event the results of the six-month merchandise plan are not satisfactory, or if they do not meet the objectives of management, the planned figures must be reviewed to determine where improvements can be made. Some possibilities might include:

- Changing the merchandise mix to improve initial markup.
- Reviewing markdown and promotional plans for possible improvements.
- Modifying the timing of receipts to reduce average inventory levels and thereby improve stock turnover, thus tying up less cash.

With the information provided by the six-month merchandise plan, managers and buyers are in a firm position to draw up their assortment and buying plans. They know where their departments have been and where they should be heading. They now can realistically determine the best means to get there.

Some of the computations necessary to develop a useful six-month plan might seem complicated at first, but most of them can be done on a computer. The retailer, however, must understand the basics of the formulas and how they work.

Based on qualitative and quantitative merchandising plans, decisions can be made with greater assurance and accuracy. Those retailers who have learned to master the numbers generally look forward each month to ever-larger figures on their bottom lines.

Six-Month Department Plan

The six-month merchandise plan is developed for each class of merchandise sold by a department. This plan can provide documentation of actual monthly results (sales, markdowns, etc.) so that comparisons between plan and performance may be made. The six-month department plan is simply a collection of the individual six-month classification plans. After the department plan is prepared, it is presented to management for review (a major part of the interactive approach described previously). Management will review these department plans and determine if they fall within the overall guidelines established.

Assortment Plan

Once the six-month merchandise plans are accepted, the next step is to decide on the actual assortment of merchandise to meet customer demand. Attempting to satisfy every customer leads to carrying too wide an assortment. After all, not all of the people can be pleased all of the time. Knowing the breadth and depth of merchandise, the sizes, colors, and price lines that will meet customer demand requires that the buyer knows the customer, studies recent history, and understands company plans for the future. For example, if a review of the figures for the past year shows that the greatest sales in sweaters were generated in the lowest price lines, the assortment plan for the upcoming season should emphasize those price lines. But if management has announced a drive to "trade up" in all departments in an effort to attract more affluent customers or to sell more items with higher markup and gross margin potential, the assortment plans will have to be developed accordingly, stressing higher price lines.

With the buying "philosophy" firmly in mind, the buyer can begin to formulate the assortment plan to assure a balanced stock. To maintain balanced stocks throughout the season, the buyer must plan for breadth, depth, and the proper mix of sizes, colors, and price lines.

Breadth and Depth

Assortment *breadth* is defined as the number of subclassifications of merchandise that will be carried within a classification. The classification sweaters, for instance, might include the subclassifications pullover—no buttons, pullover—buttons, and cardigan. To omit pullover—no buttons would not be in keeping with the balanced stock concept, unless there was a very clear reason to do so.

Having too narrow a range of subclassifications limits the customer appeal. Too broad a range might lead to unrelated groupings of merchandise that will confuse customers, hamper turnover, and destroy company image.

When breadth is too great, there is an accompanying risk of inadequate *depth*, or the proper amount of merchandise in each subclass. With only so much money to spend, a buyer can purchase only so much merchandise. Judgment is required on how much of each subclassification is needed to best match customer demand. Unit control records showing last year's sales by store can help make the decision on depth. Information on buying and fashion trends will also help determine whether or not to deviate from last year's performance.

Size

The selection of sizes in an assortment is extremely important, particularly in items for which size would be an inflexible ingredient in making a sale. In selecting drapery hardware, for instance, a shopper might buy white if brass is not available but will not switch to 64-inch drapes if 32-inch drapes are needed.

Thus depth in a variety of sizes must be part of the assortment plan. But it would be impractical, if not impossible, to carry the same depth of stock in each size. Past history and the buyer's judgment must combine in selecting the size assortments for most merchandise. Do not settle for the standard size assortments offered by manufacturers unless these have proven to be appropriate for your customers.

Buyers must concentrate the greatest inventory depth in the sizes that satisfy the greatest demand. Inactive stocks and markdowns can often be minimized when unproductive sizes are fewer. On a periodic basis, the size profile should be reviewed for every applicable department and store. This size profile analysis (see Figure 1-9) can be used to plan stock depth as a component of the assortment plan. The analysis indicates that size C sold out, while sizes A and D had relatively weak sell-throughs. The buyer may wish to revise the size distributions for the next season, giving greater weight to size C.

Color

Color is an important factor influencing customers to buy a particular item. Color preferences are not limited to fashion merchandise. For example, in many hard-goods areas, such as housewares, color preference is just as important as in ready-to-

Figure 1-9. SIZE PROFILE ANALYSIS

STORE: _____ DEPARTMENT: _____

Size	Number of Units Available During Season	Percent of Total Units Available	Number of Units Sold	Percent of Total Units Sold	Percent of Units Sold by Size
A	50	5.0%	38	4.3%	76%
B	250	25.0	215	24.3	86
C	325	32.5	325	36.7	100
D	275	27.5	220	24.8	80
E	100	10.0	88	9.9	88
TOTAL	1,000	100.0%	886	100.0%	

wear. Having the right size and color is definitely part of having the right merchandise at the right price at the right time.

While choosing the colors of merchandise is a qualitative function, determining the number of colors and the proper depth to carry them is quantitative. Often as much as 90% of sales can be generated by 30% of the colors in an assortment. The clever buyer does his homework to determine what colors in the various classifications strike a responsive chord in the department's customers.

At present, for instance, it might be that almond is the "in" color in kitchen appliances. To buy plastic kitchen accessories in avocado because that color was big in the past can cause loss of sales. Being able to determine such trends, to measure the impact on your stores, and to react on time requires alertness and judgment.

Price Lines

The analysis of price lines is another important element of assortment planning. It is critical to understand the relationship between assortment depth within the traditionally fast-selling merchandise and price lines. Summarizing unit control data by classification and price line can determine whether, based on the rate of sale, price lines need to be adjusted, whether the proportion of merchandise within each class/price line is appropriate, and whether the number of price lines carried is appropriate.

An analysis of Figure 1-10 shows how price line information can be helpful in assortment planning. The analysis shows that the $15.01 to $20.00 price line sold the best during the three-month period. The buyer would normally consider concentrating the season's classifications in that price line. But the data also indicate a growing customer acceptance for the higher-priced merchandise in this classification. The buyer must decide whether this is a trend that can be expected to continue.

The Assortment Plan

Once each classification has been considered in terms of appropriate breadth and depth, and once past performance of sizes, colors, and price lines has been analyzed, a form similar to the one shown in Figure 1-11 can be used to plan the assortment in each classification. Of course, modifications to the form must be made to suit the characteristics of the merchandise. For example, color may be a significant factor in some

Figure 1-10. CLASSIFICATION 101 PRICE LINE ANALYSIS

Merchandise Available for Sales (Units)	Price Lines (Average Price)	3-Month Sales			Total on Hand at End of Period
		1	2	3	
1,000	$10.00−$15.00	140	260	100	500
1,000	15.01 − 20.00	210	490	150	150
1,000	20.01 − 25.00	50	150	250	550

Figure 1-11. ASSORTMENT PLAN—CLASSIFICATION: SWEATERS

Subclass	% of Class Planned Sales	No. of Vendors	No. of Types	No. of Sizes	No. of Colors
1. V-neck	55	3	3	4	9
2. Crew neck	30	2	2	5	9
3. Cardigan	15	4	2	2	5

classes, weight in another; or an item might have only one style but several brands. The form should be tailored to the needs of each buyer and classification.

The assortment plan gives the buyer a rational basis on which to plan purchases. When he gets to market, new information may force him to alter the plan, but he does so only when and to the degree necessary. The buyer, not the vendors, is in control because he is concerned with increasing his company's, not the vendors', profit.

Buying Plan

The homemaker who wants to prepare balanced meals for her family goes to the supermarket with a detailed shopping list. Specials might cause her to deviate from the list somewhat and she may give in to a few impulse purchases, but because her list reflects her real needs, she sticks to it.

The buyer for a retail store benefits from the same kind of planning. The buyer already has a forecast of sales and purchases provided by the six-month merchandise plan and an assortment plan specifying the breadth, depth, sizes, colors, and price lines required to meet customer demand in each classification.

After the assortment plan is completed, the buyer prepares a buying plan—the detailed shopping list for the market trip. The buying plan is the final but crucial step in the merchandise planning process. Experience has shown that good buying plans lead to better profits.

Before drawing up the buying plan, the buyer must first make an analysis of vendors, of item profitability, and of new products.

Vendor Analysis

The vendor analysis helps the buyer determine where he gets the most for his money. Both quantitative and qualitative factors must be considered in this analysis.

Unit control records provide quantitative information indicating past success with each vendor. If last year the same number of desk chairs were purchased from Vendor A and Vendor B, what were the number of sales made of the chairs from each vendor? With which vendor are you able to obtain a greater initial markup? How many items from each vendor had to be sold at markdown? How does the maintained markup percentage of Vendor A stack up against that of Vendor B?

These figures will lead to the critical point of comparison, the gross margin contribution in relation to purchases. You might have sold more items bought from Vendor A, but because of the difference in markups and markdowns, you might have gained a greater gross margin contribution from the items purchased from Vendor B. The gross margin contribution is the buyer's ultimate concern, and it is an important consideration in formulating the buying plan.

Qualitative factors must also be considered when making the vendor analysis. What is the general customer acceptance of each vendor? The sales figures will indicate the acceptance level, but input from store personnel and from the customers themselves should give the buyer a feel for the way merchandise from each vendor is perceived. Do customers see this name as one that represents reliability, quality, low price, good workmanship, and so on?

The general quality of the merchandise received is important. In the past, has the same quality been received in stores that was viewed in the market? Has the shipment of "quality irregulars" turned out to be an embarrassment? Has damage been a consistent problem with the vendor?

Vendor adherence to your company's policies in regard to shipping, timing of incoming merchandise, terms (invoice and freight), and automatic cancellations is important. A vendor who does not comply with purchase order terms and conditions costs the retailer money. If merchandise cannot be received when you need it, it is useless, regardless of price.

Favorable freight terms and the vendor's willingness to provide funds for markdowns, promotions, and advertising are other variables to consider. So is product exclusivity. Some products, such as high-fashion jeans, are obtainable only from certain vendors, and the buyer has little choice of vendor if the item is a necessity at any cost.

Item Profitability Analysis

Item profitability must be reviewed before finalizing the buying plan. This entails reviewing all items within each classification and identifying those that are profitable and those that are not. Is the item a loss leader? What were the factors contributing to the poor showing? Is this item a good candidate for a reduction or elimination? Some items, however, might have to be kept on the buying plan, despite the lack of sales, just to provide assortment breadth or to attract customers to a department. Is the unprofitable item unique, or is a reasonable substitute available that might produce greater profit?

New Product Analysis

Each year many new products are manufactured and offered to retailers. The buyer must be aware of what those new products are and must make a reasonable

Figure 1-12. MERCHANDISE ASSORTMENT BUYING PLAN

SEASON: _____

Department: _____
Classification: _____
Subclassification: _____

MONTHLY OPEN TO BUY

MONTH	MONTH	MONTH	MONTH	MONTH	TOTAL
$	$	$	$	$	$

VENDOR NUMBER & NAME	STYLE NO. & DESCRIPTION	UNITS TO BE PURCHASED	UNIT COST	UNIT RETAIL	PLANNED PURCHASES BY MONTH AT RETAIL					TOTAL
	TOTAL		$	$	$	$	$	$	$	$
TOTAL PLANNED PURCHASES BY MONTH										

estimate of their potential sales. Information from trade journals, input from vendors and store personnel, compatibility with current merchandise, and the buyer's understanding of the customer profile and store image are all important factors in deciding on new products.

The Buying Plan

With the assortment plan completed and with vendor and product analyses made, the buyer is ready to prepare the actual buying plan. This plan lists the merchandise, by units at the style level, that will be purchased on the market trip (see Figure 1-12).

In addition to the number of units to be purchased on the trip, the expected cost and retail price of the item will be entered on the buying plan. Planned purchases and open-to-buy figures are shown monthly, and the timing of receipts is specified. This will help you receive merchandise when you want it, and pay for it when you expect to.

After the merchandise manager has approved the buying plan, the plan becomes a contract between management and buyer. The buyer proposes to buy a specified amount of merchandise at a particular price over a specified period of time. Management agrees to provide the cash needed to make those purchases on the given dates.

Before the market trip, an itinerary is developed based upon vendor priorities. The priorities are based in part on sales to date (if midseason), current inventory levels, merchandise on order, vendor lead time, and markup.

Once the buyer is in the market, the buying plan might change. New vendors might have entered the market, old vendors might have left it. Items planned for purchase might be unavailable. Prices or lead times might have changed. Terms might be different, enabling the buyer to purchase more or less than planned. The buyer modifies the plan to accommodate these changes but sticks to the plan as much as possible.

Following the market trip, the buying plan is completed when purchase orders are written, submitted for final approval, and sent to the vendors.

2

Negotiating the Purchase

OVERVIEW: This chapter highlights elements of the purchasing process that the buyer can take advantage of to save money on purchases. These elements include trade and cash discounts, dating provisions, freight terms, merchandise guarantees, and markdown and cooperative allowances. The advantages of different sets of options can be computed for easy comparison.

Negotiating the purchase of goods has direct impact on a retailer's bottom line. With the buying plan in hand, the buyer goes into the market to make the best possible buy. He has three distinct responsibilities:

- To buy enough of the right merchandise in the right assortments to meet the needs of the merchandise plan.
- To buy and sell merchandise that will meet the company's profit objectives.
- To maintain the highest possible markups and gross margins.

A particular gross margin is targeted in the six-month merchandise plan, but the buyer can improve that gross margin figure during negotiations with vendors. The language and preparation of the purchase order allow for subtle opportunities to "improve the buy." The successful buyer recognizes these opportunities and takes advantage of them with aggressive negotiating.

Specifically, these opportunities take the form of trade and cash discounts, datings, freight terms, guarantees on sale of merchandise, markdown allowances, and cooperative allowances. Let us briefly look at each of these and the way they can affect the cost of goods sold and, consequently, gross margin.

Trade Discounts

In many segments of the retail industry, vendors attempt to establish retail prices for every item of merchandise in their line. The price set by the vendor is referred to as the manufacturer's suggested list price or the suggested retail price. Although federal laws periodically change regarding manufacturers' establishing resale prices, the buyer must still be familiar with the basic concepts regarding list price.

Trade discount is the percentage of the vendor's list price that the vendor is willing to deduct and offer the retailer, regardless of when payment is made for the merchandise. Deducting the trade discount from the list price gives the *net price*, or that amount the retailer will pay the vendor. For example, if the list price of a lawn chair is $8.00 and the vendor allows a 20% discount, the buyer's net price would be $8.00 − (.20 x $8.00) = $6.40.

To encourage buying or buying in greater quantities, a vendor will sometimes offer a second and even a third discount. These are called *series discounts*. Each one is calculated on the previous net price, not on the original retail price. Using the $8.00 lawn chair of the previous example, if the series discount were expressed as 20%, 10%, 5%, the net price would be determined in this way:

$$\$8.00 - (.20 \times \$8.00) = \$6.40$$
$$\$6.40 - (.10 \times \$6.40) = \$5.76$$
$$\$5.76 - (0.5 \times \$5.76) = \$5.47 \text{ (net price)}$$

The total discount in dollars is $8.00 − $5.47 = $2.53.

For easy comparison, these series discounts are often converted into a single discount equivalent. This equivalent is found by subtracting each discount, expressed as a decimal, from 1, multiplying the results together, and subtracting the resulting number from 1. For the 20%, 10%, 5% terms in the problem above, the single discount equivalent would be calculated as shown below. The 1 in the formula represents 100%. Perform the calculations inside the parentheses first, then inside the brackets.

$$\text{Single discount equivalent} = 1 - [(1 - .20) \times (1 - .10) \times (1 - .05)]$$
$$= 1 - (.8 \times .9 \times .95)$$
$$= 1 - .684$$
$$= .316 \text{ or } 31.6\%$$

The single discount equivalent multiplied by the list price gives the total discount in dollars: $8.00 x .316 = $2.53.

Cash Discounts

Vendors like to receive payment for goods as quickly as possible and are willing to offer percentage allowances against the invoice price to gain speedy payment. This allowance is called a *cash discount*. Cash discounts are calculated on the net price of merchandise. The buyer is responsible for obtaining the best cash discount terms possible, but it is up to the financial division to take advantage of it by making payment according to those terms.

Some terms regarding dates of payments and associated discounts are defined below.

Due date Date by which payment must be made to comply with terms.

Net period The length of time during which full payment of the invoice is due.

Net X Full amount of invoice is due in X days.

Net 30; N/30; 30 net; 30N; net terms Full amount of invoice is due within 30 days.

2/10-30 extra; or 2/10-30X Vendor allows 2% discount on full amount of invoice if paid within 40 days (10 + 30) of invoice date or as otherwise negotiated on the invoice amount.

2/10 EOM Vendor allows 2% discount on full amount of invoice if the invoice is paid within 10 days following the end of the month in which the invoice is dated.

Cash discounts directly affect the purchase markup, and, therefore, the gross margin. It is to the company's advantage to take cash discounts, sometimes even when it is necessary to borrow money to do so. The buyer must work with the financial division to determine where the advantage lies at the moment.

The advantages of each discount can be seen in the analysis of the following examples.

1. What is the effective annual interest rate paid for *not* taking the cash discount that a vendor allows on terms of 2/10, net 30?

Analysis: The terms indicate the buyer will receive a 2% cash discount for payment of invoice within 10 days, but the vendor will extend credit for 30 days. To take advantage of the 2% discount therefore requires 20 days prepayment. *Not* taking the cash discount is the same as paying the vendor an interest rate of 2% over 20 days or $2\% \times \dfrac{360 \text{ days per year}}{20 \text{ days}} = 36\%$ effective annual interest. (A 360-day year is used for ease of calculation.) Looked at another way, the vendor is offering the retailer an interest rate equivalent to 36% for paying the invoice within 10 days.

2. What is the effective annual interest rate for *not* taking a cash discount on a $1,000 invoice with terms of 2/10, net 30?

Analysis: Here is a different way to analyze the same terms presented in example 1. The terms indicate the buyer will receive a 2% cash discount if payment is made within 10 days. This yields a dollar cash discount of $1,000 x .02 = $20. Net payment is then $1,000 − $20 = $980. If the buyer does *not* take the cash discount, he is in effect paying that $20 to the vendor in order to obtain $980 worth of credit over the remaining 20 days of the payment period. In other words, he is paying $20 for 20 days of credit, or a dollar a day, which can be annualized to $360 for a 360-day year. The equivalent annual interest rate, at $360 a year for a $1,000 invoice, is $\dfrac{\$\ 360}{\$1,000} = 36\%$.

Retail companies are faced with decisions like these every day. Companies are concerned with thousands of dollars of invoices, some with allowable cash discounts as high as 5% to 8%. Even at the current bank interest rates, borrowing money for payments could be a sound business decision.

Datings

Datings are the point in time or the day on which the buyer and the vendor agree as the beginning of the discount period. The buyer must have the vendor clarify the datings when the order is placed and the terms must be written on the purchase order. The following is a list of the various types of vendor datings and an explanation of each:

EOM End of month. Payment is due at the end of the month, or the discount period starts at the end of the month.

ROG Receipt of goods. Cash discount period for prepayment begins when the store receives the merchandise.

DOI Date of invoice or ordinary dating. Cash discount period for prepayment begins with the date of invoice.

Extra dating Additional amount of time in which the cash discount may be taken. Sometimes expressed as 2/10-30X. (A 2% cash discount may be taken for 40 days on the invoiced amount.)

Anticipation Vendor allows additional discount for payment before the end of the cash discount period as stated in the terms.

While dating does not directly impact gross margin, the buyer's ability to negotiate advantageous datings will result in savings for the company in terms of interest earned. These datings should be reviewed on a quarterly basis.

Here is an example purchase with an explanation of the dating and cash discount terms. The company has received an invoice of $800 dated April 30 with terms of 2/10, net 30 DOI. This means that if the company pays the bill on or before May 10, they will pay $784, taking the 2% discount. If the bill is paid between May 10 and May 30, the full $800 is due. Payment after May 30 could result in an interest charge in addition to the full amount of the invoice.

Freight Terms

After receiving the best possible trade discounts and an agreement for cash discounts, the buyer can improve the quality of the purchase by gaining favorable freight terms. The shipping and delivery of merchandise is critical, and the terms must be perfectly clear because they define who will incur cost and the liability (risk) for the merchandise in transit. Should an accident occur, the owner of the merchandise will have to absorb any loss not covered by insurance.

Ownership of goods in transit varies with the terms agreed upon. The most common term associated with shipping is FOB, or "free on board." When expressed with a location, FOB determines where title is transferred for the merchandise. *FOB origin* means the buyer owns the merchandise from the point of origin and will have to file the claim against the shipper if a problem arises. *FOB destination* means that the seller owns the goods until they reach their destination, at which point the buyer assumes ownership.

In addition to specifying the ownership in the event of a problem, freight terms indicate whether the buyer or vendor is responsible for paying shipping costs. This, then, is another area in which the buyer tries to cut costs by having the vendor agree to pay for shipping. Freight terms a buyer can negotiate depend on the size of the order, the time of season, the method of transportation, and the relationship with the vendor.

Lest buyers be surprised by delayed shipments or exorbitant costs, the method of shipment should be specified. If the goods will be shipped by truck, the buyer will expect shipment to be slower but cost less than if shipped by air.

Figure 2-1 summarizes the responsibilities of buyer and seller under different freight terms.

Guaranteed Sale and Markdown Allowances

Besides favorable trade discounts, cash discounts, and shipping terms, a buyer may wish to ask the vendor for some contingency allowances if the merchandise does not sell as well as anticipated. We may put these contingency allowances in two categories: the *guaranteed sale* and the *markdown allowance*.

When a vendor agrees to allow the retailer to return the unsold merchandise

Figure 2-1. FREIGHT TERM SUMMARY

Terms	Buyer's Responsibilities	Seller's Responsibilities
FOB origin, freight collect	Pays freight charges. Owns goods in transit. Files claims if necessary.	
FOB origin, freight prepaid	Owns goods in transit. Files claims if necessary.	Pays freight charges.
FOB origin, freight prepaid, charge back	Bears freight charges (paid by seller and billed on invoice). Owns goods in transit. Files claims if necessary.	Pays freight charges (bills buyer on invoice).
FOB destination, freight collect	Pays freight charges.	Owns goods in transit. Files claims if necessary.
FOB destination, freight prepaid		Pays freight charges. Owns goods in transit. Files claims if necessary.
FOB destination, freight collect, allowed	Pays freight charges (charged to seller by deducting amount from invoice).	Bears freight charges (paid by buyer and deducted from invoice). Owns goods in transit. Files claims if necessary.

for cash or credit, this is called a *guaranteed sale*. It differs from the concept of buying on consignment. With a guaranteed sale, the merchandise is usually paid for under the normal payment terms. With a consignment sale, the company pays for only the merchandise that is sold or reordered, and the vendor usually pays the return freight for unsold merchandise. Each store has its own policies and accounting practices for guaranteed and consignment merchandise.

It is obviously not to the vendor's advantage to allow a guaranteed sale. Therefore, the best time to ask for a guaranteed sale is when the vendor is new to the industry or to the company. It is one way of minimizing the risk of dealing with a vendor unknown to you.

Vendors may not always allow the return of merchandise that does not sell well. However, some vendors allow a rebate to defray the loss of gross margin dollars that results from the decreased price of the merchandise. In such situations the vendor is granting a *markdown allowance*. It is always easier to negotiate a markdown allowance when the order is not placed in the middle of the season, but it can be done midseason, if necessary.

Although rebates from vendors for guaranteed sales and markdowns will not affect the original cost of the merchandise, they will affect the gross margin because they reduce the cost of reductions.

Cooperative Advertising Allowances

It is also the buyer's responsibility to negotiate with vendors for allowances to partially defray the cost of advertising. This advertising can take the form of newspaper, magazine, television, or radio ads, catalogs, direct mail inserts, or in-store demonstrators. While advertising allowances may not directly improve the gross margin, the cost of advertising will affect the net profit of the company.

Some vendors allow a percentage of the invoice price of the merchandise for advertising. Others request a copy of the advertisements and rebate a portion or all of the cost of advertising directly to the company.

Most vendors have a written policy on advertising allowances and, by law, must treat each company equally. However, if management has agreed to a special ad campaign for the vendor's merchandise, there is a greater probability that the vendor will contribute to the campaign.

Domestic vs. Foreign Markets

Buyers are often faced with deciding whether to purchase goods from domestic markets or from foreign markets. While purchasing foreign-made merchandise sometimes yields a higher gross margin, there are many risks attached. Factors affecting the decision are summarized in Figure 2-2.

There are four major ways in which foreign goods may be purchased. The first is directly from the manufacturer. The second is from export merchants, who confine themselves to the export of manufactured goods. The third way is through export sales representatives, who only sell the goods of certain manufacturers but do not maintain inventory. These representatives generally make periodic trips to the United States. The fourth method is from export commission houses. These act as export departments of manufacturers and receive commissions from the manufacturer based on sales. Export houses can also help expedite paperwork for outgoing shipments.

Based on Figure 2-2, there is no clear "winner" between domestic and foreign markets. What is clear is that there are many risks associated with foreign market purchasing as well as rewards.

If no problems arise in the shipment of merchandise from overseas (*e.g.*, a dock strike), if the merchandise is of good quality, cut to specifications, and appeals to the customer, the rewards to the gross margin can be substantial.

To minimize the potential risk when dealing with import goods, stores generally add on a "load" factor to the cost of the merchandise. The load is typically a fixed

Figure 2-2. COMPARISON OF DOMESTIC AND FOREIGN MARKETS

Component	Advantage of	
	Domestic Market	Foreign Market
Lower cost prices		x
Higher initial markups		x
More reliable deliveries	x	
Quality control of merchandise	x	
Availability of invoice and shipping discounts	x	
Exclusivity of line of merchandise		x
Availability and ease of reorders	x	
Responsibility for damaged or partial shipments	x	
Ability to test market	x	
Status appeal (potential)	x	x
Permits ability to carry a more unique assortment of merchandise		x
Smaller dollar and time expenditures for market trips	x	
Shorter vendor lead times	x	
Payment for merchandise after delivery	x	
Advertising, promotion, and markdown money more readily available	x	
Return of slow-selling merchandise	x	

percentage, such as 20% of the landed cost, and is used for advertising, markdowns, and other contingencies. Typically, the load will still permit the sale of the foreign merchandise at prices below domestically produced merchandise of the same type while providing a "cushion" or protection factor. At the end of the season, the unused portion of the load is given back to the buyer as gross margin.

3

Merchandise Control

OVERVIEW: Once the six-month merchandise plan is adopted and acted upon, the buyer must track performance against plan. When discrepancies occur, the buyer applies various control mechanisms to modify the plan. These mechanisms are the open-to-buy, the replenishment system, and the movement vehicles—transfers, markdowns, and returns-to-vendor. These mechanisms help the buyer keep within budget, increase or decrease purchases as needed, reorder goods to meet demand, move goods, stimulate buying, minimize markdowns and losses, and maximize profits.

What does the retailer do if, after planning six months ahead, he finds that sales are far below plan because of layoffs that affect the families who shop his stores? Or because of a severe storm? Or because people are simply not buying as expected? Following the six-month plan to completion would mean a tremendous surplus of inventory and a drain on finances.

The six-month plan is not cast in concrete. The retailer must track actual activity and, if need be, modify the six-month plan. He must be able to control and move merchandise based on actual sales performance. The primary mechanisms of control are the *open-to-buy, replenishment, transfers, markdowns,* and *returns.*

Open-to-Buy

The chief control mechanism, once the six-month plan is actually set in operation, is called the open-to-buy (OTB). OTB represents the dollar limit to which a buyer is authorized to spend for receipt of merchandise during the month. The season begins with planned purchases. As the season progresses, OTB becomes the financial instrument for monitoring actual performance against plan. With this kind of monitoring, the retailer can take appropriate action based upon orders or plans for reorders. With the OTB, the buyer can react to market conditions and increase department profitability. Although the six-month merchandise plan indicates what a buyer's purchases will be for each month, a buyer often leaves some purchases uncommitted (that is, maintains an OTB) in order to take advantage of special purchases that become available during the month.

The specific objectives of OTB control are three: (1) to control commitments made against authorized purchasing limits; (2) to determine how much more, if any, can be purchased before the authorized dollar level for a month is reached; and (3) to highlight variances between planned and actual performance.

OTB, then, serves as a merchandise budget. OTB can be thought of as merchandise needed minus merchandise available, including on-orders. It provides a running balance from month to month of all sales, purchases, on-orders, receipts, and reductions.

To maintain an open-to-buy reporting system, the following data must be available (expressed in retail dollars):

- Planned sales (from six-month merchandise plan)
- Planned EOM inventory (from six-month merchandise plan)
- Planned markdowns (from six-month merchandise plan)
- Actual sales (from sales reporting system)
- Actual EOM inventory (from inventory reporting system)
- Actual markdowns (from statistical department)
- Open orders (from orders outstanding)

With this data, OTB can be determined at the beginning of the season or at any point within the season. The formulas for beginning and midseason differ slightly, but the basic concept is the same: OTB equals merchandise needed minus merchandise available.

OTB for the beginning of the season can be projected in conjunction with the six-month merchandise plan. It is calculated using this formula:

$$
\text{OTB} = \begin{array}{c}\text{Planned}\\ \text{EOM}\\ \text{inventory}\\ \text{for month 1}\end{array} + \begin{array}{c}\text{Planned}\\ \text{sales}\\ \text{for month 1}\end{array} + \begin{array}{c}\text{Planned}\\ \text{reductions}\\ \text{for month 1}\end{array} -
$$

$$
\begin{array}{c}\text{Planned}\\ \text{BOM}\\ \text{inventory}\\ \text{for month 1}\end{array} - \begin{array}{c}\text{On-orders}\\ \text{for month 1}\end{array}
$$

During a season, at the start of any month, you may want to calculate the open-to-buy based on actual sales performance. The formula differs from the beginning-of-season formula in that the actual beginning of month inventory is used:

$$
\begin{aligned}
\text{Midseason OTB} = &\ \text{Planned EOM inventory for month 2} + \text{Planned sales for month 2} + \text{Planned reductions for month 2} \\
&- \text{Actual BOM inventory for month 2} - \text{On-orders for month 2}
\end{aligned}
$$

If the result is negative, the buyer has overbought for the month. He has the option of either canceling orders or shifting orders to months where open-to-buy is available.

The month-by-month OTB calculations can be confusing because the buyer often places orders three to four months ahead. An open-to-buy form like the one shown in Figure 3-1 can simplify the problem of calculating multiple open-to-buys. This form can be used to calculate both the beginning-of-season OTB and midseason OTB. An example, based on the six-month merchandise plan, is presented in Figures 3-2 and 3-3. In Figure 3-2, the OTB for each month is calculated prior to the beginning of the season. In Figure 3-3, the OTB for each month is recalculated after one month of the new season has gone by. Whenever this form is used, the buyer knows exactly what the OTB is for the remainder of the season and for each month remaining in the season.

During the middle of a month, the buyer often wants to know the amount of OTB remaining for the month. The formula for midmonth open-to-buy involves checking the actual against the planned inventory, sales, and reductions. The complete formula is:

$$
\begin{aligned}
\text{Midmonth OTB} = &\ \text{Planned EOM inventory } less \text{ inventory on hand} + \text{Planned monthly sales } less \text{ sales to date} \\
&+ \text{Planned reductions } less \text{ reductions to date} - \text{On-orders for month}
\end{aligned}
$$

The difference between actual performance during the season, and planned performance will affect the open-to-buy in various ways (see Figure 3-4). If actual sales are above planned sales, for example, an increase in OTB will result. If actual sales are below planned sales, the OTB will decrease. In each instance the buyer must review open orders and current inventory levels and adjust purchase plans accordingly.

Figure 3-1. OPEN-TO-BUY FORM

Department: _____ Season: _____ Date: _____
Classification: _____

		Month 1	Month 2	Month 3	Month 4	Month 5	Month 6	Season Total
BOM inventory	Planned							
	Actual							
Sales	Planned							
Markdowns & employee discounts	Planned							
EOM inventory	Planned							
	Actual							
Open-to-receive	/////////	/////////	/////////					
On order	/////////	/////////	/////////					
Open-to-buy	/////////	/////////	/////////					

Figure 3-2. PLANNED MONTHLY OPEN-TO-BUY

Department: _____ Season: _____ Date: _____

		Month 1	Month 2	Month 3	Month 4	Month 5	Month 6	Season Total
BOM inventory	Planned	92,400	98,800	94,200	91,500	52,800	24,000	
	Actual							
Sales	Planned	44,000	52,000	42,800	41,600	35,200	24,000	239,600
Markdowns & employee discounts	Planned	6,300	3,900	3,400	3,400	4,200	3,200	24,400
EOM inventory	Planned	98,800	94,200	91,500	52,800	24,000	7,000	
	Actual	//////////						
Open-to-receive		//////////						
		////////// 56,700	51,300	43,500	6,300	10,600	10,200	251,000
		//////////						
On order		//////////						
		////////// 20,000	20,000					40,000
		//////////						
Open-to-buy		//////////						
		////////// 36,700	31,300	43,500	6,300	10,600	10,200	211,000

Figure 3-3. ADJUSTED MONTHLY OPEN-TO-BUY

Department: _____ Season: _____ Date: _____

		Month 1	Month 2	Month 3	Month 4	Month 5	Month 6	Season Total
BOM inventory	Planned	92,400	98,800	94,200	91,500	52,800	24,000	
	Actual	92,400	93,800	100,800				
Sales	Planned	44,000	52,000	42,800	41,600	35,200	24,000	239,600
Markdowns & employee discounts	Planned	6,300	3,900	3,400	3,400	4,200	3,200	24,400
EOM inventory	Planned	98,800	94,200	91,500	52,800	24,000	7,000	
	Actual	93,800						
Open-to-receive		/////////	56,300	43,500	6,300	10,600	10,200	125,600
On order		/////////	62,900					62,900
Open-to-buy		/////////	(6,600)	43,500	6,300	10,600	10,200	61,700

Figure 3-4. FACTORS AFFECTING OPEN-TO-BUY

Changes to Plan	Effect on OTB	Comments/Analysis
Sales above plan	Increase in OTB	Review open orders and current inventory levels.
Sales below plan	Decrease in OTB	
Markdowns higher than plan	Increase in OTB	Markdowns above plan are not desirable. There is a negative effect on the maintained markup and the gross margin.
Markdowns lower than plan	Decrease in OTB	Better than anticipated merchandise acceptance.
		Markdowns below plan may be due to increased retail sales (desirable).
		Failure to take markdowns on a timely basis.
Purchases above plan	Decrease in OTB	Desirable if sales are over plan, but not desirable if overstocking occurs.
Purchases below plan	Increase in OTB	Review stock-to-sales ratio to determine if this is desirable.
Receipts over plan	Decrease in OTB	Not desirable if sales are under plan.
Receipts under plan	Increase in OTB	Should be consistent with trend of sales.

Making this type of analysis for every component of the open-to-buy (*i.e.*, EOM inventory, sales, reductions, BOM inventory, and on-orders) can greatly improve management of the inventory investment. Retailers will be able to react quickly to market conditions. Furthermore, because they can see the effect of one component on another, the retailers will be able to apply corrective measures to the appropriate factor and to the right degree.

An OTB analysis also permits playing "what if" situations to see what adjustments are required to various OTB components if purchases are increased, if sales decrease, if markdowns are taken, etc. Each change will affect the overall OTB. Thus the OTB is an invaluable merchandising management tool. It permits the buyer to take advantage of special offers that could yield a substantial profit and, perhaps more importantly, to respond to changing market conditions in an orderly way.

Stock Replenishment

Another vital merchandise control mechanism is stock reordering. Careless reordering can bring in too much merchandise at the wrong time or keep you out of stock at the peak of a season. Either way, your profitability will suffer. Reordering, or replenishment, must be an outgrowth of a good ordering plan, against which the buyer measures actual sales data and his knowledge of developing trends in consumer purchasing patterns.

Because reordering strategies differ depending on a company's warehousing practices, we will look at replenishment at both store and warehouse.

Store Replenishment

Stock replenishment is affected by the following factors:

1. Predicted rate of sale: How fast an item will sell is more difficult to predict for some items than for others. Nevertheless, such a prediction, based on the buyer's judgment and an analysis of past sales performance, is necessary in planning a reordering strategy.

2. Frequency of information from the stores: How often will the stores furnish sales figures? Will inventory counts be possible every two weeks? Every three weeks? The more frequent the reporting of information, the greater the ease and accuracy of determining reorders.

3. Lead time for an order: How much time elapses between writing an order and placing the goods on the shelf? Consider the time needed to process the order in your office and transmit it to the vendor, who must process it, possibly manufacture it, pack it, and ship it to your store, where it is received, unpacked, marked, and shelved.

4. Presentation stock: A buyer must know how much stock is needed to display an item effectively. The quantity needed for display is an important factor in establishing the minimium stock required for an item.

5. Customer service level: Management decides what its customer service level will be. How many times out of ten will it be acceptable to say, "Sorry, we're out of that item"? To be never out of stock on any item requires a great inventory, probably greater than would be profitable. Too many out-of-stocks, however, and customers will find another store to shop in. The store image is strongly affected by this customer service level, so it must be determined with care and become part of the reordering strategy.

6. Safety stock: Tied to lead time and customer service level is safety stock. How many units are needed on hand to prevent an out-of-stock situation in the event of unusual demand or extreme delay in receiving a reorder?

7. Standard pack of item: Vendors will often pack items in particular quantities only, such as dozens. Your reorder must be sized and timed accordingly.

Reordering Methods

Three methods of reordering stock are the fixed reorder cycle method, the fixed reorder quantity method, and the model stock replenishment method.

In the *fixed reorder cycle method*, an order is placed at fixed intervals. For example, every two weeks an order will be placed, and the quantity ordered varies. The amount ordered is the difference between a predetermined maximum and the stock on hand. The maximum on-hand level (the order up to level) for the fixed reorder cycle is determined by defining the order cycle, establishing the lead time, estimating average weekly sales (rate of sale), and defining the safety stock requirement.

With the *fixed reorder quantity method*, an order is placed whenever the on-hand inventory drops to a certain level (the reorder point). Under this method, the same quantity is always reordered and the time between placing orders varies. This method requires maintaining a perpetual inventory system.

In the *model stock replenishment method*, a target level of stock for each store or ordering unit is determined. As merchandise is sold, a reorder is placed to refill the model stock. Orders are generated automatically based on the actual sales movement. Replenishment frequency can either be as sold or on the next scheduled store order, depending on the nature of the item.

The model stock replenishment method requires a perpetual unit inventory system based on capturing detailed sales information with point of sale equipment. This method generally results in the closest control over store inventories.

Short of a fully computerized model stock system, the most commonly used manual system is the fixed reorder cycle method. In this system the maximum on-hand level can be calculated as follows:

$$\begin{array}{c}\text{Maximum} \\ \text{on-hand} \\ \text{level}\end{array} = \left(\begin{array}{c}\text{Order} \\ \text{cycle}\end{array} \times \begin{array}{c}\text{Average} \\ \text{weekly sales}\end{array}\right) + \left(\begin{array}{c}\text{Lead} \\ \text{time}\end{array} \times \begin{array}{c}\text{Average} \\ \text{weekly sales}\end{array}\right) + \begin{array}{c}\text{Safety} \\ \text{stock}\end{array}$$

Assuming the order cycle = 2 weeks, lead time = 1 week, average weekly sales = 3 units/week, and safety stock = 2 units, the maximum would be:

$$\begin{aligned} \text{Maximum} &= \left(2 \text{ weeks} \times \frac{3 \text{ units/}}{\text{week}}\right) + \left(1 \text{ week} \times \frac{3 \text{ units/}}{\text{week}}\right) + 2 \text{ units} \\ &= 6 \text{ units} + 3 \text{ units} + 2 \text{ units} \\ &= 11 \text{ units} \end{aligned}$$

The fixed-reorder cycle and its relationship to inventory on hand is depicted in Figure 3-5. At the end of week 1, the merchant has five units on hand and orders six units to achieve the maximum on-hand level of eleven. Three more units are sold by the time the order is received a week later, leaving two units on hand (i.e., the planned safety stock) at the beginning of week 2. When the order was received, the stock was replenished up to eight units. By the beginning of week 3, three more units were sold and stock on hand was five units. Again six units were ordered, and at the beginning of week 4, two units were on hand when the reorder was received. During week 4, five

Figure 3-5. FIXED REORDER CYCLE REPLENISHMENT

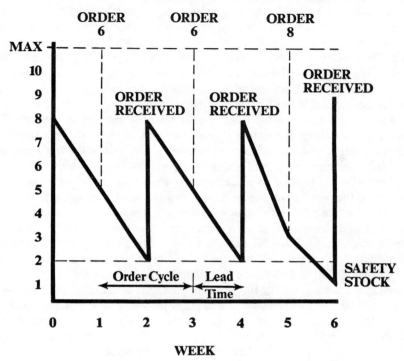

units were sold, leaving only three units on hand at the end of the week. Consequently, eight units were ordered to achieve the maximum of eleven. In week 5, only two units were sold and there was only one unit on hand before the reorder was received in week 6. Due to the increased sales in week 4, inventory on hand had dipped into the safety stock.

Warehouse Replenishment

The major differences between store and warehouse replenishment are in the areas of rate of sale, lead time, reorder cycle, on-orders, pack size, space utilization, and throughput (the rate at which goods are processed through the warehouse). Each of these factors is calculated differently for warehouse replenishment.

At the warehouse, the rate of sale considered is the *sum* of all the individual store rate-of-sale figures for an item. Warehouse replenishment considers how many stores will order an item instead of how many customers will buy this item from a department. This estimated rate of sale is often statistically determined, based on past sales and projected future sales.

Vendor lead times are much more uncertain at the warehouse level than at the store level because when the order is placed, it is frequently not known whether the goods are in the vendor's finished inventory or whether they have to be manufactured. If the items have to be manufactured, the vendor's lead time will be drastically increased. The efficiency of order processing also varies from vendor to vendor and will significantly affect the overall delivery time to the warehouse. Vendor shutdowns during specific periods, as well as busy seasons when shipments or order processing are delayed, must also be considered in predicting lead time.

Most warehouses use the fixed reorder quantity method of ordering. That is, the warehouse stock status is constantly monitored and, as the stock approaches a reorder point, an order is placed. The amount ordered is based upon the frequency of reorders, the lead time, outstanding orders, and the potential future sales.

Typically, the buyer uses a stock status report that provides the current inventory position in the warehouse, a past history of total sales or shipments for the item, and an indication of a minimum stock level or reorder point.

The warehouse stock status reports permit the buyer to analyze the seasonal variation in rate of sale. Data for the last three to six months will reveal developing trends, and data for last year will reveal a fall-off or acceleration in this year's performance. Seasonal demands occur even in a staple stock environment. August, for example, is typically a strong month for paper and pencils because of the back-to-school season, and the buyer must consider this in plans for warehouse replenishment.

In determining the reorder quantity, the buyer must also consider the total costs involved in purchasing the inventory and maintaining the inventory in stock. The objective for the buyer is to minimize the total cost incurred. This total cost includes factors such as order processing costs, inventory investment costs (interest), quantity discounts, and warehousing costs.

In making practical replenishment decisions, the buyer must also consider the level of service maintained. Level of service is a measure of the percentage of the time the retailer is guaranteed being in-stock. No one can expect to be in-stock 100% of the time, but management usually sets a policy that will prevent the stores from losing customers. As the level of service increases, the average level of inventory on-hand also increases. This increase in inventory level also increases the inventory investment and the carrying costs associated with financing that inventory. The objective for the retailer is to utilize sound inventory management policies to maintain the minimum level of inventory for a given level of service.

Advantages of Warehousing

In some instances, considerable savings can result from warehousing certain items instead of stocking them in the store. These savings result from:

1. Reduced inventory level—Because merchandise is kept at a convenient, centrally located warehouse, individual stores can reduce their safety stocks

without a deterioration of the service level. Response to unusual demand patterns can be maintained.

2. Minimizing out-of-stock conditions—Out-of-stock seldom occurs if the merchandise is centrally located and available for distribution on demand.

3. Inventory control—Merchandise at retail stores usually cannot be controlled as efficiently as central warehouse stock because many employees work part-time. The warehouse has a fulltime staff whose sole responsibility is stock control and distribution.

4. Reduction of interstore transfers—By distributing merchandise to the point of sale in response to customer demand, redistribution or interstore transfers are reduced or eliminated.

5. Optimizing freight costs—Warehousing permits consolidating small shipments (which would have been delivered by separate trucks to individual stores) into a large shipment delivered to one location at advantageous freight rates. Shipments to the stores can also be arranged efficiently, resulting in an additional savings.

Merchandise for the Warehouse

Warehousing certain types of merchandise can result in increased margins, but the pooled merchandise must be selected carefully. The following criteria should be applied in assigning items to pooled stock.

1. Items with moderate sales volume—Items that sell at a moderate pace are best for pooled stocks. Pooled stocks minimize the on-site inventory needed to maintain customer service level in multiple retail locations and also reduce costs for transportation through consolidated deliveries. On the other hand, items that move very fast can often be ordered in large enough quantities to gain advantageous freight rates, making direct shipment from vendor to store economical. With fast movers, it makes sense to locate goods at the point of sale to avoid an out-of-stock situation and loss of sales. With slow movers, it is often possible to have an entire inventory on display at retail. Stock inventory is not really a problem with slow-moving items.

2. Bulky merchandise—Space utilization at the point of sale is an important consideration for the retailer who wants to maximize the profitability of each square foot of the store. Using this space to stock large bulky items such as snow blowers can be a waste of a valuable resource. Pooling stock of bulky merchandise in a central warehouse frees space in the store. Bulk and size, therefore, are criteria to consider when deciding upon where to stock an item.

3. Long lead time from vendor—If an item has a long lead time from vendor to store, that item is a candidate for pooled stock. Generally, pooled stock affords a short lead time from warehouse to store.

4. Store order quantities less than vendor pack—With pooled stock, vendor master cartons can be broken into demand lots at the warehouse, thus providing balanced stock and appropriate assortments at the point of sale. This flexibility will eliminate out-of-stock or over-inventory conditions at the store, while still meeting customer demands.

5. Nonperishable and nonprecious merchandise—Merchandise that is subject to spoilage, such as plants, and items subject to a high degree of pilferage, such as jewelry, are not good candidates for pooled stocks. Pooled stocking should be reserved for merchandise that is nonperishable and nonprecious.

6. Large number of selling locations—As the number of stores increases, so does the amount of inventory. Pooling stocks permits better inventory control as well as greater freight savings in a growing company. Any operation with a large number of selling locations should consider the advantages of pooled stock.

Reordering Staple, Decorative, and Seasonal Goods

Staple goods present the least difficulty in reordering. For such merchandise, which must be on hand all year, week in and week out, the numbers are determined once, and then the orders are repeated either at fixed intervals or by fixed quantity. Past experience with a staple item permits reasonable accuracy in projecting how many will be sold in a given period of time. Working with the vendors on a regular basis, the buyer knows how much time is needed to process and receive orders and how much safety stock is needed to meet customer demand in spite of unusual delays and selling spurts.

Decorative and fashion items present a more difficult reordering problem than staple goods. Sales of such items are more erratic than staples and more judgment is required of the retailer in setting reorder quantities. Sales of decorative goods must be watched closely and those items that sell well must be reordered quickly. The buyer pays particular attention to the colors, styles, and sizes of items that are moving. The quantity reordered will vary from item to item, even from color to color. Reordering tapers off as the selling does; as the season progresses, the buyer places fewer and fewer reorders.

Judging when the season for decorative and fashion goods is ending can be a major problem for the inexperienced buyer. Particular styles of wall coverings and ceiling tiles, for example, may lose popularity as quickly as they gained it. Reordering at the crest of demand, and receiving the order within a short lead time, will make a great purchase and turn high profits. Reordering or receiving merchandise when the demand is fading results in a case of too much too late.

Standard reordering methods cannot be used as readily for decorative fad goods as they can for staples. Decorative or fashion items are unique and must be tracked individually to determine the reorder and markdown candidates. The percentage sell-off in a given period of time can provide an indication of a fast seller, but experience and judgment are required to determine what rate of sell-off represents a fast seller.

Seasonal goods present still another reordering problem. For the span of the season, these goods should be treated like staple goods with a "never-out-of-stock" label. But because their season is not very long, the fixed reorder cycle method cannot be used for seasonal items, or at least not to the same degree. Seasonal merchandise requires careful monitoring and quick, decisive reactions to the selling patterns.

Garden hoses, for example, would be a staple item from March through September. A certain level of stock must be maintained during these months or considerable sales will be lost. Processing and receiving reorders during this time can be difficult since all stores are probably buying from the same vendors whose peak production will not be sufficient to meet total demand. The retailer, therefore, must set a minimum stock figure and consider the limitations of vendors when planning reorders. Studying past sales data can help determine the date at which to reduce that minimum figure and the date to stop all reorders completely.

Keeping a minimum stock requirement for too long can result in an excess of garden hoses on your half-price table. While some merchandise can be held until next year, doing so means taking up valuable warehouse space and tying up capital that could be used for purchasing new merchandise.

The retailer's judgment is required in reordering many items in the store. With thousands of items for sale, however, as many items as possible should be reordered by a standard reordering method. This makes the process more efficient and systematic and reserves the retailer's time for the unique items.

In many stores, reordering is done by computer. In some of the more sophisticated systems, the computer automatically prepares reorders. Some systems even deduct the purchase from the store's or buyer's open-to-buy.

Regardless of the method, though, reordering is a critical element in merchandising and requires as much thought as original merchandise plans. Attention to detail, as painstaking and routine as it may be, does pay dividends.

Merchandise Movement Decisions

Other means of controlling merchandise are available besides the OTB and reordering. The analysis of sales reports, unit control information, fast and slow seller reports, and in-season stock counts provide the buyer with valuable information on the performance of a department. Three basic decisions can be made from the analysis of this information:

- Transfer
- Markdown
- Return-to-Vendor

Transfers

The decision to transfer merchandise between stores is based upon store-to-store comparisons of the trend in sales and sell-off, store-to-store comparisons of the weeks of stock remaining in inventory, and the number of weeks remaining in the season. Any imbalance in the inventory or weeks of stock among the stores in the chain suggests stock transfer opportunities. Those stores with poor sales patterns and a large inventory can transfer merchandise to a store needing inventory, rather than having the better-selling store order the merchandise directly from the vendor. For merchandise of a seasonal nature, the retailer must be cautious in analyzing data early in the season; sufficient time should be allowed for sales trend information to develop.

Markdowns

Markdowns or price changes may be required when customers will not pay the original retail price for an item. Lowering the retail price represents a reduction in the market value of the merchandise but not in the invoice cost or the replacement cost of the merchandise. The effect of markdowns is to decrease the gross margin and the maintained markup.

The need for markdowns can be minimized if the retailer is aware of the factors that lead to price changes, knows which ones are controllable and acts accordingly. Those factors that are controllable include:

- Setting an unrealistically high initial markup.
- Failing to take markdowns at the most advantageous time.
- Overestimating customer demand.
- Failing to realize when a fad has peaked.
- Purchasing unwanted merchandise.
- Using a high stock/sales ratio (slow reaction to reverses in trends).
- Carrying too many styles or items within a specific code or class (over-assortment).
- Failing to know the customer.
- Failing to fill in merchandise on the floor properly.

Uncontrollable factors include severe, unanticipated weather conditions, shopworn merchandise, unexpected drops in demand, and carrying items that are traditionally sold at markdown prices, such as furs.

Other factors contributing to markdowns that may or may not be controlled depending on circumstances include:

- Desire to stimulate store traffic in connection with a holiday or special event or promotion.
- Poorly made merchandise.
- Desire to maintain an established company image by offering markdowns on certain merchandise at specific times.
- Late deliveries (foreign and domestic).

- Nondeliveries that were replaced with secondary selection or vendor.
- Mismates.

Returns to Vendors

A return to vendor (RTV) should be considered as an alternative to deep markdowns. Vendor practices, past experience, product history, and current overall economic conditions have major impacts on whether or not a vendor will allow a return. A return is more likely to be allowed at the beginning of the season or early midseason when merchandise can be sold to other retailers. This is especially true if the "merchandise problem" appears to be unique to the particular retailer, as when test merchandise not normally carried by the store is rejected by the customers. However, if the merchandise has wide customer rejections at a number of retail outlets, the vendor might provide a markdown allowance to the retailer realizing that, once returned, the merchandise will probably never be sold to another retailer.

4

Computer Systems and Merchandise Management

OVERVIEW: The computer is an invaluable aid in processing the large number of transactions and items of information involved in managing a retail operation. The amount of data needed for merchandise planning, for example, would require hundreds of man-hours to produce, whereas a well-programmed computer can generate the information in seconds. Not only does the computer store, process, and generate sales and purchase information, but it can assist in creating and revising merchandise plans. Computerized Purchase Order Management systems are also an integral part of modern merchandise managing.

In the previous chapters, we have looked at methods of planning merchandise purchases, tracking inventory, and replenishing stock. Most retailers would probably agree that the concepts behind these activities reflect basic common sense. To implement such planning and control procedures, however, is a major undertaking. Consider the thousands of purchase orders, the volume of merchandise, the number of stores and distribution centers in a chain, and the repeating cycle of buy-ship-receive-sell-buy. The number of transactions, steps, and decisions is staggering.

Enter the computer. Although many retailers have been slow to recognize the value of the computer, experience has proven that this electronic wizard is a boon to the industry. Tasks that would have required hundreds of man-hours can be done in minutes by a properly programmed computer. In this chapter we will take a closer look at computer-aided systems of merchandise planning, performance analysis, and purchase order management.

Computer-Aided Merchandise Planning

Most retailers recognize the need for some sort of unit or dollar plan to control inventories and purchases. But few companies have successfully implemented a formal merchandise planning process. The reason is that even a simple merchandise planning process requires a carload of information from a variety of sources. The information has to be collected, stored, manipulated, and conveyed in a way that is meaningful to the users. A great deal of time, energy, and, consequently, dollars are required to do that manually.

For serious planning, retailers must automate the merchandise planning process. The obstacles that make merchandise planning difficult on a manual basis are the very things that the computer is good at overcoming. Specifically, the computer takes on the burden of storing data, updating it, performing complex calculations, and producing useful reports. More and more companies are realizing the benefits of using an automated merchandise planning system (MPS) to improve the quality of merchandise management. The tasks involved in planning include:

- Collecting prerequisite information
- Creating a base plan
- Revising the plan before the season
- Updating and revising the plan during the season

How an automated MPS can facilitate each step of the planning process is examined in the following pages.

Step 1: Collecting Prerequisite Information

The computer is invaluable in the first step of merchandise planning—collecting prerequisite information. The minimum information requirements for a merchandise planning process include:

- Sales and inventory history at the planning level.
- Current orders at the planning level.
- Reductions (markdowns, employee discounts, shortages) history at the planning level if planning is to be done in dollars.

The more information to be tracked and reported on, the more information must be supplied. The sheer volume of data to be collected makes the computer a must.

Consider, for example, a company with two six-month seasons and ten departments. Each department has ten classes, each of which is broken into ten sub-classes. In the simplest case, for monthly unit planning for the chain, data on sales, inventory history, and current orders must be collected. This amounts to 36,000 individual figures annually [12 months x 10 departments x 10 classes x 10 subclasses x 3 information categories (sales, inventory, current orders) = 36,000]. To do weekly dollar planning by store for a ten-store chain and include information on the three types of reductions, the number of start-up figures soars to 312,000.

Many retailers already have these figures in existing computerized sales, inventory, and purchase order management systems. To translate the data manually into meaningful form for merchandise planning is a Herculean task. But by feeding the existing systems into the MPS, that mammoth clerical effort can be reduced to a simple file conversion job that the computer can run in seconds.

Step 2: Creating a Base Plan

After collecting the requisite information, the second step in merchandise planning is the creation of a base plan. The base plan is the plan for sales that are flat on a per-store (or per-square-foot) basis as compared to last year. The sample base plan in Figure 4-1 shows a chain-wide monthly unit plan for the socket set subclass of the XYZ Company. In Figure 4-1, let's assume that the number of stores (and hence chain-wide sales) has risen 10% since last year's spring/summer season. Therefore, the sales plan figures (line 3) are 10% greater than those of last year (line 2). The base plan assumes the weeks-of-supply (WOS) plan (line 11) is a copy of last year's WOS (line 10) and generates the inventory plan (line 7) to support that WOS. Stock/sales (S/S) ratios (lines 14 and 15) are computed by the system. Current orders (line 17) are taken from the purchase order management system. Finally, the computer calculates open-to-buy (OTB) on line 18 through the usual "need minus have" equation.

Of the 82 numbers on the plan, none requires manual input. Last year's sales and inventory and this year's current orders (21 entered figures) are fed in from existing automated systems. Even the single figure store growth (10% in Figure 4-1) can be computed if a two-year file of store counts or square footage is available to the computer. The MPS computes and reports the remaining 61 figures in a fraction of a second.

Could this particular plan be prepared without an automated system? Consider again the example in step 1 of monthly planning for 1,000 subclasses. Creating base unit plans at the subclass level each year would require entry of 42,000 numbers and 122,000 computations. Even the most efficient clerical team would not attempt this job manually. Without automation, the would-be planner must resort to a less formal, less detailed plan and a lot of guesswork.

Step 3: Revising Plan Before Season

The base plan is unlikely to satisfy serious buyers. They undoubtedly will want to revise their plan according to the economic climate, market or fashion trends, and changes in company merchandising policy. Sample types of revisions include:

Figure 4-1. BASE PLAN BEFORE SEASON

XYZ COMPANY MERCHANDISE PLAN (UNITS)

Merchandise Mgr: Jones   Buyer: Smith
Year: 1983   Season: Spring/Summer   Dept.: Hardware   Class: Tools   Sub-Class: Socket Sets

	Pre-season	Feb. (4 Wks)	March (5 Wks)	April (4 Wks)	Qtr. 1	May (4 Wks)	June (5 Wks)	July (4 Wks)	Qtr. 2	Season
1. Sales										
2. Last year	10	20	20	20	60	30	30	30	90	150
3. Plan	11	22	22	22	66	33	33	33	99	165
4. Actual										
5. Inv.—EOM										
6. Last year	40	30	35	60	—	60	30	0	—	—
7. Plan	44	33	39	66	—	66	33	0	—	—
8. Actual										
9. Weeks of supply—EOM										
10. Last year	9	7	6	9	—	9	4	0	—	—
11. Plan	9	7	6	9	—	9	4	0	—	—
12. Actual										
13. Stock/sales—avg.										
14. Last year	2	1.8	1.6	2.4	—	2	1.5	0.5	—	—
15. Plan	2	1.8	1.6	2.4	—	2	1.5	0.5	—	—
16. Actual										
17. Current orders	45	10	20	20	50	0	0	0	0	50
18. Open-to-buy	10	1	8	29	38	33	0	0	33	71

- Exchange weeks in the plan (*e.g.*, Easter comes one week earlier than last year) and recompute WOS, S/S, and OTB.
- Change sales plan, hold WOS constant, and recompute required inventory, S/S, and OTB.
- Change inventory, hold sales constant, and recompute WOS, S/S, and OTB.
- Change WOS, hold sales constant, and recompute required inventory, S/S, and OTB.

Since most of the revisions affect calculations in months both before and after the month(s) changed, the calculations must be redone for the entire season. For example, a change of June's planned sales in Figure 4-1, holding inventory constant, changes May's WOS; a change of June's inventory, holding sales constant, raises July's S/S ratio. Without a computer system to do this work, even our simple XYZ Company scenario becomes unwieldy because each revision requires so many calculations.

Once freed from the number-crunching chore, the buyer/planner can not only make the plan more realistic but can also answer "what if" questions quickly. For example, "What happens to my monthly OTB if sales fall 15% short of my plan? If I lower my opening inventory? If management restricts me to 6 WOS? If I cancel half of my April order? If I achieve double June's sales plan with a successful promotion?" Without an automated system, the manual computations required consume so much time that such exploratory questions are rarely asked. Buyers are left with only their intuition to cover these real possibilities in their buying plans.

Step 4: Updating and Revising Plan During Season

Once the season is in progress, actual sales, inventory, and current order figures should update the plan each week. Planned figures are the prediction, actual figures the reality. Open-to-buy and resultant buying decisions must be based on actual conditions.

As before, updating the plan with actual figures affects calculations in months other than the current month. Figure 4-2 continues the example from Figure 4-1, showing actual results for the preseason period and February. Although updates have been made only through February, OTB has changed for March from 8 to 21. Actual WOS and S/S figures are computed and reported, enabling the buyer to compare plan to actual and to spot trends in progress. In Figure 4-2, actual sales are exceeding the plan, which may result in an out-of-stock condition in socket sets. If the buyer believes this trend will continue, he can quickly use the MPS revision tools described in step 3 to raise the sales plan and compute the corresponding increased inventory and OTB while there is still time to place orders with vendors.

As in the previous steps, the computer is indispensable in collecting actual figures from other systems, updating the planning reports automatically, computing and reporting resultant changes in WOS, S/S ratio, and OTB, and helping the buyer revise plans based on the latest selling performance.

Figure 4-2. PLAN UPDATED DURING SEASON

XYZ COMPANY MERCHANDISE PLAN (UNITS)

Merchandise Mgr: Jones   Buyer: Smith
Year 1983   Season: Spring/Summer   Dept.: Hardware   Class: Tools   Subclass: Socket Sets

	Pre-season	(4 Wks) Feb.	(5 Wks) March	(4 Wks) April	Qtr. 1	(4 Wks) May	(5 Wks) June	(4 Wks) July	Qtr. 2	Season
1. Sales										
2. Last year	10	20	20	20	60	30	30	30	90	150
3. Plan	11	22	22	22	66	33	33	33	99	165
4. Actual	15	30								
5. Inv.—EOM										
6. Last year	40	30	35	60	—	60	30	0	—	—
7. Plan	44	33	39	66	—	66	33	0	—	—
8. Actual	40	20								
9. Weeks of supply—EOM										
10. Last year	9	7	6	9	—	9	4	0	—	—
11. Plan	9	7	6	9	—	9	4	0	—	—
12. Actual	6.3	4.5								
13. Stock/sales—avg.										
14. Last year	2	1.8	1.6	2.4	—	2	1.5	0.5	—	—
15. Plan	2	1.8	1.6	2.4	—	2	1.5	0.5	—	—
16. Actual	1.3	1.0								
17. Current orders	—	—	20	20	40	0	0	0	0	40
18. Open-to-buy	—	—	21	29	50	33	0	0	33	83

MPS Refinements

The MPS presented above is a simple model. Several refinements and variations can be introduced to customize the merchandise plan or provide additional tools to the buyer/planner.

First, planning can be done in dollars instead of units. Unit planning is helpful in year-to-year comparisons because units are constant and not subject to price inflation. But because the buyer's OTB is ultimately a measure of how many dollars he can spend, dollar planning becomes very important. Dollar planning, however, requires more data collection, updating, and calculating than unit planning. For example, in addition to sales, inventory, and current orders, the reports and the OTB must also include markdowns, employee discounts, and shortages.

Planning can also be done at a more detailed level than the chain level. For example, for a chain with only a few stores, where distribution decisions are made by buyers, plans can be developed by store. The increased detail in the plan demands that the sales, inventory, and purchase order systems track by store to feed the MPS. It is easier to generate plans by subclass by store if subclasses are defined as percentages of classes and if stores are defined as percentages of the chain. This allows the planner to specify higher level plans and then have the system automatically break them down to the more detailed levels.

Some retailers prefer to add sales and merchandise flow information to the plan reports for a more complete analysis of how goods are moving. The analysis might include:

- Store counts or square footage for this year and last year by week to show store growth.
- Breakdown of the sales plan between new and established stores to permit more conservative planning for stores that are building their clientele.
- Comparative ratios for sales, inventory, WOS, and S/S, such as actual-to-plan for this year and last year, last year to this year for plan and actual, per store averages for last year and this year, plan and actual.
- A second current orders line for planned (not yet official) orders and a second OTB line showing what OTB will be if those orders are placed.

Another refinement is to factor lead time into the system. The typical planning report tells the buyer how much to buy to support sales and inventory in a given month. If a list of lead times by vendor (or style, class, etc.) is maintained as part of the MPS, the system can report when to buy, as well as how much.

The Microcomputer

Automated MPS's do not necessarily require large computers. A case in point is a major ladies apparel chain that made very effective use of a simplified MPS on a personal computer (microcomputer). The system enabled the firm to reduce excessively high inventories. While working with this smaller system, management also refined its requirements for a more comprehensive MPS on a large, centrally located mainframe computer.

Whether on a microcomputer or a mainframe, merchandise planning is essential to controlling a company's buying activity. With intelligent use of a computerized MPS, buyers are freed from the chore of sifting through and manipulating mountains of data. They can, instead, concentrate on the qualitative and creative aspects of their jobs.

Analyzing Store and Merchandise Performance

Merchandise planning is at one end of the retail cycle. Assessment of performance is at the other. The retailer must know how the plans hold up in the marketplace. Like the battlefield tactician, the retailer must be able to change targets, modify approaches, and reassign resources to meet current demands and expectations. This kind of flexibility requires up-to-date information on what is actually happening. Equipped with software customized to the needs of the retailer, the computer can generate a variety of up-to-date performance analyses. Once the retailer knows where the problems in performance are, corrective measures can then be taken.

Performance Ranking

One type of report that can lead to improved store operations ranks each store on predefined sets of merchandise information such as profits, sales, gross margin, variance from sales plan, sales per square foot, markdown percentage, maintained markup, number of out-of-stocks, salesperson productivity, and so on. Reporting performance in a ranked listing (best at the top, worst at the bottom) can develop a healthy competitive spirit among store management at all levels. No one likes to be at the bottom of his peer group, especially when all peers know where each of the others stands. Any good manager will take positive steps to improve his or her performance and move up the ranking ladder.

To develop an effective reporting system based on store performance, ranking requires some planning. First, performance criteria must be selected that are equitable and can be translated into action steps for corrective measures.

Secondly, not all stores can readily be compared together. That is, while a geographical grouping is helpful in measuring performance of regional and district operations, a different categorization is probably more useful in evaluating individual store performance. A better measure of performance results when stores are placed into categories that match the merchandising concept for that group. For example, if merchandise is planned differently for downtown stores and rural stores, or for large stores and small stores, then the stores should be placed into those categories when performance is evaluated.

Figure 4-3. STORE PERFORMANCE BY REGION/DISTRICT

Region 01—East   District 05—New York

Store	Units or $	Sales (Thousands) STD Act.	STD Plan	Last 4 Wks Act.	Last 4 Wks Plan	Last Week Act.	Last Week Plan	Average Transaction Amount STD	PTD	LW	Average Unit Retail Amount Sales STD	PTD	LW	On-Hand Inv.	Inventory Ship LW	On-Hand LW	Units Sq/Ft	Markdowns STD	LW	Gross Margin $ Plan	Act.	Variance
21	U	42.6	40.8	6.2	6.8	3.5	3.9	1.6	1.2	1.25					360	1,486	1.3	4,367	443			
	$	430.8	412.3	67.6	71.2	37.4	43.5	20.4	18.7	19.4	8.7	7.2	7.5	14.3	3,651	15,261	10.2	8,764	906	28	25	(3)
22	U	25.1	30.5	4.0	4.8	1.5	1.6	1.9	1.5	1.4					300	1,200	2.5	3,800	425	—	—	—
	$	405.4	394.1	38.1	40.0	10.4	15.0	21.0	20.0	19.5	8.1	6.5	6.8	12.0	3,890	6,200	18.1	7,811	879	25	21	(4)

STD = Season to date; PTD = Plan to date; LW = Last week.

(District, Region and Company totals would follow store detail lines.)

Ranking stores within their own categories will produce results that more closely match merchandising plans. Ranking by relevant category also makes it easier to see differences that can be traced to operational problems. This means that corrective action can more readily be taken.

Store Performance by Region

A report on store performance by region or district can provide a summary of actual overall store performance versus plan objectives. This report can rank stores on sales, the average transaction amount, average limit retail amount, inventory, markdowns, and gross margins. With this information (see Figure 4-3), management can see at a glance how each store is doing compared to the others in the same region or district. Such a comparison will help store operations assess the ways the stores are run.

Some companies want all stores in a region to adhere strictly to a uniform operational program, while other companies encourage flexibility in dealing with factors unique to particular stores. Thus company policy and the manager's judgment must be applied in determining whether or not differences between the performance of one store and another represent operational problems.

Merchandise Performance by Store Type

Reporting merchandise performance by store type permits an analysis of the departmental selling mix in various stores. The report provides sales and inventory by department by store within a group of stores (see Figure 4-4). Since all stores do not have the same potential, more equitable evaluation is possible if stores can be classified by size, by volume, by climate (tropical area, cold weather), or by location (downtown, strip, mall). Companies using these breakdowns will most often do their buying accordingly, with all stores within a specific classification receiving essentially the same merchandise.

A report on merchandise performance by store type might reveal that not all stores within the aggregate are performing in the same way. The sales pattern in one small store may be more like that of the downtown stores. In this case the store would be reassigned to a more appropriate category. In many cases, merchandising is not the problem. If the problem is one of poor display or inadequate staffing, store operations would also be involved in analyzing the reasons for the deviation and correcting the situation.

Store Variance

A store variance report is basically exception reporting on merchandise by department. It alerts management of store performance that varies significantly from plan. Such reports can be produced on a company-wide basis or in more manageable and meaningful breakdowns by region, district, type of store, or even by individual stores.

Figure 4-4. MERCHANDISE PERFORMANCE BY STORE TYPE

DEPARTMENT

Store Type	Store		10		20		30		40		50		60		All Merchandise	
			Sales	% of Dept.	Sales	% of Dept.	Sales	% of Dept.	Sales	% of Dept.	Sales	% of Dept.	Sales	% of Dept.	Sales	% of all Merch.
Downtown	1	Sales	513	32.6	141	25.8	84	15.4	212	34.6	—	—	—	—	2,599	38.0
		% of Store	32.0		8.8		5.3		13.3		—		—		100.0	
	2	Sales	475	30.1	196	35.8	214	39.2	195	31.9	—	—	—	—	1,765	26.0
		% of Store	26.9		11.1		12.1		11.0		—		—		100.0	
	3	Sales	275	17.4	96	17.6	145	26.5	121	19.8	—	—	—	—	1,582	23.0
		% of Store	25.4		8.9		13.4		11.2		—		—		100.0	
	4	Sales	313	19.9	114	20.8	196	35.8	84	13.7	—	—	—	—	911	13.0
		% of Store	22.2		8.1		13.9		6.0		—		—		100.0	
Total Downtown		Sales	1,576	100.0	547	100.0	639	100.0	612	100.0	—	—	—	—	6,857	100.0
		% of Downtown	22.9		7.9		9.3		8.9		—		—		100.0	

Example of type of report useful to store operations.

Stores are ranked by total sales.

Figure 4-5. STORE VARIANCE

Region 01—East   District 05—New York   Attribute: Urban High Volume

	Sales (Thousands)					
	STD		Last 4 Wks		Last Week	
Store	Act.	Plan	Act.	Plan	Act.	Plan
35	40	50	10	11	3	3
36	80	100	12	14	3	2
37	50	100	12	12	5	4
38	96	120	20	25	4	4

(District, region, and company totals would follow store detail lines.)

Let us assume that the variance report of four stores categorized as "urban—high volume" shows that three of the stores are 20% below plan in the camera department, but one store is 50% below plan (see Figure 4-5). Merchandising would use this information to alter its plan for this aggregate of stores, but store operations could act on that information and try to determine why that one store is so far below the others in its group. Store operations could look into areas such as deliveries, mishandling of goods due to poor or insufficient help, theft, or poor display. Perhaps the poor performance can be explained by something as simple as emergency maintenance that made that department inaccessible for a period of time. If store operations can determine the reason, then a remedy can be tried or an explanation given. The key is that peer ranking will help promote corrective actions by the personnel responsible for the store that is performing poorly.

Other worthwhile variance reports that can be generated by a good computerized merchandise information system include variance in gross margin, open-to-buy, markdowns, cumulative markdown, and shrinkage.

Creating Dialog

Another benefit of performance reports and rankings is that a healthy dialog can be spurred between store operations and merchandising, with the result that store operations will have more involvement in planning. Store managers, for example, will now have documentation on which to challenge buying decisions that might negatively affect performance in their stores. This dialog can result in a more compatible blend of merchandising and store operations objectives, a blend that can only help to improve company performance.

Purchase Order Management

The computer plays a critical role in purchase order management (POM). Because of the pivotal role of the purchase order in the merchandise system, automated POM is an integral part of the total retail information system.

POM has a direct bearing on open-to-buy, inventory management, receiving, and accounts payable. The purchase order, whether produced manually or automatically, notifies the vendor to ship goods, alerts the receiving and checking functions to accept merchandise and prepare it for sale, allocates a department's open-to-buy, and notifies accounts payable of the impending liability.

Automating the purchasing function affects several processes besides purchase order preparation. The integrated POM system provides input to receiving, marking, inventory control, and accounts payable. It adjusts open-to-buy amounts and, if purchase orders include store distribution breakdowns, tells the distribution department how much to ship to each store.

Ultimately, POM facilitates getting the goods to the right place at the right time. To do that, POM speeds up a number of intermediary steps:

1. POM provides a method of input into the automated unit inventory system. This keeps the warehouse or distribution center alerted.

2. POM provides basic input into store inventory accounting systems. Out-of-stocks and overstocks are reduced.

3. POM provides accurate and current information for open-to-buy and on-order. Buyers work with up-to-date information.

4. POM increases buyer and administrative productivity. Accurate, timely data reduces phone calls, double-checking, reordering, and canceling.

5. POM controls paper work. Information is keyed into the PO once and the data is transmitted automatically to the various functions.

6. POM improves the flow of merchandise to the selling floor. This is the end result.

Phases of POM

There are four phases in the POM system: purchase order entry, merchandise processing, distribution processing, and invoice processing.

Phase I of the system is Purchase Order Entry (Figure 4-6). The buyer decides to purchase and makes the PO entry. In doing so he selects a vendor and issues special instructions for each purchase. A key point in this phase is order approval. It is important that purchasing be kept in the hands of management, not the computer.

Once the order is approved, it enters the POM system. At that point, the PO data is processed to generate the documents and reports needed, including vendor analysis, open orders, PO status, and exception reports.

Figure 4-6. PURCHASE ORDER ENTRY

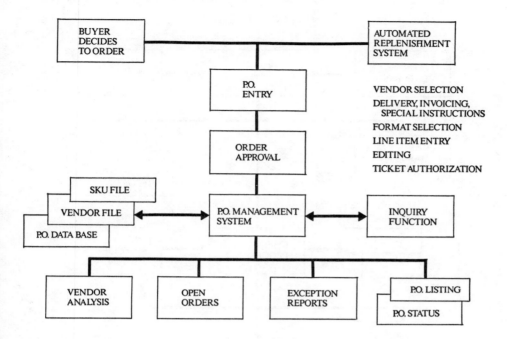

Phase II, Merchandise Processing (Figure 4-7), begins when the merchandise arrives. With the information generated by the PO, merchandise is received, checked for exceptions, ticketed, and prepared for distribution.

In Phase III, Distribution Processing (Figure 4-8), merchandise is allocated and shipped to the store. This is the key point for controlling the billing to stores.

Phase IV, Invoice Processing (Figure 4-9), produces the invoice, using information from the original PO and the exception reports. The invoice is adjusted to reflect actual receipts. As it is paid, the account payable is reduced accordingly.

POM Enhancements

A number of companies have been able to add state-of-the-art enhancements to their POM systems. One such enhancement is on-line interactive purchase order development and entry. The computer is programmed to guide the buyer through the entry of the PO by querying him for the data needed—vendor, style, quantity, cost, retail price, and so on.

Automated distributor-planner functions is an enhancement especially important to specialty shops and departments with post-distribution. The system uses histor-

Figure 4-7. MERCHANDISE PROCESSING

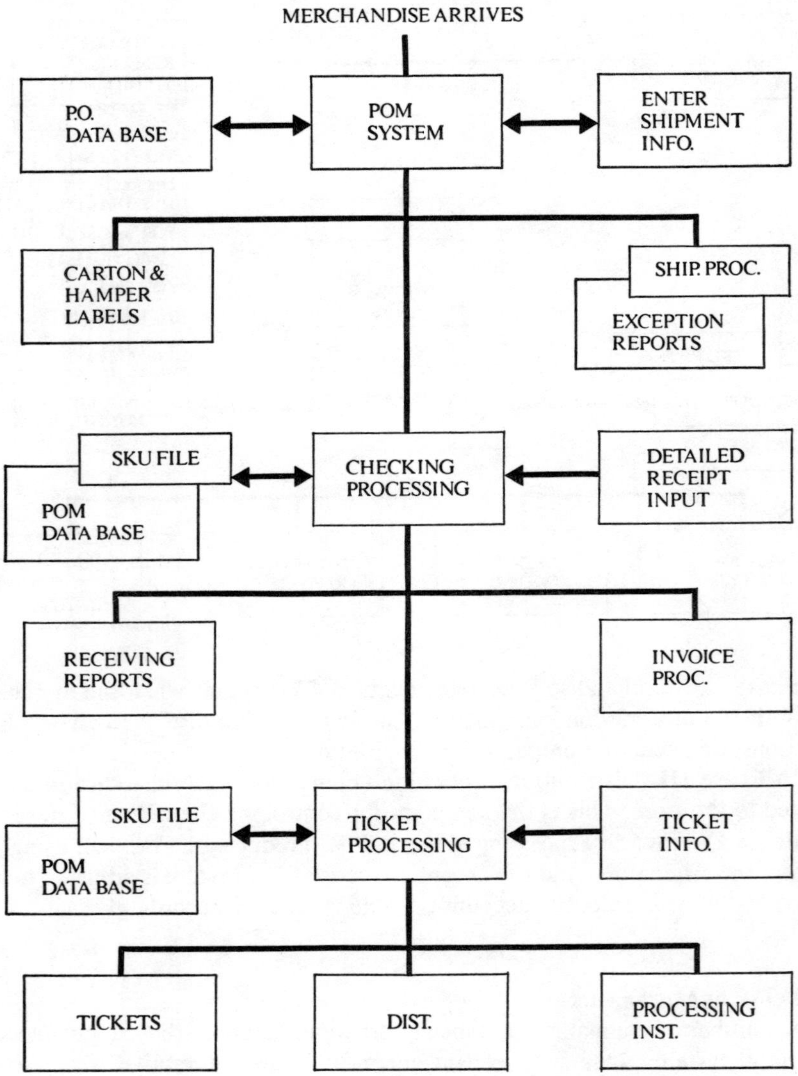

MERCHANDISE ARRIVES

```
┌─────────────┐        ┌─────────────┐        ┌─────────────┐
│ P.O.        │◄──────►│ POM         │◄──────►│ ENTER       │
│ DATA BASE   │        │ SYSTEM      │        │ SHIPMENT    │
│             │        │             │        │ INFO.       │
└─────────────┘        └─────────────┘        └─────────────┘

       ┌─────────────┐              ┌─────────────┐
       │ CARTON &    │              │ SHIP. PROC. │
       │ HAMPER      │          ┌───┴─────────────┐
       │ LABELS      │          │ EXCEPTION       │
       └─────────────┘          │ REPORTS         │
                                └─────────────────┘

   ┌─────────────┐    ┌─────────────┐    ┌─────────────┐
   │ SKU FILE    │◄──►│ CHECKING    │◄───│ DETAILED    │
┌──┴─────────────┐    │ PROCESSING  │    │ RECEIPT     │
│ POM            │    │             │    │ INPUT       │
│ DATA BASE      │    └─────────────┘    └─────────────┘
└────────────────┘

   ┌─────────────┐              ┌─────────────┐
   │ RECEIVING   │              │ INVOICE     │
   │ REPORTS     │              │ PROC.       │
   └─────────────┘              └─────────────┘

   ┌─────────────┐    ┌─────────────┐    ┌─────────────┐
   │ SKU FILE    │◄──►│ TICKET      │◄───│ TICKET      │
┌──┴─────────────┐    │ PROCESSING  │    │ INFO.       │
│ POM            │    │             │    │             │
│ DATA BASE      │    └─────────────┘    └─────────────┘
└────────────────┘

   ┌─────────────┐    ┌─────────────┐    ┌─────────────┐
   │ TICKETS     │    │ DIST.       │    │ PROCESSING  │
   │             │    │             │    │ INST.       │
   └─────────────┘    └─────────────┘    └─────────────┘
```

Figure 4-8. DISTRIBUTION PROCESSING

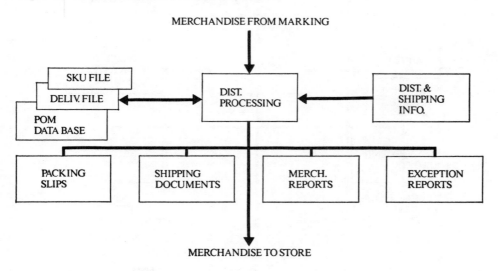

MERCHANDISE FROM MARKING

SKU FILE		
DELIV. FILE	DIST. PROCESSING	DIST. & SHIPPING INFO.
POM DATA BASE		

PACKING SLIPS	SHIPPING DOCUMENTS	MERCH. REPORTS	EXCEPTION REPORTS

MERCHANDISE TO STORE

ical performance such as turnover to recommend (but not dictate) a breakdown of merchandise to individual stores.

Automatic replenishment has been sought by many companies to reduce inventory levels and improve productivity. This involves establishing minimum stock levels and having the system order merchandise to replenish as needed.

Pre- and post-distribution system interfaces entail sending instructions to the warehouse and distribution operations regarding storage location, break-packing, and priority shipping.

Electronic purchase order transmission permits instantaneous communication between retailer and vendor. Basic PO data, as well as promotion announcements, changes, and other information, is transmitted from computer to computer.

Benefits of POM

The benefits of an integrated POM system are many. First, POM leads to a more efficient operation. The buyer spends less time on routine functions such as tracking merchandise; revising orders, receipts, and invoice information; modifying orders; and recalculating open-to-buy. The buyer's time is then freed for the vital aspects of merchandising that require human judgment. Operations become more efficient because of the reduced clerical effort needed to check orders, match invoices, and control orders. Buyers can react more quickly to problems. Tickets can be printed automatically, relieving congestion in the receiving area. As a result, merchandise flows much faster to the stores.

Improved management information is a second benefit of POM. With access

Figure 4-9. INVOICE PROCESSING

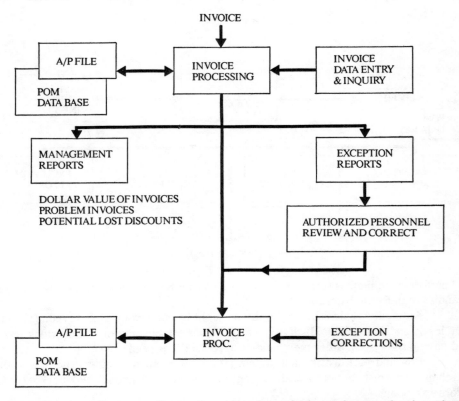

to accurate open-to-buy, on-order, and receipts data, the buyer knows what is on-hand and what is needed. Therefore, buying decisions will be more in line with real needs. Better information brings problem areas to management's attention faster. For example, problems with outstanding orders or unmatched invoices will surface more quickly. Through improved merchandise tracking, the buyer has better control of merchandise through the pipeline, and fewer sales will be lost because of out-of-stock situations.

The financial benefits of POM include automatic printing of vendor and freight carrier claims, which enhances the processing of claims. The finance division can take advantage of discounts because of faster input to accounts payable. The investment in inventory is reduced by the reduction in safety stocks, which occurs when merchandise moves more quickly. There is also improved markups maintenance because tickets reflect the most recent changes.

Merchandise planning, performance reporting, and purchase order management are only three of the areas in which the computer has revolutionized merchandise management. Other areas of retailing have been equally affected, with significant effects on the bottom line. These are detailed in Part Two.

Part Two

TECHNOLOGY AND RETAILING

5

Management Information Services in Retailing

OVERVIEW: The computer has many applications in almost every aspect of retailing, including accounting, credit, payroll, merchandise and inventory control, and personnel. The computer-based system which processes, organizes, and reports the information in a useful manner is called Management Information Services (MIS). An effective system issues reports on a graduated scale of detail, designed to give individuals at different levels only as much detail as they need.

The costs of MIS are controlled by allocating expenses to the various users (departments or offices) who pay for time, equipment, and personnel. With detailed records, management can determine when new systems actually save money or speed up a process and what the net effect and cost of MIS is.

Developing new computer systems requires detailed planning. Critical to the planning process is the interaction of users, MIS personnel, and top management. Needs, benefits, alternative solutions, costs, and potential problems should be analyzed before the project is begun.

MIS in Perspective

The retail companies at the top of the profits charts are often those making the most efficient use of the computer and electronic data processing. The deeper and broader merchandise assortments, the variety of transactions, the swelling numbers of personnel, and the intensity of competition make it necessary for retail management to digest thousands of pieces of data in order to have the right merchandise at the right price in the right place at the right time. With competing retailers selling similar merchandise at similar prices because they all buy from the same vendors, the key to success has become information. The difference between the very profitable retailer and the others is often the accuracy and timeliness of merchandise decisions. Management Information Services (MIS) is indispensable to making those decisions.

The speed, capabilities, and seeming complexities of MIS have put many in awe of its celebrated wizardry. However, we must separate the myths from the reality. For starters, we must realize that the computer is not an electronic counterpart of the human brain. It is a complex electronic machine. The primary operations of the machine are:

1. *Computing*—adding, subtracting, multiplying, and dividing.
2. *Comparing* one number, letter, or symbol with another to determine if they are the same or different.
3. *Recognizing* three types of numbers—positive, negative, and zero.
4. *Performing additional calculations* based on the results of the computations and comparisons.
5. *Issuing* messages, the results of its calculations.

The human brain performs the same operations but with one major distinction. The brain is an aware intelligence, able to understand and manipulate concepts by creating symbols that represent those concepts. The computer, a mass of electronic circuits and magnetic components, must be told by a human being the symbols that have been created. The computer does not understand the concepts that lie behind the symbols.

While lacking understanding, the computer does have a tremendous capacity for recording, assembling, manipulating, and disseminating vast amounts of information. Because it is a machine and not a human, the computer does not weary of absorbing millions of symbols and processing them in countless routine patterns in very short periods of time. Herein lies the fundamental merit of the computer.

Many critics of MIS are those who receive too much data too often in a form they cannot read. This shows a lack of human control, the control needed to make the machine produce what the human beings want. The information and reports generated by the MIS must be specially geared to the particular needs and responsibilities of the people who receive and use them. Identifying and responding to those information needs is a critical first step in implementing a successful MIS.

Uses of MIS

Management must have accurate, timely, and meaningful information to plan, organize, coordinate, operate, and direct the many different divisions and activities in a retailing enterprise. Hundreds of decisions must be made, some over a long period of time, some almost instantly, but all affecting considerable sums of money. Sales figures, personnel data, merchandise information, and financial updates are needed for decision making at various rungs on the management ladder. MIS can provide this data with great speed.

Many companies develop management information systems to meet an immediate need. Some make long-range plans and implement MIS in phases, developing it into an integrated network. The more sophisticated uses for sales forecasting and replenishment generally follow a gradual progression from other uses, many of which have minimal effect on merchandising decisions.

Some of the uses of MIS in retailing are outlined below.

Accounting

Because of the highly structured and repetitive nature of accounting procedures, the accounting department is usually one of the first to convert to MIS. The computer is well-suited to process the equivalent of mountains of tedious, redundant paperwork. The computer requires fewer people and releases others to review and check the source documents for accuracy. Typical applications are for accounts receivable, sales audit, general ledger, and retail inventory. In addition, automated accounts payable enable a company to squeeze cash by controlling debit balances, to realize all cash discounts, to improve the accuracy of financial information, and to make the audit easier.

Credit

More and more customers are using credit cards for their purchases. MIS enables the register clerk to speed up these transactions, thereby improving customer service and increasing the potential for more sales. By simply entering in the card number, the clerk is able to determine the viability of the customer's credit. With the information from credit transactions, the retailer is more readily able to determine the trading area and mobility of his customers and to plan selective sales promotions based on customer locations and buying habits.

Payroll

The computerized payroll is usually faster and cheaper to process than a manual system. With the ever-increasing demand for government reports, computerized payrolls are doubly useful. From a merchandising standpoint, payroll data can be used in analyzing expenses by department, by store, or by merchandise type. The computer can also be programmed to identify employees for periodic review.

Merchandise and Inventory Control

Merchandise is of primary interest to the retailer, and MIS has been a boon to the intelligent control of goods for sale. The great assortment of items, multi-store operations, and the variety of customer preferences require an efficient means of gathering and interpreting reams of merchandise information. The retailer must balance inventory to meet customer demand, pinpoint trends, reduce the cost of markdowns, allocate the inventory investment, analyze the company's resources, evaluate merchandise performance, and improve customer service and profitability. All of these activities can be performed better and faster if the information on which they are based is accurate and timely. And the input, analysis, and reporting are faster if the data is processed electronically.

Unit sales, stock-to-sales ratios, on-hand inventory, and other information, when quickly obtained, put the retailer in a better position to identify fast movers for reorders and slow movers for markdowns. Timely transfer of one store's excess supply of an item to cover depletion in another store can increase profits, reduce inventory, free up cash, and increase the open-to-buy. But the key is rapid retrieval and analysis of the data.

On the sales floor, the computer can help the sales clerk, particularly with big items. The customer interested in the bathroom vanity wants to know now when he can have it. If the department is plugged into the computer, the sales clerk can determine almost immediately if the vanity is in stock, at the warehouse, or deliverable in two weeks.

With a good two-way communication network, a buyer can often get last week's sales information on Monday morning and can prepare markdowns by the afternoon. On Tuesday morning the store receives the notification, makes the changes, and informs the buyer. By Wednesday morning, the markdowns, based on an interpretation of fresh sales data, are in effect.

This rapid retrieval of sales data has been made possible largely through the installation of the point-of-sale (POS) terminal and the use of computers that enable identification of items by SKU (stock keeping unit) number. In a finely tuned MIS system, when an item is sold, its SKU number goes into the POS terminal. Sales data are collected daily and reports for each SKU can be produced weekly to guide buyers. For staple items, many systems provide automatic replenishment. As soon as the sales data indicate that stock on the item has reached a predetermined point, the computer automatically prepares a purchase order to bring stock back up to a specified inventory number. A paper copy of the order is printed for the buyer, who still maintains control and can release or override the order as necessary.

Once the order is released, the computer produces a vendor purchase order, tickets, and receiving documents that are generally neater and more accurate than those prepared manually. When the merchandise arrives at the store, the shipment is matched against the receiving documents, and the paperwork is sent back. Receipts of purchase orders are fed into the computer for verification, giving the retailer the important control factor.

In the allocation and distribution of merchandise, the computer can be programmed any way the buyer desires. Goods can go out in equal quantities to all stores or in different quantities according to store class or in proportion to need, based on forecasted sales and inventory on-hand.

Personnel

Some organizations use computers to rate job applicants in quantifiable factors and to help match qualified candidates with specific needs of the company. In evaluating the performance of employees, MIS provides hard statistics which make this process much more objective. Total sales, total sales per hour, number of transactions, number of multi-item sales, number of credit applications taken, and other vital data help make employee evaluations more objective and fair, complementing the supervisor's judgment, and help justify promotions and increases.

Matching Reports to Information Needs

People at different levels have different functions and different information needs. Why spend time and money giving people information they do *not* need? Why run the risk of hiding the information they do need among pages of data which, though relevant to someone else, is useless to them in their function? And why bother producing reports on stable items, vendors, or conditions which are the same week after week, year in and year out?

What management needs to be alerted to are the deviations from plan, the changes, the unexpected. The useful reporting systems are those that can focus attention on the "need-to-know" information.

Responsibility reporting is a valuable service of MIS. The idea behind responsibility reporting is to provide managers with the information they need to support decisions at their level of responsibility or authority. A well-designed MIS system will generate reports that vary in degree of detail and in frequency depending on the function or responsibility of the people who use them. The higher the level of authority in the organization, the more summary in nature will be the report; the lower the level, the greater the detail.

To design an effective reporting system, the information requirements for each level of management must be determined. How much information is too much or too little? Who is responsible for doing what? The answer to that question provides the guidelines for deciding who needs what kind of information.

The chief executive officer (CEO), by nature of the position, must receive a summary report on each division in the company. With respect to the merchandising

**Figure 5-1. MERCHANDISING REPORTING SYSTEM—
CHIEF EXECUTIVE OFFICER**

CHIEF EXECUTIVE OFFICER

INFORMATION REQUIREMENTS	• Profitability by Store/Department • Profit Contributions • Comparison to Industry • Comparison to Business Plan

BENEFITS	• Evaluate Operating Expenses • Measure Performance

reporting structure, the CEO must have information on which to evaluate operating expenses and to measure performance. To do that, he needs data on profitability by store or department, profit contributions, and company figures compared to the rest of the industry and compared to the company's plan (see Figure 5-1).

The vice-president of merchandising, however, has a number of very different functions, so the report the vice-president receives must be considerably different from that of the CEO. This report must have enough detail so that the vice-president can

**Figure 5-2. MERCHANDISING REPORTING SYSTEM—
VICE-PRESIDENT OF MERCHANDISING**

V.P. MERCHANDISING

INFORMATION REQUIREMENTS	• Profitability/Sq. Ft. by Store/Dept. • Return on Investment • Buyer Expenses & Operating Costs

BENEFITS	• Evaluate General Merchandise Manager Performance • Measure Division Profitability • Evaluate Return on Investment • Determine Trends in Expenses

evaluate performance, measure division profitability, evaluate the return on investment, and determine trends in expenses. To perform these functions, the vice-president of merchandising would need figures showing profitability per square foot by store and department, the return on investment (for the company and the industry, for this and previous years), as well as buyer expenses and operating costs, again with comparative figures (Figure 5-2).

The buyer is responsible for evaluating stock turnover, for knowing performance at SKU level, and for planning purchases, transfers, markdowns, and returns to vendors. In order to make these judgments, the buyer needs accurate figures on performance by department, inventory, category, style/class, and price range. Information on markdowns, gross margin, and open-to-buy must be up-to-date and specific (Figure 5-3). Note that both the buyer and the CEO evaluate performance. They do so, however, on much different scales and therefore require different kinds of information or different amounts of detail.

Once the degree of detail necessary for various reports is determined, the next step is to gather that detail. Since profitability is the ultimate concern of each individual

Figure 5-3. MERCHANDISING REPORTING SYSTEM—BUYERS

at every level, merchandise profitability must be analyzed in a fashion suited to each management level.

To analyze the profitability of each department, the following data are necessary:

- Name of department, number of square feet, and percentage of total square feet.
- Sales in total dollars and per square foot.
- Gross profit in total dollars and in percentage of contribution.
- Inventory in total dollars at the end of month and per square foot.
- Annual turnover specifying the number of turns.
- Profitability in dollars and in dollars per square foot.
- Return on investment in dollars and dollars per square foot.

These data can be used to generate reports for previous years and the current year and to plan budgets for future years. These data can yield a variety of comparisons of stores by region or type, or comparisons of departments within or among stores.

The success a company has with the goods from each vendor can also be analyzed to effect decisions about the desirability of the vendors. Vendors can be ranked after weighing these factors: total dollar amount of purchases, total markdowns in dollars, the percentage of purchases resulting in markdowns, gross margin in dollars derived through goods of each vendor, and the gross margin percentage.

Similar reports can be generated to analyze the effectiveness of each item. Which items sell first? Which are profitable? What is the profitability of each per square foot? This kind of merchandise reporting enables management to determine which items should be given more or less space, more or less advertising, a greater or lesser percentage of the departmental budget. These decisions can be made by department, by store, or by region and will be based on specific information for each item.

In conjunction with item analysis is price line analysis. Studying performance according to price lines not only affects buying plans but can also tell much about the store's customers. When summarized for CEO reports, this kind of information can help top management see that the company's customer today is more of a bargain-hunter, or is trading up a good deal more than in the past. This information will affect basic company planning and strategy.

Merchandise reporting can be done at the most minute level of detail in the merchandise structure. That information will not only affect day-to-day decisions, but when summarized, it can have significant impact on company policy. It is this kind of bottom-up input that gives top level planners the solid information base they need.

The scheme of reporting outlined here for the merchandising division can be followed in each of the company's divisions. Titles, functions, and types of data are different, but the hierarchy, types of responsibilities, and relative need for information are the same.

Reporting and Allocating MIS Expenses

As data processing has become more sophisticated, the investment in and cost of management information services has increased accordingly. Nevertheless, while management endeavors to make the entire retail operation cost-efficient, MIS is an area that often escapes close and meaningful scrutiny. In fact, return on investment analyses are seldom applied to MIS decisions. In simple terms, this means that management does not or cannot control its MIS department.

One symptom exhibited by companies in need of tighter MIS control is an overloaded computer center. As soon as capacity is increased to relieve the situation, the computer is overloaded again. In these companies, workload always tends to fill capacity. As expenditures for increasing the capacity of and operating such huge systems escalate, management begins to doubt the cost-effectiveness of the system.

Many companies do not know how to determine the cost-effectiveness of their MIS operation and simply let "industry figures" determine how much they spend on data processing. If their MIS budget falls within 1/2 to 3/4 of one percent of sales, they feel they are competitive and are less inclined to reduce that total cost and maintain the same level of productivity. Worse, they are not aware that if they were to increase the cost by 10%, they might increase productivity by 40%. In other words, they never really know what they are getting for their money.

A second symptom of an uncontrolled MIS system is increased demands by user departments for data processing in their daily activities. These users want more and more services and become frustrated by the lack of control over the MIS activities related to their area. This frustration may be a result of several problems:

- Lack of a structured method for defining and prioritizing user requests for MIS services.
- Lack of a standard method for estimating the cost of fulfilling such requests.
- Failure to charge for MIS services, causing unchecked demand on MIS resources.
- Inequitable chargeback of MIS services, resulting in allocation of costs to users disproportionate to actual usage.

Expense Reporting

Accountability for data processing activities of the MIS department and of user departments *is* possible and is attained by a number of successful companies. To have accountability, though, the company must be able to measure its total MIS expenditures. This requires that all MIS expenses within the company be completely and accurately identified. Every expense should be properly placed within either the personnel or equipment category, and within the proper subdivision within either category.

Figure 5-4 lists MIS resources and typical units of measurement for the purpose of compiling costs. The MIS resources in Figure 5-4 are those typically used in

Figure 5-4. TYPICAL MIS RESOURCES AND EXPENSES

Resource Personnel	Unit of Measure	Comments
MIS management	Hours	
Systems and programming	Hours	New application development and maintenance
Operations	Hours	Operates systems under development and in production
Data entry	Hours	Database, telecommunications, systems
Technical support	Hours	Programming

Equipment		
Central processing unit	Seconds used by computer job	
Input/output devices	Records read or written	Tape, disk, drum units
Memory	Kilobytes of memory used	
Card reader/punch	Cards read or punched	
Printer	Lines printed	
Plotter	Seconds or feet of paper	
Disk/on-line storage	Track days	Number of tracks used per day, summed over the accounting period
Magnetic tape/storage	Tape days	Number of reels used per day, summed over the accounting period
Computer terminals	Connect time	Time user is logged onto system
Communications	Miles × Seconds	Distance and time covered by telecommunications lines between computer devices
Point-of-sale terminals	Transaction	Can also charge flat monthly fee
Credit authorization equipment	Transaction	Can also charge flat monthly fee

allocating to users the costs of developing and using systems. They do not, however, constitute the universe of all expenditures for the MIS department. There are many fixed expenses, such as rent, that must be included in the department's overall budget. There are variable costs, too, such as supplies (printer ribbons, paper, forms) that are paid for by the MIS department but which are not pragmatically allocated to a single user. Thus, a subset of the objects of expenditure are used to define the allocation of the total departmental costs.

For example, say that the XYZ Company purchases a $120,000 line printer and that it plans to use it for three years. Does the cost to be allocated equal $40,000 per year? No, because the printer will use paper, printer ribbons, and electricity, and it will probably require some maintenance during its life. Estimates (based on history and/or projected use) of the total costs associated with the device must be prepared. The total cost is the figure that XYZ's MIS department must allocate to its user community.

Each subdivision can be broken down further so expenses can be pinpointed. Costs associated with the data entry function, for example, would include costs of all personnel who operate data entry equipment both on-line and off-line, as well as salaries for the manager, supervisors, clerks, and secretaries of that unit. Other costs might include supplies, travel, services purchased, and some miscellaneous expense items. A similar breakdown of expenses can be done for every subdivision in the personnel and equipment categories. By itemizing data entry expenses under these accounts, management knows exactly where the money is going. This kind of reporting is crucial if decisions are to be made about altering that flow of money.

A consistent and orderly means of MIS expense reporting will provide an accurate total of MIS expenditures. It not only tells how much is being spent on MIS, but also accurately apportions those expenditures to the personnel or equipment incurring the expense.

Chargeback

With MIS expenses identified, management is now in a position to allocate a portion of the total MIS expenses to the various departments in the company. This means that each user department will be charged for the MIS personnel, equipment, and time used to perform a particular service for the department.

Of the various subdivisions of MIS expenses, some, such as those for POS and telecommunications equipment, generally are absorbed by the MIS department and considered overhead. Other expenses, such as the cost of MIS personnel developing a new system for a user department, can be allocated to the user. Still other expenses, such as the cost of computer hardware, can be shared by the MIS department and the user departments according to a utilization formula developed for the company by the MIS department. In this formula, the user pays a certain amount per resource unit, such as $1.00 per CPU second or .001 per line printed.

Measuring the actual utilization of shared MIS resources is possible through the use of *data entry logs*, which record the amount of time required to prepare a particular job for entry into the computer; *timesheet reporting systems*, which measure the amount of time that each programmer/analyst spends on a particular project for a given period of time; and *computer job accounting packages*, which analyze and report on the computer activity as measured by the operating system. These systems typically report costs by the items in Figure 5-4, thus facilitating the costing of a particular computer run or development project.

The MIS chargeback system is usually set up by the MIS department with help from and approval by the users on the MIS steering committee. Once the charge rates are agreed on and the MIS department's expenses have been listed, the MIS department allocates the cost of its services to all system development projects and production systems run for users. (Note that for some of the services the user is MIS itself; for example, the EDP chargeback system run on the computer is an MIS overhead.) The components of the chargeback are the resource units listed in Figure 5-4. Each user group (*e.g.*, accounting) is assigned a charge number and all personnel time and equipment usage benefiting that user is charged back to it.

At the end of each chargeback period (*e.g.*, a month), the MIS department generates reports detailing the charges to each user. These charges are subtracted from the revenues of profit center departments and added to the costs of cost centers. Users with budgetary authority analyze their "bills" to better learn where their MIS expenses are going and decide whether they are good financial investments. For example, a system that costs $10,000 a year to operate but saves $15,000 in personnel costs is showing a 50% ROI and is cost-effective. One that is costing more than it returns should be considered for termination unless it is necessary for compliance or produces nonfinancial benefits.

Systems Planning

The MIS department in many retailing companies uses the latest technology, demands a hefty share of the annual budget, and plays a vital role in company operations. Yet user departments and management often express dissatisfaction with MIS, pointing to incomplete systems, the long and expensive process of developing new systems, and on-again off-again projects. Very often these complaints can be traced to poor systems planning rather than to the inefficiency of the MIS. In too many companies, long-range, detailed plans necessary for a successful information system are never drawn up; consistency between systems activities and company priorities is not assured; and systems costs and benefits are never evaluated.

A sound information system requires thorough planning. The purpose of systems planning is to determine how computer-related resources will be used to meet the needs and objectives of the company. Computer-related resources include computer equipment (hardware), computer programs or sets of instructions that run the equipment (software), and personnel to develop and maintain programs and operate the equipment.

Successful systems planning requires:

1. Interaction among users of data processing services, the computer systems department, and top management.
2. An assessment of needs, expected benefits, alternative solutions, and costs.
3. Avoidance of the known pitfalls associated with systems development and planning.

Interaction

MIS is a service organization and cannot function effectively when isolated from the feedback of user departments and top management. The user departments, not the MIS department, must determine the systems support they need, when they need it, and the benefits of those systems to departmental functions and to the company as a whole. The MIS department determines what must be done to provide the systems support requested by users, how long it will take, and what it will cost.

Top management must decide which user needs are most important, which projects justify the cost, which requests can be delayed, and which alternatives are most consistent with overall company objectives. Interaction of these three groups results in more productive evaluation of company problems and sounder decisions on immediate and long-term goals.

Figure 5-5. INTERACTION AMONG SYSTEMS PLANNERS

USERS

- Define needs
- Request system solution
- Identify benefits

MIS

- Analyzes needs
- Proposes solutions, staffing, schedules, and costs
- Reviews benefits

MANAGEMENT

- Establishes priorities of needs
- Evaluates benefits vs. costs
- Decides on solution
- Allocates resources

Figure 5–6. THE SYSTEMS DEVELOPMENT PROCESS

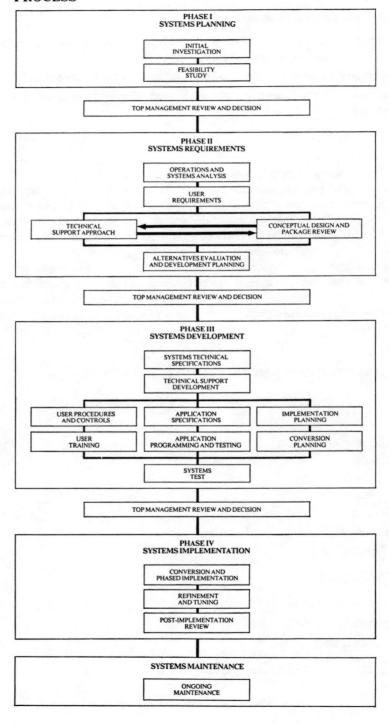

The Steering Committee

The steering committee is central to the systems planning process. This committee is composed of vice-presidents, major MIS users, and the director or vice-president of MIS, and it is responsible for the management and control of MIS. This committee defines long-range and short-range MIS plans, ensuring compatibility with company plans; sets priorities and timetables for implementation; monitors the use of personnel and equipment; initiates system/site reviews and audits; and makes budget decisions.

The MIS director is the bridge between the retail personnel and the systems personnel and must be able to communicate with both. The director must understand the needs of the retailers and be able to translate these into directives for the systems staff. The director must also realize when the retailers' expectations are unrealistic and say so. The director must be sensitive to the difficulties of effecting change and to the limitations of the people who are learning to work in a new environment.

Representatives of user departments are also members of the steering committee. It seems only natural that those people who use the system have input into it. But this is not always the case. Systems have been developed by systems staffs working in a vacuum. The odds that such systems will satisfy the users are slim.

Assessment

Planning decisions must be based upon sound information. Each major project or system development must be defined, researched, and analyzed before management decides to undertake it. (See Fig. 5-6.)

First, specific objectives of each system must be defined. What functions, reports, and services will the user receive when the system is operational? Which needs and problems will be addressed by a new system? Which needs will *not* be met by the system?

How does the system translate into benefits for the user? Will it save $40,000 per year in labor costs? Increase throughput at checkout by 40%? Reduce average outstanding accounts receivable by ten days? Increase sales of big ticket merchandise by 10%? Reduce warehouse dollar inventory by 15%? Qualitative benefits can include improvements to customer service, issuance of more accurate and up-to-date merchandising information, and reduction of shrinkage. These benefits can have indirect financial impact that is difficult to measure.

Once the objectives and benefits are defined, the MIS department should propose a computer solution and describe generally how the system will function. Will an existing package meet the needs of your company? Will the system require on-line update or inquiry capability? What special and specific functions are required? Are microfiche reports needed? What interfaces with other systems are necessary? How current must information be? How critical is the data to operations at the store? Is special equipment required, such as a badge reader for security, an optical scanner for OCR, bar code or magnetic encoding on tickets?

There is often more than one way to meet the user's needs. The advantages, disadvantages, and cost of each alternative must be identified. To determine a system's cost, the MIS department must account for the required hardware and software to be purchased, leased, or rented, the manpower expense to develop and implement the system, and the ongoing expense of operating the system after it is developed. These new system costs should be compared to the costs of the system to be replaced, whether automated or manual.

Planning Pitfalls

Some of the pitfalls present in systems planning listed below are unique to computer-related activities. Many, however, are symptomatic of poor planning in any area of business. Avoiding these pitfalls will help ensure a plan that is reasonable, achievable, and meets the needs and objectives of your company.

1. Developing a plan, then ignoring it. No plan should be rigid because user needs change. Management must be prepared to react to change by modifying and updating the plan as needed. A well-constructed plan should be capable of modifications so that the plan need not be scrapped when needs, priorities, or financial considerations change.

2. Ignoring the users. When the user departments are not asked for input, or when that input has little impact on plans, important needs will go unmet. Ideally, systems are developed through an understanding of user needs enhanced by the experience of data processing personnel.

3. Failing to update plans periodically. Good MIS systems plans should be updated at least once a year to acknowledge progress, to adjust to new priorities and conditions, and to reschedule projects accordingly.

4. Establishing too long a planning cycle. A manageable and realistic period of time for a systems plan to cover is three to five years. It is best to start with a shorter time frame, then expand each year to the three-to-five year planning horizon. Eventually, the cycle of updating the three-to-five year plan should become a normal routine.

5. Failing to identify system interdependencies. An information system will spread its tentacles in many directions—operations, merchandising, finance. Failure to identify and plan for all interfaces can result in overly complex systems, contradictory reports, delays in processing of shared data, redundant files, duplicated effort, and unnecessary expense.

6. Taking a narrow-minded approach to solutions. A systems plan should be viewed as a beginning, an opportunity to improve operations through growth and change. An approach that is limited to performing an old task with new tools can result in an inefficient system. Often an opportunity for innovation in marketing strategies, operational effectiveness, or improved information reporting is overlooked due to this nearsighted attitude.

7. Failing to take existing systems or procedures into account. Failure to thoroughly understand existing systems can result in wasted expenditures for reinventing the wheel or for creating procedures that are not consistent with current operating procedures and needs. Existing manual or computerized systems and their strengths and weaknesses must be well understood before developing a replacement.

8. Failing to identify the risks of various alternatives. Sounder decisions can be made when all interested parties are aware of all alternatives and the potential benefits and risks of each. For example, investing in new, unproven hardware products can jeopardize a project's success and may even have significant financial impact on a business.

9. Failing to completely analyze the cost of implementation. Too many otherwise well-constructed plans are aborted when management discovers how much its implementation will really cost and when users discover how much of their time and resources are required. Even if they are not aborted, these projects almost always take longer to implement and therefore to benefit the users.

10. Underestimating development and implementation time. Very often, because of eagerness to undertake a project or to get management approval, or through a lack of experience, system planners underestimate the time needed for implementation. There is no benefit to this. All parties to the planning effort should scrutinize and challenge the project timetable to assure the greatest possible accuracy. Exceeding the time for development and implementation is the most common cause of project cost overrun.

11. Overestimating the capacity of the MIS department. Many pressures are placed on the MIS department, and user requests almost always exceed its resources. Frequently more work is undertaken than can be accomplished, and everyone loses. The users wait longer than expected, data processing employee morale drops, and systems are implemented inefficiently.

12. Establishing systems priorities without considering company-wide needs. Users that are the squeaking wheels often receive systems help regardless of their actual need or relative place in the company's overall scheme.

13. Failing to specify the products the system will provide the user. Unrealistic expectations can exist in the minds of users unless the major end products are identified clearly during systems planning. If this isn't done, a project viewed by the data processing department as nearing completion is often seen as incomplete or deficient by the user. Large, complex systems are usually implemented in phases. In this case, the end products of each phase must be clearly defined for data processing and for the user.

6

Point-of-Sale:
The Core of MIS

OVERVIEW: The electronic point-of-sale system (POS) is the center of the retailer's management information system. While serving as sales register to speed up the sales transaction, electronic POS also provides the critical data for most other computerized information systems. POS hardware and software must be selected with the element of interaction in mind. This requires a thorough review of the company's current systems, its needs for information, and its plans for system enhancement. POS selection is facilitated by submitting requests for proposals (RFP) to several vendors. This allows all vendors to respond to the same requirements and to be evaluated on the same criteria. The retailer gains a wealth of information and can choose the vendor and system best suited to the company's needs.

The Point-of-Sale System

POS, or electronic point of sale system, is pivotal to the modern retailer's data processing system. POS serves a dual role in the retail operation. First, the terminal functions as a cash register in completing the sales transaction. Second, it provides much of the data for other computer systems. All other primary retail functions become eligible for automation because POS can provide the accurate, timely data such automation requires.

POS affects three levels of operation—selling floor, store, and backroom. Let us look at each of these in turn.

At the selling floor level, POS facilitates four key functions: cash sales, credit sales, recording merchandise data, and obtaining information for customers. The focus of all retailing is the sales transaction. POS helps speed these transactions and ensure accuracy. Clerks at the register are guided by the POS terminal through all steps of the transaction and are aided in calculating taxes, discounts, markdowns, and other variables that could affect the exchange of money. In credit sales, POS provides the same assistance, as well as verification of the customer's identity and credit line.

A vital by-product of the sales transaction is the instantaneous recording of merchandise data. As the sale is entered into the register, POS is recording information on the purchased item that can be used for merchandise control. This data includes the number of the department, vendor, classification, style, size, color, quantity, and price of the item.

With this kind of up-to-date record keeping, selling floor personnel are in a better position to give customers accurate information about merchandise. They can tell the customer quickly if an item is out-of-stock, on-order, or available at another location. Thus POS can facilitate the sales transaction as well as customer interaction.

At the store level, POS assists store management in completing a number of important tasks. The daily compiling of sales data can be done automatically by the POS device and transmitted to the data processing center. The sales audit is another routine, whereby store management balances registers, deposits cash, calculates salesperson commissions and productivity, clears and resets cash registers, reviews sales checks and credits for accounts receivable, prepares store flash sales reports, and extracts tax information. With POS, many of these tasks are automated, and the audit can be done more quickly and more accurately.

In providing information for the sales audit, POS can also generate store management reports on current sales, merchandise status, productivity, and customer service. These timely reports enable the store manager to react quickly to problems or changing conditions.

A third level of operation is in the backroom or central office where point-of-sale data from the store are processed and analyzed. Not all retailers have reached this level of sophistication, but many are working toward this extension of POS. With it, the data can be used for meaningful decision making.

Accounts receivable uses POS data for credit authorization, customer billing, and bill collection. Accounts payable works with more timely data to pay bills promptly, to take advantage of discounts, and, when tied into the purchase order system, to pay only for merchandise received.

The merchandisers in the buying office rely heavily on POS data to replenish stock quickly, to take advantage of special offers, and to plan purchases. Sales analyses can be made daily, even hourly if necessary, with the timely reports provided by POS.

POS holds a central place in the retailer's information system. Consequently, selecting the proper POS equipment and implementing the system requires careful planning and a thorough understanding of the interfacing of POS with other systems.

POS Selection and Implementation

Components

Since POS was first introduced in a significant manner in the early 1970s, its capability and flexibility have expanded substantially. In the early days, POS was little more than a cash register capable of some data entry checking and improved data capture. Today the most sophisticated systems are small computers with substantial flexibility and processing capability. In addition, a variety of components can be incorporated in the system.

The major components of the POS system include:

Terminal The basic unit of the POS system on the sales floor. Today's terminals either have small computers (microprocessors) within them or they are hooked up to a small computer in the store.

Wands or scanners Devices which can be attached to the system or terminal for reading merchandise and/or price information encoded on the tags.

Collectors or concentrators Components that store the data from one or more terminals.

Store controllers or computers Components that provide data collection and processing capability. Store controllers and computers have been increasing in capability and sophistication.

Modem The device resembling a telephone, that connects the store's POS terminal, controller, or concentrator with the central site.

Central computer The computer, usually located at company headquarters, that performs the company's data processing.

Software Computer programs that tell the store computer and the central computer how to process and report the data from POS.

Types of Systems

There are four major types of POS systems, each with different capabilities and levels of sophistication.

The lowest level of sophistication is an *electronic cash register (ECR)*. The ECR is not truly a POS terminal or system because it lacks data capture capability. ECRs perform the basic sales functions, usually with limited flexibility to change the way the functions are performed. The ECR has many more totals available for sales and merchandise information than does the traditional cash register. Some ECRs also have the capability to store and retrieve item prices for a price look-up function. Many of the ECRs on the market have a limited store management reporting capability, although advances are being made in this area.

The POS *store-and-forward terminal* comes next in capability. Store and forward means data is collected (stored) during the day and forwarded to the central computer at night. In addition to the ECR functions, these terminals usually allow for one or more terminals to be tied together. They are POS terminals because they have the capacity for detailed data capture on sales and nonsales transactions. Administrative-type information such as merchandise receipts or payroll data can usually be entered on the terminals via non-sales transactions.

The administrative features of these terminals vary from POS to POS. This terminal can usually generate in-store reports based on information processed at the terminal or print out reports produced by the central computer. Price look-up and negative credit authorization are also common features.

Building on the store-and-forward terminal is an *on-line inquiry system* with store-and-forward data collection. In this system, detailed data is captured for later transmission to a central site. Many of these systems are larger than the store-and-forward systems, and the greater store reporting capability permits the use of customized software. These systems also have an on-line inquiry capability that permits rapid communication with the store or central computer for such functions as credit authorization, price look-up, and big ticket systems.

The most sophisticated system is an *on-line interactive system* with two levels. The first level is on-line to a store computer; the second is on-line to a central computer. The on-line interactive systems are fully on-line for all transactions. The inquiry capability is usually more extensive than in the on-line inquiry system. This system provides for transmission of messages both to and from the store. In addition, this system usually has the capability for extensive integrated non-sales functions, such as ticketing, purchase order receiving, etc.

As POS systems have evolved, the distinctions among the four types have become less and less clear. It is difficult at times to determine in which category a particular system fits. The groupings described above are simply intended to provide some idea of the general capabilities and differences among systems.

POS and Existing Systems

The type of system selected must be coordinated with the existing hardware and systems in the company. Companies that have converted to POS indicate that the benefits they expected to realize but did not are those that require other systems to process the information captured by POS. It is very important, then, to consider the existing hardware, functions, and systems before looking at POS and its capabilities. The POS must be compatible with mainframe hardware, the credit authorization system, manual and batch systems, coding and marking procedures. POS alone is not the answer. There must be other systems and an enlightened management to support and properly utilize the POS system in an integrated network.

Importance of the Vendor
As the industry has matured in its understanding of POS, primary criteria for system selection have shifted from terminal functions to vendor service. Respondents to a Touche Ross POS survey felt vendor-related factors were more important than factors of cost, equipment characteristics, and functions (see Figure 6-1). Issues such as software and system architecture are becoming more important as the concern for technological obsolescence increases. It is becoming a vital question whether the system purchased today will be adaptable to the innovations of five years from now.

Defining POS Requirements

We have said that the POS system must be an integral part of your total information system. Therefore, before defining your POS requirements, you should have defined your overall systems plan. This plan should include a conceptual design of the applications to be developed or major enhancements to be added, with a priority listing for implementation. Within this plan, consideration should be given to those applications to which POS can provide input.

POS Project Team
With the systems plan in hand and a concept of the role of POS in it, the research on POS requirements can begin. To conduct the requirements analysis and to direct further activities, a POS project team should be created. The POS project team should be comprised of representatives from store operations, merchandising, finance, training, and data processing divisions. The project team leader should be an EDP/ MIS manager or an operations manager.

Figure 6-1. POS TERMINAL SYSTEMS SELECTION CRITERIA

- VENDOR SUPPORT
- VENDOR CREDIBILITY
- VENDOR STABILITY
- VENDOR INDUSTRY EXPERTISE
- COST
- TERMINAL FUNCTIONS
- SYSTEMS ARCHITECTURE
- SOFTWARE

One of the first tasks of the project team is the requirements analysis. Even if a company has had a POS system installed for a few years, this step is a necessary one because system capabilities and requirements may have changed.

Store Activities Analysis

In order to define POS requirements, the first step is to review all store activities. This review should look both at sales and at administrative operations. In the sales area, the review should include an analysis of:

- All sales transactions, including information entered, field sizes (*e.g.*, the number of digits identifying a department or SKU), printout requirements, and totals requirements.
- Difficulties in using the current system, whether POS or not, and where errors are likely to occur.
- Authorizations required.
- Forms used.
- End-of-day register balancing procedures.
- Totals or information currently produced or that would be beneficial.

In the administrative or non-sales area, review the types of functions performed, forms used, data mailed to a central office, and reports prepared. This review should emphasize understanding of priorities and timeliness of information to assist in determining what should be included in a POS system.

Central Site Applications Analysis

After store operations are analyzed, the central site applications that use data from the store are reviewed next. The object of this review is to understand:

- Who uses what data and why.
- What types of edits or checks are performed on the data by the various software systems.
- What the frequent errors are.
- What the level of priority of the data is and the necessary timing of receipt.

Specifying Requirements

At this point, if the team does not have an understanding of the general capabilities of POS terminals, the team should review some of the vendor literature and arrange short meetings with two or more vendors. Even with an understanding of POS systems, an update on new products is worthwhile. Then the team is ready to define POS requirements.

The definition of POS requirements can be divided into two major areas: POS transaction requirements and general POS system requirements. A typical requirements outline might be as follows:

I. Sales Transactions and Non-sales or Administrative Transactions

    A. Overview of sales transactions
    B. Description of sales transactions
    C. Files and tables required
    D. End-of-day register balancing
    E. Totals
    F. Administrative transaction descriptions
    G. Summary of transaction priorities
    H. Explanatory charts and tables

II. General POS Requirements
    A. Interfaces to existing systems—hardware and software
    B. Physical characteristics (*e.g.*, size)
    C. Data collection media
    D. Communications
    E. Software requirements (*e.g.*, polling and reformatting)
    F. Security features (*e.g.*, keys and security codes)
    G. Printers and printing
    H. Other terminal features (*e.g.*, time and date stamping, prompting, etc.)
    I. Other devices (*e.g.*, wands, scanners)
    J. Installation considerations

Each of the requirements should be given a high, medium, or low priority. High priority requirements are ones the vendor must be able to provide. Medium ones would be highly desirable. Low ones are nice to have but are expendable. In addition, a gradual phasing in of the requirements may be desirable and necessary. The requirements document should therefore include a timetable of implementation for the terminals as well as for other components.

Charts and tables can be an excellent tool for defining POS requirements. Sample charts are shown in Figures 6-2 to 6-4. Similar types of tables and charts can also be used for the administrative transactions. These are not the only charts that may be needed. Elements included on the chart are typically identified as "required" or "optional." The column heads in Figure 6-2 indicate the data that need to be entered in the POS for each type of sales transaction.

Figure 6-3 describes the data fields contained in Figure 6-2 in more detail. The information in this chart tells the POS vendor how to validate and check information

Figure 6-2. DATA ENTRY REQUIREMENTS FOR SALES TRANSACTIONS

SALES TRANSACTIONS   R = Required
                                  O = Optional
                                  — = Not Needed

DATA FIELDS

Transaction Type	Associate Number	Department/ Class	SKU	Retail Amount	Payment Amount (1)	Quantity	Old Balance	Amount Tendered	Customer Account Number
Cash	R	R	O	R	—	O	—	R	—
Check	R	R	O	R	—	O	—	R	—
In-house charge	R	R	O	O	O	O	R	O	R
Visa (2)	R	R	O	R	—	O	—	O	O
Mastercard (2)	R	R	O	R	—	O	—	O	O
American Express	R	R	O	R	—	O	—	O	O
Layaway or gift certificate	R	R	O	O	O	O	R	O	R
No sale	R	—	—	—	—	—	—	—	—
Optional									
Payment	R	O	O	O	R	O	R	R	R

NOTES:
(1) It is desirable to be able to identify the type of tender used in making a layaway payment and to update tender totals for making deposits.
(2) May decide to include VISA and Mastercard together.

Figure 6-3. DESCRIPTION OF SALES TRANSACTION DATA FIELDS

Data Field	Alpha Numeric	Min/ Max Size	Edit Checks	Look-up	Description	MPF Form	Ledger Card	Tear Receipt	Journal Tape
							To Be Printed on:		
Associate number	Numeric	4	—	Table would be desirable by store	Employee identification number (unique throughout chain)	Required	Required	Required	Required
Department	Alpha or numeric	1 2	A–Z 01–29	Table	Classifies types of merchandise	Required	Required	Required	Required
Class	Alpha or numeric	1 2	A–Z 01–29	Table	Identifies types of merchandise within a department	Required	Required	Required	Required
Retail amount	Numeric	%	N/A	N/A	Amount merchandise is sold for	Required	Required	Required	Required

Figure 6-4. KEYS FOR SALES TRANSACTIONS

Action Keys[1]	Description/Comments
Return/refund	Changes the sign on the amount, for either the entire transaction or the next item. Updates returns total.
Nontaxable	Identifies either the entire transaction or an item as nontaxable. Updates nontaxable total.
Void	Nullifies data being entered.
Payment	Identifies dollar amount as a payment reducing the old balance by that amount. Updates payment total.
Subtotal	Calculates running total.
Total	Calculates tax and total.

Data Entry Keys	
Department/class	Alpha or numeric classifications of merchandise.
Miscellaneous income	General ledger account number to which income should be credited (*e.g.*, repair sales).
Quantity	Number of items with the same merchandise ID and retail price.
Amount tendered	Amount customer gives to cashier. Concludes sales transaction sequence. If key depressed without amount entered, amount tendered is assumed to equal the amount due.

1. It is acceptable to use either action keys or different transaction codes to accomplish the same actions.

when it is entered and where it should be printed when entered. The table shows the following:

1. Alphanumeric—Where the data has to be either alphabetic, numeric, or either.
2. Min/max size—How many characters the field can have, or the minimum and maximum number of characters it can have.
3. Edit checks—This column describes the type of editing (checking) that must be performed, such as whether the data entered falls within a predetermined numeric range.
4. Look-up—This column tells if the data entered is to be checked in a table to see if it is valid.
5. Description—Contains a definition of the field.

6. To be printed on—Describes which paper or forms should have the data field information printed on it when it is entered. In this example, there are four forms.

Figure 6-4 describes the keys on the POS terminal needed for various sales transactions. There are two groups of keys shown: action keys (those that cause actions) and data entry keys (those that are used to enter data).

Final Review and Sign-Off

The POS project team should review the defined requirements with other representatives from store operations, merchandising, distribution, finance and accounting, top management (the MIS steering committee), and data processing to identify any necessary changes or adjustments to the priorities and timing. After the changes have been made, the requirements should be finalized and a formal sign-off obtained. With the approved and agreed-upon requirements, proceed into vendor selection.

Figure 6.5. CONTENTS OF A REQUEST FOR PROPOSAL

I. Introduction
   A. Purpose
   B. Date for Responses
   C. Contact for Questions
   D. Priorities on Requirements
   E. Format for Responses
   F. Proposal Acceptance

II. Overview of Company
   A. Background
   B. Current POS and Computer Equipment
   C. Number of Stores and Location

III. Goals and Objectives for New POS System

IV. POS Terminal and System Requirements
   A. Introduction and Overview
   B. Sales Transactions and Non-Sales Transactions
      1. Overview of sales transactions
      2. Description of sales transactions
      3. Files and tables required
      4. End-of-day register balancing
      5. Totals
      6. Administrative transaction descriptions
      7. Summary of transaction priorities
      8. Explanatory charts and tables

Selecting a POS Vendor

The first step in POS vendor selection is to become familiar with a number of vendors by sending each a summary of requirements and asking each to make a brief presentation on its ability to meet the requirements. Based on these presentations, the project team is in a position to make an initial screening and thereby limit bidding to those vendors that have the potential to do the job.

The Request for Proposal

The bidding revolves around the request for proposal (RFP). The RFP is a formal document that details all of a company's POS requirements, minimum and maximum expectations, scheduling, and other conditions. A sample outline for an RFP is shown in Figure 6-5. The RFP spells out for vendors exactly the kind of company you are, what your needs and requirements are, and what you expect from POS and a POS vendor. Vendors then know if they can meet your needs and if they should bother bid-

Figure 6.5. (*Continued*)

    C. General POS Requirements
       1. Interfaces to existing systems—hardware and software
       2. Physical characteristics such as size
       3. Data collection media
       4. Communications
       5. Software requirements such as polling and formatting
       6. Security features such as keys and security codes
       7. Printers and printing
       8. Other terminal features such as time and date stamping, prompting, etc.
       9. Other devices such as wands and scanners
     10. Installation considerations

V. Preliminary Implementation Schedule

VI. Vendor Requirements
    A. Implementation Support
    B. Training
    C. Documentation
    D. Warranties
    E. Maintenance
    F. Future Enhancements
    G. References

VII. Pricing Terms and Conditions

ding on the project. The RFP, then, helps to screen out vendors who cannot meet your needs, and saves time in the vendor selection process. By receiving vendor proposals in the same form, that is in response to the RFP, management can more readily compare the relative merits of each candidate.

A major component of the RFP is the vendor requirement section. This deals with the kind of service one expects from the vendor. Since a POS system is a method of gathering data, time wasted in implementing or servicing the system can mean the loss of valuable merchandise information. This data loss can be translated into serious sales and profit losses.

In listing vendor requirements in the RFP, it is important to stress the following items:

Implementation support What assistance will the vendor provide during implementation?

Training What type of instructional materials or support will the vendor provide for systems personnel, management, and cashiers?

Documentation What manuals, pamphlets, and other literature are provided for hardware, terminal, and systems, and how many copies of each?

Warranties What warranties or other protection will the vendor offer? (Warranties, *per se*, are not common.)

Maintenance Where are the vendor's service representatives located, what is the response time for service calls, what are the hours of service, etc.?

Future enhancements What are the vendor's capabilities and policy on future upgrading of hardware and software, and what are the costs likely to be?

References What retail companies similar to yours in size, location, or merchandise are now using this vendor's system, and who can be contacted at those companies for information about the system and vendor?

The RFP should be mailed to the vendors that pass the initial screening. Minimum response time should be four weeks. The name of a contact person within the company should be included in the RFP so interested vendors can call with any questions they may have.

Try to get the list of references before the complete RFP is returned and call on other retailers for their experience with various vendors. This reference check is important because it can uncover problems or successes that will influence your choice of vendor. In addition, this information can be useful during implementation to help avoid mistakes others have made. The major focus of discussion with other users should be on:

- Maintenance support
- Frequency of systems problems

- Quality of maintenance and support personnel
- Flexibility or ability to upgrade
- Installation problems
- Response on software problems
- Ease of use and change
- Meeting of commitments
- Training support and problems

Direct competitors might not be as free with this kind of information as other retailers will. So for service response, discounters, for example, can check with specialty retailers in the same geographic area. For merchandise aspects, discounters can check with other discounters whose markets do not cross their geographic lines, and who, therefore, are not competitors.

Reference reviews should be documented and, where possible, be conducted by the same person to ensure consistency and a valid interpretation of information. If possible, conduct the reference checks on-site, rather than over the phone or through the mail, to ensure a fuller understanding of each situation.

Criteria for Evaluation

It is essential to develop a list of criteria for evaluating vendor proposals. Ultimately the project team will want a ranking of responding vendors. This ranking should reflect those elements that are most important in meeting the company's needs. Usually these elements will include meeting POS requirements, meeting implementation schedule, ease of use, flexibility and upgradeability, maintenance and installation support, and vendor stability. Each company must develop its own evaluation criteria and determine which of these are most important.

Placing these criteria on a matrix and grading each vendor on a scale of 1 to 5 for each criterion is a convenient way to perform the evaluation. If need be, create a weighted system, so that for more important criteria, the grades are doubled. The total score for each vendor indicates that vendor's relative ranking.

The vendor evaluation will be based on the relative rankings as well as the information from reference checks. Review the proposals and rankings, noting any inconsistencies, questions, or doubts. Vendors can be called to speak to specific points that come up.

The final rankings should identify the vendor and system best suited to the identified needs. If no clear-cut choice emerges from the analysis, review the two or three vendors at the top of the list. If no objective differences exist, then subjective factors must determine the vendor. Rest assured, though, that as a result of the efforts thus far a good decision will be made in selecting a POS vendor.

POS Trends in the 80s

To determine the extent of POS in retailing at present, and of its potential for the future, the National Retail Merchants Association (NRMA) commissioned Touche Ross & Co. to conduct an extensive study. The result was a volume of statistics, observations, conclusions, and opinions entitled *POS Trends in the 80's*. A look at some of this data provides a perspective on the role POS plays in the industry. The study details the widespread use of POS, the variety of applications retailers have found for it, and practical concerns of vendor selection and implementation.

The study clearly shows that retailers who install POS equipment primarily to improve their merchandising and operating decisions have realized their expectations. POS does in fact provide more accurate and useful information, and in much less time. That information enables retailers to operate with reduced inventory levels and markdowns, while increasing inventory turns and gross margin.

Supporting these major conclusions are responses to a 35 page questionnaire completed by more than 500 retail companies representing more than 56,000 stores. Their combined sales exceeded $140 billion in 1980. The respondents came from five industry segments—specialty, department, discount, variety, and full-line national chains.

Equipment

Many companies are into their second generation of POS equipment, upgrading their systems for a number of reasons. They have discovered other needs that can be met through the system, and they have seen the enhanced capabilities of newer equipment. Some companies are changing equipment due to dissatisfaction with the support they receive from the vendor.

Of those respondents that have POS systems, 94% either have their own in-house mainframe computer or use an outside service bureau. (A recent development among smaller and non-department stores is the use of the small, personal computer.) The mainframes and service bureaus perform sophisticated retail functions involved in sales analysis, sales audit, accounts receivable, flash sales, and accounts payable systems. Open-to-buy, inventory control, and purchase order management are other common applications of POS in the purchase cycle.

Many of these applications are now on-line. For instance, credit authorization is on-line at 72% of the companies responding, and positive credit at 71%. In the purchasing cycle, 55% of survey participants show purchase order management and big-ticket inventory on-line.

Benefits

At one time retailers were reluctant to install POS because they felt its benefits did not justify the cost. Today, however, retailers are confident that POS pays for itself.

The justification for the conversion may differ from one situation to another.

Most retailers feel, however, that POS helps to "improve merchandising and operations decisions." More than half of the companies in the survey see management information benefits as a reason to go to POS. Department stores see credit authorization as a big plus of POS, whereas specialty and discount stores do not consider credit authorization a major factor.

Among companies without POS, cost is still the principal obstacle. Some companies feel they do not have the data processing capabilities needed to make POS worthwhile. A small number, which seems to be decreasing all the time, do not feel POS "meets their needs."

Uses

Widespread operational uses of POS include cash register, register balance, communications to host, item description printing, and report preparation. Among merchandising uses, the survey cites SKU data capture, markdowns, layaways, and inventory. One reason for the correlation between POS and merchandising information is that communication between POS terminals and a central facility takes place daily in 80% to 100% of the responding companies.

In terms of satisfying companies' expectations, POS has received high marks. Most of the companies expected—and realized—more accurate and faster information, additional sales information, an ability to handle peak seasons, a reduction in bad debts, and increased cash flow.

Implementation

Most companies take a store-by-store approach to installing POS. This method seems more manageable than a department-by-department approach. Larger companies and specialty stores often install POS simultaneously at several stores. Depending on the size of the company, the rate of conversion can vary from one store per year to more than ten.

Since POS installation is a major undertaking, most stores create project teams just for this purpose. The typical team, prior to installation, usually consists of five persons. An MIS person generally heads the team, aided by representatives from each of the divisions—store operations, finance, merchandising, and training. Often the team includes someone from the chief executive's office.

Some companies need more members on the team than others, largely depending on the level of sophistication in the company's existing systems. That is, the POS team sometimes must do more than install terminals if backup computer systems must be developed at the same time.

Costs

The largest portion of the total conversion cost – about 70% – is in the cost of the terminals. The remaining costs are divided among in-store processors, the project team, mainframe computer processing, training, software, and other items.

Maintenance

Once the POS system is up and running, it needs staff to maintain it. Typically this means two people, most often from MIS.

Training

For any POS system to work well, its users must be well-trained. Some companies designate store trainers who travel from store to store giving instruction. Some companies have the store managers do the training. Others create a training lab at a central facility and train all users there. It seems that in-store training, with users being trained where they work, is most effective.

Learning from Experience

When asked to comment on their experiences with POS, retailers cited as their biggest mistakes:

- Waiting too long before implementing
- Not understanding or using the system's full capability
- Not planning thoroughly
- Believing vendor claims
- Planning or formatting software poorly
- Not training users adequately

When asked if there were any viable alternatives to POS, most respondents said, "POS is the only way to go."

The Future

POS systems are already expanding into total store information systems. The POS system provides the computing capability in the store that can be expanded for use in administrative functions, energy control, security, and customer inquiry. The Store Information System is discussed in more detail in the Epilogue.

7

Merchandise Marking

OVERVIEW: The information fed into the POS terminal depends on the way merchandise is marked. Each retailer must determine the information desired, the best marking option, and best reading alternative to meet specific information needs. Selecting a marking system, therefore, depends on the company's merchandise and information systems.

At one time, a merchandise ticket served only one purpose—to indicate to the customer the price of the item. Gradually, however, more and more information has been printed onto the ticket, so that today the ticket is the key link in many merchandise management systems. As such, the merchandise ticket must be designed to be both cost-efficient and of maximum use to the retailer. That is, the retailer wants the merchandise ticket to provide as much information as is needed in that particular merchandise system. Too little information can mean loss of valuable data or require collecting the same data through other, more costly means. Too much information for a particular system represents a waste of time and money.

Depending on the organization, any combination of the following pieces of information might be marked on the merchandise ticket: price, department, class, vendor, style, color, size, season, and cost code. Retailers with a preponderance of softgoods, fashion, and seasonal merchandise tend to require that more of these items be identified. Basics and hardgoods require fewer. The retailer must decide what information is necessary and, therefore, is to be marked and read. This subject is dealt with in greater detail later in this chapter.

In the interest of economy and efficiency, the retailer should review his options in determining a marking procedure. A recent count of marking and reading technologies shows no fewer than 52 possible combinations. Besides this myriad of combinations is the complication of source-marked goods with two different standards and technologies, UPC (Universal Product Code) and OCR-A (Optical Character Recognition—Type A).

The Stock Keeping Unit

After deciding on what information is needed on the ticket, the next step is to select one of the two basic approaches to indicating this information on the ticket—the long or short SKU (stock keeping unit). Most companies use one or the other.

The long SKU has its origins in the manual era when tickets were either stubbed and mailed to the home office for manual recording in black books, or stock was periodically counted. The long SKU usually contains all the information necessary to identify an item uniquely in an easily understood format. Therefore, all nine information categories listed above might be represented on a single ticket and can be from 20 to 30 characters in length. In the long SKU, each category of information normally contains a minimum of two characters, some numeric and some alphabetic.

The short SKU came into being via the computer. The short SKU is basically a meaningless number, but one with sufficient digits to identify an item uniquely. The computer is programmed so that the same number cannot be repeated within a company. The short SKU, usually a seven- to ten-digit number, identifies for the system the record, which is stored in the computer, that contains the information normally held in a long SKU.

The short SKU requires less room and therefore can be put on a smaller ticket. The short SKU can be keyed more quickly and can be read more easily.

A variation on the short SKU is the inclusion on the ticket of a department and/or class number with the short SKU. This approach permits collecting sales totals at the department and/or class levels using cash register, ECRs, or POS terminals. This combination of numbers is still shorter than the long SKU (compared to a long SKU or short SKU alone).

Marking Options

There are six basic merchandise marking methods currently in use by major retailers. A POS survey published by the National Retail Merchants Association (NRMA) in 1981 showed the percentage use of each of these six technologies in the department store chains. They are:

- Print only: 70%
- OCR-A: 26%

- Print/punch: 21%
- Magnetic: 6%
- UPC: 5%
- Bar code: 2%
- Other: 5%

Other non-food industries paralleled the department stores in their use of these technologies. In the food retail segments, print only price marking or UPC are the two major methods in use.

Each marking technology has pros and cons that make one more suitable to some environments than others. Other factors affecting a retailer's selection of marking systems are:

- The current status of his own merchandise systems.
- The number of unique items carried.
- The level of detail desired in information reporting.
- The capture method to be used.
- The reading technology to be used.

Careful analysis of these factors must be made before deciding upon a particular marking method.

OCR-A, VUVM, and UPC

The retailers represented by the NRMA have selected OCR-A as a voluntary standard for marking merchandise. The OCR-A technology was chosen because:

- The ticket is both human- and machine-readable with one technology.
- The technology can be used by large and small companies.
- Tickets can be created with machines or hand-held ticket markers.
- Tickets can be key-entered, batch read, or wand read.

Extensive progress has been made with OCR-A in terms of acceptance and use by retailers and manufacturers, the variety of equipment available to make and read OCR-A tickets, and equipment cost.

When used in the standard format shown in Figure 7-1, the OCR-A ticket becomes Voluntary Universal Vendor Marking (VUVM). VUVM is source-marked by the manufacturer prior to shipment to the retailer. VUVM offers tremendous potential to reduce both store and backroom costs because the manufacturer does more of the marking. VUVM will probably appear on softgoods, both fashion and staple, toys, luggage, and many other items in discount stores.

Figure 7-1. SALES TICKET IN STANDARD OCR-A FORMAT

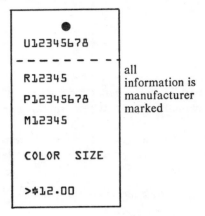

Some stores also receive goods bearing the food industry's Universal Product Code (UPC). Created in a joint effort by food retailers and manufacturers, the UPC is a black and white bar code placed on grocery hardgoods, health and beauty aids, and other items. In its basic form, UPC is a ten-digit number in two five-digit segments. The digits are shown in OCR-B below the bars. The ten-digit numbers are assigned uniquely. The manufacturer receives a number representing the company and assigns numbers to the products within that number. Product numbers are drawn from and maintained in the UPC Council.

The UPC is a part of the label on more than 90% of the items sold in food stores, appearing on both food and non-food products. UPC labels can be marked in the store for produce and meats. The UPC can be key-entered, wand read, or scanned. The symbol was chosen because it can be marked economically, it can be accurately incorporated into labels, and it has accurate first-time read characteristics.

Since some retailers receive some items marked by OCR-A and other items marked by UPC technologies, a word about compatibility of the two technologies is in order. Current equipment cannot read both symbols, so some method of modifying existing equipment to allow both standards to be marked and read is required. Since retailers have made substantial investment in one technology or the other, changing would be a substantial investment. A few manufacturers have already been able to produce a UPC symbol with a line of OCR-A information beneath it that can be read with a scanner. So the capability does exist and, sometime in the near future, more and more manufacturers will have it and be using it.

Other Marking Technologies
Other marking technologies include print only, print/punch, magnetic tape, and bar codes. A brief description of each is given below.

- Print only—The merchandise information is printed on the ticket in standard letters and numbers.
- Print/punch—The merchandise information is both printed and encoded in a series of holes punched in the ticket.
- Magnetic—The information is encoded in the ticket using magnetic tape similar to the stripe on a credit card.
- Bar code—The information is encoded in a series of bars of different sizes. Bar codes are either black and white or three color (usually green, black, and white).

Reading Technologies

There are nine basic methods of reading or capturing merchandise information on sales. They are:

1. Human readable only
2. Stubbing and batch reading
3. Key entry at POS
4. Key entry with portable terminals
5. Key entry back office
6. Wanding back office
7. Wanding at POS
8. Wanding with portable terminals
9. Scanning

Non-food retailers have traditionally used stubbing (removal of a portion of the ticket) and batch reading (grouping the tickets to be read by a machine) or wanding. Key entry of short SKUs, however, has gained in usage with department and specialty retailers. Portable terminals and back office wanding have applicability in certain types of specialty operations, especially where most of the merchandise is stored in the backroom, as is the case with shoe stores.

Food retailers predominantly use scanning to capture UPC information. Wanding may be used in smaller stores where scanning is too expensive, but the use of scanning has been increasing rapidly.

The most effective reading techniques in mass merchandising are key entry of short SKUs, wanding, and scanning. These methods have been proven to give the most accurate readings of more information at the most reasonable cost.

The choice of a merchandise reading or capture technique depends largely on the individual retailer's objectives for merchandise information. The type of data and the timeliness and accuracy required are a part of these objectives. Also critical to this choice is the company's policy with respect to centralized or decentralized control. The choice of a reading method is also affected by factors such as marking technology, the percentage of manufacturer- or source-marked goods, the number and type of checkout facilities, and the cost of checkout personnel.

Determining Ticket Information

The information contained on a ticket can range from the price only to a long SKU with all the data needed to uniquely identify an item. How does the retailer, then, decide which information he needs? In making that decision, he must consider the following factors:

1. What is the status of the merchandise system?
    If the merchandise system is still largely manual and detailed information is required, serious consideration should be given to a long SKU. If the merchandise system is automated or in a state of flux, then the full range of options is available, depending on the difficulty and cost of modifying the current system.

2. What is the price range of the items to be marked?
    Generally, the higher-priced items should be marked with a short or long SKU. Small, low-cost items such as candy, pens, and pads, should be marked with only price, or price, department, and/or class, unless they are source-marked. The reason for the distinction is the cost of developing and maintaining SKU information on the item and the cost of marking.

3. What percentage of sales and inventory is represented by the items?
    The 80/20 rule of retailing has definite applicability to marking. When 80% of sales come from 20% of the items, it is important to identify and track those items in detail. These items, therefore, should have tickets bearing a good deal of information. To prevent inventory build-ups, it is also important to identify in detail slow-selling but required items.

4. Are the items reorderable?
    If the item can be reordered, and will be, it should be identified to the detail level needed for reordering. If a shelf-count or eyeballing is sufficient, less information is needed than for fashion or big-ticket items that must be identified in detail. Items that are not reorderable need to be identified down to style level, so that fast-sellers can be replaced with similar styles. Very often in softgoods, color and size are important for balancing stock or for determining future color and size distributions, so these categories must be marked on such merchandise.

5. Are the items source-marked with VUVM or UPC?

    Because of the economics involved in marking and capturing merchandise information, the status of source-marking is another major factor to consider. If items are source-marked and you can make use of those markings, then it is wasteful not to take advantage of it.

Item Analysis

With the factors outlined above in mind, the retailer then begins an item analysis to determine how much information should be gathered from each item. The analysis should start with those departments representing the highest percentage of sales or the highest inventory investment.

For each item the following information should be logged:

- Current marking method
- Current capture method
- Price
- Source-marking
- Reorderability
- Merchandise system used (manual, automated, centralized, decentralized)
- Level of information required by the buyer

This analysis will help determine what detail is desirable on the ticket. Cost considerations then dictate what is realistic. Generally, though, if detailed SKU information is required in an automated system, serious consideration should be given to the short SKU because of its cost, ease of key entry, ease of marking and reading, and capability for price look-up on POS.

As we have indicated, not all goods need to be marked with the same level of detail. However, for practical reasons, the number of different levels should be limited to two or three. A very workable grouping of three types of tickets would be (1) price only, (2) department and/or class and price, and (3) short SKU and price.

Marking and Capture Alternatives

After analyzing the information needed on each item, attention then shifts to marking and capture alternatives. To determine which of the more than fifty possible combinations of marking and reading is best for you, a detailed cost/benefit analysis is required. The forms shown in Figures 7-2 and 7-3 can be used to facilitate this analysis.

The first step is to collect the costs of the current marking system (see Figure

Figure 7-2. TANGIBLE COST/BENEFIT WORKSHEET

Cost Element	Current System	Alternative 1	Alternative 2	Alternative 3
Distribution Center				
Ticket stock				
Ticket making equipment				
Ticket making personnel				
Checking personnel				
Marking personnel				
Ticket attaching equipment				
Maintenance				
Subtotal 1				
Point-of-Sale				
Stock counting				
Courier service for stubs				
Wands (includes installation)				
Wand maintenance				
Change in no. of POS terminals				
Subtotal 2				
Ticket Conversion				
Unit control personnel				
Ticket converter or reader				
Data entry equipment				
Ticket converter operator				
Data entry clericals				
Supplies				
Maintenance				
Subtotal 3				
Conversion Cost				
Personnel				
Systems				
Subtotal 4				
Grand Total				
Net Difference from Current System				

Figure 7-3. INTANGIBLE BENEFITS WORKSHEET

	Alternative 1	Alternative 2	Alternative 3
Merchandise information accuracy and timeliness			
Better stock balance			
Inventory reductions			
Reduced stock outs			
Increased sales			
Compatibility with a source marking standard			
Improved customer service			
Higher ticket accuracy			
Improved distribution center flow			
More detailed marking			

7-2). These costs should include costs of distribution center ticketing, in-store ticketing, back office and other ticket-reading methods, as well as costs for stock-counting, POS and other terminals, and so on. While collecting current costs, be sure to log the number of items which are source-marked and the type of technology that is used. This information is very important in the analysis of the potential marking and reading techniques which may be practical for the company.

In addition, any rating of intangible benefit should be done using the Intangible Benefits Worksheet (see Figure 7-3). These intangible benefits can be in such areas as merchandise information, inventory control and performance, improved customer service, and higher ticket accuracy.

For example, portable readers or back-office readers are probably not practical unless most of the stock is in the backroom, as it would be in a catalog operation.

Next, enter each marking and reading alternative being considered into a column on the cost/benefit worksheets. The projected costs must then be calculated and entered. Alternatives that are compatible with UPC or OCR-A should include reductions in marking costs for those goods which are source-marked. Wanding or scanning at POS may also reduce the number of registers or checkout counters required. A moderate amount of source-marking will normally reduce stock counting because items that otherwise might not be marked will be source-marked and read.

With the Tangible Cost/Benefit Worksheet completed, the investment and ongoing costs can be used to perform an ROI analysis and comparison. If the cost/benefit analysis results in an obvious answer, the intangible benefits do not need much analysis. If the results are close, then the intangible benefits analysis can be used to make the final decision.

8

Electronic Data Interchange

OVERVIEW: A logical outgrowth in the use of computers in the retail industry is electronic transmission of purchase orders, invoices, and other kinds of business data outside the company. Some retailers are already communicating electronically with their vendors. The reduction in effort, time, and error results in substantial savings. A number of industries have established committees to create the common standards (forms of data entry) needed for large-scale computer-to-computer communication.

A tremendous amount of information flows back and forth between retailers and vendors to get the right merchandise into the stores at the right time. All too often, however, data blockages in the form of delays and errors can keep a retailer from receiving materials when they are needed. Because of the volume of data passing between retailers and vendors, any improvement in this area is looked upon as a major source of savings and increased productivity. Electronic transmission of business data is one of the most important areas in which progress is being made.

Sending and Receiving

Currently, purchase orders and invoices for most vendors are either written manually and then keyed into an automated system, or they are generated directly by an automated system. In either case, the paper is then mailed, which entails a time lag and potential loss. When the purchase order is received, the vendor reviews it manually, adds the appropriate data required for processing, and enters the order into the system. Retailers follow the same basic process upon receiving invoices.

These processes result in duplicate keying of data, with substantial potential for errors. The combination of mail delays and manual processing can result in three to ten days' lag in the actual processing of orders or invoices.

In contrast, orders sent electronically can be received, processed, filled, and shipped in the same day with a low potential for error. Depending on the retailer's payment policy, an invoice sent electronically can be processed and paid within one or two days, again with few, if any, errors. This kind of invoice processing can improve the vendor's cash flow.

If shipping advice is added to order transmission, the retailer can receive immediate confirmation on orders, with notations made regarding substitutions, exceptions, and back orders. At this point, prior to shipment, the retailer can accept or reject changes as he or she sees fit, thus precluding wasteful shipments and return of unwanted goods. In addition, if an item is back-ordered, the items can be left to stand or be cancelled, and the open-to-buy can be adjusted accordingly.

By shortening the lead time between orders and receipts, reductions in inventory are possible, without the corresponding negative impact on service levels or sales. In today's economy, this benefit is of major importance.

The advances in electronic transmission have been made possible by a reduction in the cost of electronic communication, as well as by the recognition of the potential benefits. These benefits can be accrued without major systems development and investments, since most of the information to be transmitted is already contained in the retailer's existing computer system.

Benefits to Retailers

The electronic purchase order and invoice can result in significant savings as well as in intangible benefits in inventory control, data processing, and improved vendor relations.

Increased sales can result from several factors. For example, the improved ordering process will create fewer stock out situations, even with reduced inventory levels. With open-to-buy being freed up sooner, dollars will be available to purchase goods that can be obtained to meet customer demand. And, because of the reduction in stock inventory, shelf space can be used more effectively and efficiently.

The total order processing cycle is made more efficient because there should be no errors at the vendor's end in converting the orders to machine-readable form. Consequently, the retailer's personnel will not be required to sort out and process errors that occur in a manual system. Also, using the order confirmation received from the vendor, the retailer can print the receiving document in the same sequence, reducing checking time in the distribution center.

The electronic invoice can produce several benefits to the retailer. These include:

- Savings through complete elimination of data entry costs.
- Greater ease in matching purchase orders and invoices, resulting in faster problem detection, follow-up, and correction. The invoice can be used as a receiver and it can even be prechecked against the purchase order prior to receipt.
- Reduction of "lost" invoices and costly personnel follow-up and correspondence.
- Since the items on the invoice should be in the same sequence as that in which the goods are packed, line-by-line receiving is made possible in many areas, such as cosmetics, where it has not previously been feasible.

Benefits to Vendors

Vendors also obtain substantial benefits from the use of electronic purchase orders and electronic invoices. As with the retailer, if the vendor has existing automated systems, the additional development for use of electronic transmission is minimal.

Specific vendor benefits from the use of the electronic purchase orders and invoices include:

- Receipt of timely and accurate data with the resulting reduction in clerical time to track lost purchase orders and correct errors.
- Savings in data entry costs through the elimination of this function.
- Reduction in field personnel time to take and write orders in person or by phone.
- Improved cash flow through quick processing of orders and invoices.
- Increased sales due to improved retailer relations. Substitution or back order sales and confirmations are handled more efficiently.

The Status of Electronic Transmission

Electronic transmission can be achieved through a variety of means including magnetic tape or diskette, direct company-to-company transmission, or a clearing house.

Magnetic tape or diskette can be mailed between the vendor and retailer. This approach does not eliminate mail delays but retains most of the other benefits of electronic communication. Direct company-to-company communication uses no intermediary. The clearing house is an intermediary between the retailer and vendor. The retailer transmits data for one or more vendors to the clearing house. If the retailer transmits information using one of the industry standard formats, the clearing house splits the transmission by vendor and files the data for each vendor for later inquiry by the vendor. If one of the industry standards is not used, the clearing house puts the data into the standard format. The effort to develop standards is proceeding on several fronts concurrently.

The NRMA Information System Division Board of Directors established a retail system task force to look at electronic purchase orders and invoices. As a result of this committee's efforts, a voluntary standard was published by NRMA in October 1980. This voluntary standard uses a data dictionary to define the data elements to be transmitted with a combination of fixed and flexible message formats. The voluntary standard provides for communication of order information, invoices, and sales data via several alternative communications media. Several member retailers are currently transmitting data, with plans for expansion to additional companies.

In a joint effort among food distributors, manufacturers, brokers and their trade associations, the food industry conducted a feasibility study of electronic data interchange. This study identified major benefits for all participants and led to standards development and guidelines for systems implementation. The draft standards have been completed, and a pilot implementation has been conducted at several sites.

Called UCS (Uniform Communication System), the food industry's electronic transmission venture is expected to produce net industry savings of $300 million annually at 50% industry participation. This saving represents 0.2% of retail grocery sales. In a food distributor with sales of $100 million, net savings could be up to $200,000. A manufacturer with a direct sales force and $300 million in annual sales could save as much as $850,000 a year through electronic data transmission.

The American National Standards Institute has established the ANSC X-12 committee for business data interchange. This committee includes representatives from retailing, food, banking, steel, transportation, and other industries and is working on the development of standard message formats and communications methods. The NRMA has decided to shift from a unique industry standard into the ANSC X-12 standards. Representations from NRMA have worked with ANSC X-12 to ensure the retail industry needs are being met. Other industries such as transportation and wholesale druggists are also pursuing standards and systems for transmission of business data.

In summary, the electronic transmission of business data between retailers and vendors offers substantial benefits to both groups, with a low capital investment and development cost. Electronic data transmission has the potential to revolutionize the way retailers and vendors conduct their business.

9

Planning for Technological Obsolescence

OVERVIEW: Computer technology is advancing so rapidly that retailers must be concerned about the life of any equipment they purchase. They must look to its potential for accepting new and different software and for meeting new or expanded needs. Leasing equipment as opposed to purchasing it can be very advantageous.

Retail management is looking increasingly to automation as a means of improving productivity. In recent years, technological innovations have been introduced into the retail environment with great success. But technology, as many retailers know, can be a two-edged sword, with as many potential risks as gains. The risks today are greater than ever before, and the reason is technological obsolescence.

To Lease or Buy:
The Costs of Technological Obsolescence

The feeling in the early 1970s was that buying computer technology was much more cost-efficient than leasing. Today, rapid obsolescence makes more retailers hesitant about buying. Ten years ago systems professionals were still fairly confident that computer lease/buy decisions could be based on realistic assessments of the "life" of a particular system. A common opinion among many in the MIS field was that the rate of technological change was slowing down and it was unlikely that a new machine would be technologically obsolete within six to eight years.

Figure 9-1. PURCHASE/LEASE ANALYSIS FOR MINICOMPUTER SYSTEM

CUMULATIVE AFTER TAX CASH FLOW DISCOUNTED @ 15%

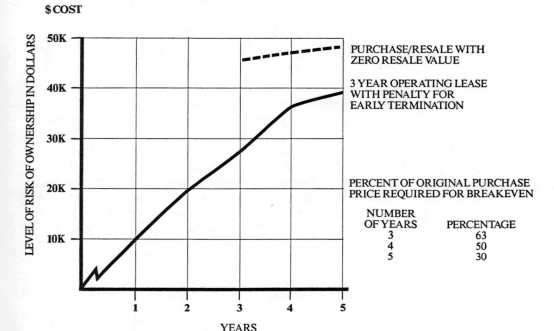

$ COST

LEVEL OF RISK OF OWNERSHIP IN DOLLARS

PURCHASE/RESALE WITH ZERO RESALE VALUE

3 YEAR OPERATING LEASE WITH PENALTY FOR EARLY TERMINATION

PERCENT OF ORIGINAL PURCHASE PRICE REQUIRED FOR BREAKEVEN

NUMBER OF YEARS	PERCENTAGE
3	63
4	50
5	30

YEARS

Working on that basis, a retailer might have analyzed a lease/buy acquisition in this way. Let's say the purchase price is $61,000, investment tax credit can be used by the retailer, the corporate tax rate is 50%, the discount rate is 15%, the purchase is funded by available cash, depreciation is accelerated over five years to zero residual, and maintenance and lease payments remain constant over the life of the analysis. Clearly the optimum choice between purchase or lease is a function of both the time frame and the anticipated resale value of the hardware. In this example, the five-year breakeven point requires an $18,000 (30%) resale value after five years (see Figure 9-1). Under these assumptions, one would buy the machine if the company could afford the cash flow requirements.

Based on recent developments, however, even a five-year residual value of 30% is an overly optimistic requirement. An even more important consideration in this case would be the investment that the retailer had to make in all the nonhardware aspects of the system acquired. It is the hidden costs of technological obsolescence that can potentially be the most damaging. These hidden costs include:

- Initial conversion costs (including one-time installation and training costs).
- Cost of change once installed, such as the cost of technology management moved from vendor to buyer, and the movement of service quality cost from vendor to buyer.
- Cost of living with the system as the company grows.
- Costs due to loss of competitive position, systems replacement, and conversion to replacement if new technology significantly undercuts previous cost and performance assumptions.

These hidden costs become paramount when we realize how rapidly technology is developing and, therefore, how frequently change will be mandated in the retail environment. Contrary to many people's expectations, the data processing industry experienced a continuing explosion of new products and services throughout the 1970s. In fact, whole new industries have developed; and there is every indication that the rate of technological change and improvement of the past decade will continue throughout the present one. As an illustration, the IBM 308X, presently one of the the company's larger mainframe computers, has a performance rating of millions of instructions per second (MIPS) and a volume measured in cubic yards. IBM has recently postulated a late 1980s machine with 70 MIPS performance and packaged in a six-inch cube.

Other developments, many of which will make present technology obsolete, are the following:

External Communications

- Replacement of telephone lines with microwave communication via satellite for long-distance communications.
- Substitution of fiber optics for copper cables.
- Availability of all digital communications between major metropolitan areas.
- Replacement of mechanical switching with computerized switching.

Software

- Improved capability of systems software in fields such as teleprocessing and data base management.
- Availability of retail application packages for small businesses.
- Reduced dependency of software on specific pieces of hardware.

Hardware

- Increased capability of micro- and minicomputers.
- Integration of bubble and other memory as storage media.
- Integration of many computers into large-scale national and international networks, permitting users to inquire into each other's data bases.

- Improvements in data acquisition using optical character recognition and voice recognition devices.
- Incorporation of capabilities formerly handled by software into the design of the hardware.

Human Engineering

- Improved understanding of how to develop effective man/machine interfaces.
- More effective development tools for implementing systems projects on time and within budget.

Internal Telecommunications

- Implementation of business computer systems that replace many voice-based systems such as message storing and routing systems.
- Implementation of office communications systems that replace or augment voice-based systems such as electronic mail coupled with storage of voice data.
- Introduction of new internal and external voice and digital data mixed systems.
- Introduction of personal amplification appliances as replacements for telephones.

This rapid development has three effects. First, the expected life of computer hardware is dropping, so, for competitive reasons, hardware must be replaced sooner. Second, the cost of people and software is rising. This increases the probability that the software will have to be designed to last through several rounds of hardware change. Third, the systems contemplated for automation are increasing in complexity. For example, we have moved from accounts receivable to purchase order management, which potentially touches all the money-making operations in the retail store.

Technology Acquisition

The risk of obsolescence has altered the way a retailer evaluates what technology to purchase or lease. The decision to acquire expensive technology is not just an economic one. In most cases, the retailer must make at least a matching investment in the management of change to utilize the new technology. This management or systems development process has its own lead times, resulting in a maximum rate at which new technology or ideas can be absorbed by an individual company. We have already reached the point where technology is moving ahead faster than the individual company's ability to take advantage of it, and traditional evolutionary management techniques will be inadequate to close the gap.

In evaluating the potential acquisition of state-of-the-art technology, four sets of factors must be considered:

Economic

- Are sufficient funds available to acquire the technology?
- Is the technology profitable as measured by payback period and cash flow analysis?
- How much is at risk in the event of failure or cancellations?

Technical

- Will the technology operate satisfactorily in the intended environment?
- Do the envisioned short-term advantages of this technology actually represent a technical blind alley?

Management

- Does the company have the management talent in place to effectively install and utilize the technology?
- Do the economic and business plans allow for installation lead times and adequate learning curves?

Rate of Change

- Where does the technology fit into the company's strategic business and systems plan?
- Are there potential developments that could make this technology obsolete in the foreseeable future?

Assuming that the application of a technology is profitable, the key issue in determining how to acquire it is obsolescence. The five- to seven-year period of useful life over which a 50% improvement in technology was perceived as likely has now shortened considerably. Since trying to determine technological obsolescence is an imprecise exercise, the decision-maker can best deal with this environment of uncertainty by choosing those technologies that have short payback periods (two to three years) or by leasing or renting equipment.

Part Three

RETAIL
MANAGERIAL
ACCOUNTING

10

Retail Accounting: Retail Inventory Method and FIFO/LIFO

OVERVIEW: Most retailers prefer to use the retail method rather than the cost method in determining the cost value of inventory. The cost method uses the actual or average cost of merchandise to the merchant as the basis for determining inventory value. The retail method uses the relationship of retail price to cost for purchases to determine the cost of inventory. As the number of items and transactions increases, the cost method becomes increasingly cumbersome and expensive to apply. The retail method is an averaging method and is more convenient for most types of merchandise. It enables the retailer to determine profits without taking frequent physical inventories. In computing taxable income, retailers have traditionally used either the FIFO (first in–first out) or LIFO (last in–first out) method of accounting. The impact of inflation on inventory costs has caused many retailers to switch to LIFO because it reduces taxable income.

Retailers invest great sums of money in merchandise and must know at all times the value and quantity of their inventory. Merchandisers need this information to make day-to-day merchandising decisions. For example, they need to know the current retail and cost values of inventory in order to modify actions called for in merchandising plans. The accounting and information services departments are responsible for providing this information. Since profits are based on inventory costs, and merchants and management are measured according to profits, inventory cost is of concern to many people in the organization.

How, then, is a cost value placed on inventory in a retail operation? Basically there are two methods: the retail method, preferred by most retailers, and the cost method.

Cost Method

The cost method provides an evaluation of inventory using only cost figures. This means that all inventory records are kept at the cost of the merchandise, either by specific identification or by some averaging technique. Other retail statistics, such as initial markon and subsequent price changes, are maintained in supplementary records and are not necessarily a part of the accounting system. A physical inventory is taken based on unit counts, which are then extended at cost values. Cost of sales is determined in one of two ways: either by assigning a cost to all individual units sold, or by starting with the beginning inventory at cost, adding purchases at cost, and subtracting ending inventory at cost. Shortage is automatically included in cost of sales since ending inventories will reflect shortages.

Under the cost method, a separate computation must be performed to determine the "lower of cost or market" value. (The retail method, on the other hand, automatically produces the "lower of cost or market" value, provided timely markdowns are taken.)

The cost method is well-suited to departments and stores with high dollar value items, where it is important to keep unit control. These items are easier to track as they move through inventory. There generally are fewer stockkeeping units (SKUs) and fewer transactions. Consequently it is easier to follow the flow of each item and to monitor records of their actual cost.

Retail Method

Most retail organizations use the retail method to track the dollars invested in inventory. This method was developed because it was becoming increasingly difficult for retailers to keep track of the large number of items carried in inventory. As companies grew, it was not practical to track each inventory unit or SKU and its cost. The retail inventory method is an averaging method that assumes that the cost complement (the percentage relationship of cost to retail for merchandise purchases) of actual items in ending inventory is representative of the cost complement of purchases. The retail method provides a means for reasonably estimating at any time the cost value of inventory that is stated at retail selling prices. This method expresses all percentages, such as initial markup and gross profit, *relative to the retail price*, rather than to the cost price, of the merchandise.

A simple example will explain the principal difference between the cost and retail inventory methods. In the cost method, a dress is purchased for $50. The item retails for $105. The markup is $55, or 110% of the cost price. In the retail method, the same dress is purchased for $50, and retails for $105. The markup is $55 or 52% of the retail price.

Under the retail method, the total cost of merchandise on hand is determined by first calculating the sum of current retail prices. The dress will be listed at its selling price of $105 and reduced to cost value by multiplying the selling price by the cost complement of 48% (the inverse of the markup percent). This produces a cost of $50 (48% X $105). Under the cost method, the dress would be valued by direct reference to the $50 cost. This is obviously a simplified example but one can see that when many items are involved, it is easier to use the cost complement percentage rather than the cost method. The reason is that perpetual inventory records are more easily maintained at retail selling prices.

If the dress is marked down by $25, in the retail method the cost complement of 48% would be applied to this new retail selling price. This produces a cost of $38 ($105 - $25 X 48%). The retail markdown of $25 therefore produces a cost write-down of $12 ($50 - $38 = $12). This step also values the inventory at "lower of cost or market," as required by accounting rules.

There are many benefits to the retail inventory method, and these benefits are the reason it is used by most organizations. They include:

1. The retail method is the most efficient method of keeping track of many items, since all transactions, such as sales and markdowns, are done in terms of retail values.

2. Periodic determination of inventory cost and gross profits can be made without taking physical inventories. However, physical inventories are generally taken twice a year to check the accuracy of the perpetual inventory.

3. All merchant-oriented inventory information is expressed in terms of retail dollars so that the buyer can plan sales, stock levels, gross margins, markdowns, desired merchandise turnover, and open-to-buy in a consistent manner.

4. The taking of physical inventories is simplified because the count can be taken at the readily available retail prices and compared to corresponding book amounts.

5. The retail method permits an accurate determination of inventory shortage by referring to retail values without having to compare unit counts to unit records.

6. The retail method automatically produces an inventory at the "lower of cost or market," provided appropriate markdowns are taken on a timely basis.

7. This method records the reduction in gross profit when the price reduction is taken, rather than waiting until the sale is made.

The retail method is not without its disadvantages. These include:

1. It requires a large amount of record keeping to accumulate price changes, markups, and markdowns.

2. It is an averaging method and as such smooths extremely high or low relationships of cost to retail for individual purchases.

3. It is also subject to a certain amount of distortion. For example, deferred markdowns will cause an overstatement of inventory. In addition, the method assumes a homogeneous markup percentage for purchases in a given department. It also assumes that ending inventory is representative of total purchases throughout the period. Since neither assumption always applies, distortion can occur.

Applying the Retail Inventory Method

The retail inventory method can be applied in step-by-step fashion. The steps are:

1. Calculate total inventory available for sale at retail and cost.

2. Calculate the department's cumulative markup percentage and cost complement.

3. Calculate the total retail reductions (sales, markdowns, employee discounts, and shortage provision) from inventory.

4. Determine the ending inventory at retail and cost.

5. Calculate the cost of goods sold.

6. Determine the gross margin.

The procedure may seem complicated, but it can be learned easily if viewed as a series of six steps, each one building on and using the information gathered in the previous steps. Facilitating the retail inventory method is the *retail stock ledger*, represented in Figure 10-1. This is the accounting report that details the book inventory or dollar totals for each merchandise department.

Let us illustrate the retail inventory method with sample figures. The retail

Figure 10-1. RETAIL STOCK LEDGER

	Cost	Retail	Cumulative Markup Percent	Cumulative Cost Percent
Beginning inventory	$100,000	$208,000	52.0%	48.0%
Add: Purchases, net of returns	60,000	120,000		
Freight	2,000			
Less cash discount (2%)	(1,200)			
Additional markups		5,000		
Net additions	60,800	125,000		
Total merchandise available for sale	160,800	333,000	51.7%	48.3%
Less:				
Net sales		100,000		
Markdowns, net		20,000		
Shortage		2,000		
Employee discounts		1,000		
Total retail reductions		123,000		
Ending inventory	101,430	210,000		
Cost of goods sold	59,370			
Gross margin:				
Net sales		$100,000		
Less cost of goods sold		59,370		
Gross margin		$40,630		

stock ledger shows the result of the complete process. As you complete each step, locate the data from that step in the ledger.

1. *Total Inventory Available for Sale at Retail and Cost*

Beginning inventory plus purchases represents the inventory to be accounted for in the period, at both cost and retail. The elements that constitute merchandise received at both cost and retail are: vendor invoice cost less cash discount and returns to vendors, freight-in charges at cost only, assigned retail for all purchases, and additional markups at retail only.

In Figure 10-1, total inventory available for sale at retail and cost is calculated as follows:

	Cost	Retail
Beginning inventory	$100,000	$208,000
Purchases, net of returns	60,000	120,000
Less cash discount	(1,200)	—
Freight-in	2,000	—
Additional markups	—	5,000
Total inventory available for sale	**$160,800**	**$333,000**

2. Cumulative Markup and Cost Complement

Cumulative markup is the difference between the retail selling price and the otal cost of merchandise. In our example this is:

Total retail	$333,000
Total cost	− 160,800
Total markup	**$172,200**

Cumulative markup percentage is the total markup in dollars divided by the total retail price. Knowing the cumulative markup as a percentage of retail is very useful in comparing actual and planned figures and the current period's performance against the prior period. In the example, cumulative markup percentage is:

Cumulative markup %
= Markup dollars ÷ Retail dollars
= $172,200 ÷ $333,000
= .517 or 51.7%

Cumulative cost complement is cost divided by retail, or 100% minus the cumulative markup percentage (100% - 51.7% = 48.3%).

3. Total Retail Reductions from Inventory

In this step the total reductions from the inventory at retail will be calculated. Total reductions represent the cumulative retail value of net sales, net markdowns, shortages, and employee discounts. Each of these elements is defined below.

Net sales are the audited sales figures for the accounting period that are prepared by the sales audit department. Net sales consist of customer purchases less customer returns.

Net markdowns are markdowns less markdown cancellations. **Markdowns** reduce merchandise from its original marked and recorded retail price to a reduced retail price at which it is marked and finally sold. After merchandise value has been reduced at retail (marked down), the retailer may want to restore it to its original retail price or some intermediate higher price. This action to restore the item to a higher retail would be a markdown cancellation.

Stock shortage is the difference between the actual physical inventory at retail and the retail amount in the stock ledger. A provision for estimated shortage is usually made as a percentage of sales for the periods between physical inventories. The provision is adjusted to actual when a physical inventory is taken.

Employee discounts are the difference between recorded retail price and price at which merchandise is sold to employees.

Continuing with the example, total retail reductions would be calculated by adding the four categories detailed above:

Net sales	$100,000
Markdowns, net	20,000
Shortage	2,000
Employee discounts	1,000
Total retail reductions	$123,000

4. *Ending Inventory at Cost and Retail*

In this step, ending inventory is calculated at both cost and retail. Ending inventory at retail is calculated by subtracting total retail reductions from the retail value of the merchandise available for sale during the period. In our example, total merchandise available for sale is $333,000 and total retail reductions are $123,000, so the ending inventory at retail is $333,000 - $123,000 or $210,000.

Ending inventory at cost is determined by multiplying ending inventory at retail by the cumulative cost complement percentage. In our example this is $210,000 X 48.9% = $101,430.

5. *Cost of Goods Sold*

The merchandise cost of goods sold is calculated by subtracting ending inventory at cost from total merchandise available for sale at cost. In our example, the total merchandise available for sale at cost is $160,800 and the ending inventory at cost is $101,430. So the cost of goods sold is $160,800 - $101,430 or $59,370.

6. *Gross Margin and Gross Margin Percentage*

Gross margin and gross margin percentage are statistics that measure the profitability of a department. All of the components needed for calculating gross margin and gross margin percentage have been determined in previous calculations.

To calculate gross margin, subtract total cost of goods sold from net sales. In our example, net sales are $100,000 and the total cost of goods sold is $59,370. So the gross margin is $100,000 - $59,370 = $40,630.

To calculate gross margin percentage, divide gross margin by net sales. In our example, this is $40,630 ÷ $100,000 = .406 or 40.6%.

Applying the retail inventory method requires discipline. Nevertheless, retailers have found the results to be worth the effort. Though it is an averaging method, applied consistently it is the best method available for controlling the elements of gross margin.

FIFO/LIFO

A major objective in accounting for inventories is to determine income by properly matching appropriate costs against revenues. Two methods used in that computation are FIFO (first in–first out) and LIFO (last in–first out). FIFO matches the oldest cost of items purchased with revenue from current sales. LIFO matches the most recent cost of items purchased with the revenue from current sales. Since most retailers expect inflation is here to stay, they have been switching from FIFO to LIFO in order to deal with continually rising costs.

Tax Impact
The LIFO method of inventory valuation saves tax dollars in periods of inflation. Since LIFO enables a retailer to match most recent, and higher, inventory costs with current sales, it reduces taxable income and, consequently, the company's tax payment. Conversely, using FIFO during an inflationary period, the retailer is matching current sales against older and lower costs. The result is greater taxable income and higher tax payments than under LIFO.

Let us illustrate with an example (Figure 10-2).
Column 1—Retail Inventory. The initial data required is identical to that used in converting to cost under the retail method—namely, the retail inventory value as indicated by the balance in the inventory records.

Note that in the first year, the values for the opening and closing inventories are listed. The reason is that the price levels at the beginning of the first year in which the LIFO election is made acts as the base level and all future years are measured against this level.

Also note that in subsequent years' computations, each year's retail inventory valuation, from the base year on, is listed separately. This is necessary to determine the inventory layers which will comprise the year-end LIFO valuation. Each year's inventory represents a layer or level of inventory valuation which is used as a segment of the whole of the LIFO valuation. Since each layer must be calculated by the same factors that created it, it is essential to segregate the information on a yearly basis. If inventory level decreases at year end (as shown in Year 3), the decrease is taken from the immediately preceding inventory layer.

Figure 10-2. COMPUTATION OF LIFO INVENTORY

Year Ended	(1) Retail Inventory	(2) Index (Base = 100)	(3) Retail Inventory at Base Year Prices (1) ÷ (2)	(4) Retail Layers Increase or (Decrease)	(5) Retail Layers at Base Year Prices	(6) Retail Layers at End of Period Prices (2) × (5)	(7) LIFO Cost Complement	(8) LIFO Cost at End of Period (6) × (7)
1st Year:								
1/31/80	$25,000	100.0	$25,000	$25,000	$25,000	$25,000	66.4	$16,600
1/31/81	36,000	108.4	33,210	8,210	8,210	8,900	65.3	5,812
					$33,210	$33,900		$22,412
2nd Year:								
1/31/80	$25,000	100.0	$25,000	$25,000	$25,000	$25,000	66.4	$16,600
1/31/81	36,000	108.4	33,210	8,210	8,210	8,900	65.3	5,812
1/31/82	40,000	110.0	36,364	3,154	3,154	3,469	66.0	2,290
					$36,364	$37,369		$24,702
3rd Year:								
1/31/80	$25,000	100.0	$25,000	$25,000	$25,000	$25,000	66.4	$16,600
1/31/81	36,000	108.4	33,210	8,210	6,304	6,834	65.3	4,463
1/31/82	40,000	110.0	36,364	3,154			66.0	
1/31/83	36,000	115.0	31,304	(5,060)			65.8	
					$31,304	$31,834		$21,063

Column 2—Index. The index column indicates the level of price change that occurs from the beginning of the first fiscal year under the LIFO method. Thus, in the illustration, January 31, 1980 bears the index of 100.0 and this is the point in time against which all future years will be measured.

An appropriate index must be used and is subject to challenge by the Internal Revenue Service. In our illustration, the index of each year has been assumed. As a practical matter, department stores generally use the Bureau of Labor Statistics (BLS) LIFO index, which has express IRS approval. This index was first published in 1948 with price level data from 1941; it is now published monthly. To facilitate the use of the index for those taxpayers who elected LIFO later than 1942, in which case a base level other than 1941 is needed, the BLS also publishes the index information in a form that gives the relative change in the price level from month to month.

The BLS index is presently broken down into 23 groups: 20 individual merchandise groups, a soft goods group, a durable goods group, and a store total group. Because the computation of LIFO is made on a departmental grouping basis for department stores, the BLS groupings must be matched with the generally accepted department classifications as suggested by the Financial Executives Division of the National Retail Merchants Association.

Column 3—Retail Inventory at Base Year Prices. To continue with the illustration, by dividing the inventory at retail at each year end by the appropriate index factor, we have now eliminated the influence of the price level change and have restated the various retail valuations in common units of base year dollars. Thus, we have a unit of measurement by which one can compare year-end balances and determine variations due to physical quantities.

Column 4—Retail Layers' Increase or Decrease. By subtracting each year's inventory at base-year dollars from the preceding year's inventory at the same base-year dollars, the yearly retail increase (incremental layer) or decrease (liquidation of layer) starting from the base year total is established. Since Column 3 eliminated differences attributable to price level, the amounts in Column 4 represent changes in quantities for each year.

Column 5—Retail Layers at Base Year Prices. The amounts for each year in Column 5 are derived from those in Column 4 and project the various layers of inventory sufficient to cover the base dollar valuation indicated in Column 3, plus each year's increase. Decreases (as shown in Column 4) are eliminated by applying them against increases in the immediately preceding year or years until fully eliminated. At the end of the first year there was an increase of quantities. This increase and the base layer at the beginning of the year are listed in Column 5 at base-year dollars. The layers for each period subsequently will be priced out individually by use of the index identified with the period during which each layer was created (Column 6).

The second year shows a similar increase in physical quantities and, again, a layer, at base-year prices, is added to the inventory valuation. During the third year, however, there occurred a decrease in quantities. This decrease, therefore, has to be offset against the inventory layers built to that point, the latest one being used first. As the term LIFO (last in—first out) implies, the liquidation of layers is started with the last layer and proceeds to each immediately preceding layer as needed. Using this procedure, the January 31, 1982 layer is completely eliminated and a portion of the January 31, 1981 layer is also liquidated to absorb the January 31, 1983 decrease. Once an inventory layer has been depleted in this manner, it can no longer be utilized for future year's computations.

Column 6—Retail Layers at End of Period Prices. Here the retail layers at base-year prices, as obtained in Column 5, representing the quantitative composition of the LIFO valuation, are restated at the price levels existing at the time each layer was created. This supplies the LIFO valuation at retail, which must now be converted to cost.

Column 7—LIFO Cost Complement. The procedure for converting the LIFO valuation at retail to cost is substantially the same as the conversion done under the retail inventory accounting method. However, the FIFO cost complement used in the retail method is based on gross markup (without including markdowns in the computation), whereas tax regulations require the use of a cost complement based on a "net" markup (i.e., markups net of markdowns) for LIFO purposes. The lower percentages used in the FIFO retail method result in a lower of cost or market valuation, and this is not permitted under LIFO. The use of the net markup percentages eliminates this and provides the cost complement required for LIFO.

Column 8—LIFO Inventory at Cost. By use of the LIFO cost complement (Column 7), in conjunction with the retail layers at their respective period prices (Column 6), a LIFO cost valuation is now obtained.

Impact on Earnings

LIFO is one of the few tax elections that must also be used for financial reporting. This regulation is known as the "LIFO Conformity" rule. Therefore, along with the reporting of lower taxable income and lower tax payments, LIFO results in lower financial earnings. Lower reported earnings might concern a retailer's stockholders or credit grantors, but knowledgeable business people are familiar enough with LIFO to take into account its effects on earnings.

Principal Advantages and Disadvantages

LIFO does offer the retailer a distinct tax advantage during periods of inflation. There are, however, some disadvantages.

A reduction in income taxes is the most tangible advantage of using LIFO. In effect, the tax impact of the cumulative difference between the FIFO and LIFO inventory is an interest-free loan from the government. This method, however, accrues only with continuing inflation. The anticipated tax advantage is reduced if there is a drop in price levels below those at which the base inventory is priced.

Reduction in financial earnings is seen by many as a disadvantage. However, this is offset by the easing of the conformity requirement that allows disclosure of non-LIFO information and the growing familiarity of readers with these disclosures.

11

Tracking Real Performance and Profits

OVERVIEW: More sophisticated barometers than sales figures must be used if retailers are to measure accurately their companies' performance. Many variables can negate even healthy sales growth -- inflation, disinflation, rising overhead, additional store openings, for instance. Unless retailers are aware of the possible effects of these variables, they can be misled by historical patterns of growth in sales. Overall company performance can be impeded by less-than-adequate performance at individual stores. Retailers must be able to study performance on a regional and store-by-store basis to discover the weak links that might threaten the strength of the chain. To evaluate performance, retailers must be able to measure sales per square foot and profit per square foot.

Measuring Profit Performance

Changes in the economic environment make it imperative that retailers review the way they measure profit performance. Slowed population growth, shifting population centers, inflationary and recessionary pressures on consumer demand, changes in and curtailment of consumer credit, continuing high interest rates, and overstored conditions in many parts of the country have combined to change the game and the method of scoring in retailing today. Traditionally, sales increases have been the retailers' goal and principal benchmark. Comparing sales from one year to the next was generally a valid indicator of a company's performance. But with fluctuating rates of inflation and overhead, the comparison of sales is no longer a trustworthy measure of performance. In the next few pages we will discuss methods of performance evaluation that are better indicators because they take into account such variables as inflation, disinflation, overhead and selling expenses, return on equity, and sales and profit per square foot. As a result, these methods focus attention on the real meaning of the bottom-line figures.

Although retail sales in current dollars have increased, profits have been lagging behind this growth. A Touche Ross analysis of the published data for 17 general merchandise retail companies representing $67 billion in sales and $2.4 billion in pre-tax profits revealed that, over the six years from 1975 to 1980, retail sales increased almost 60%, but pre-tax profits, although peaking in 1978, showed no gain 1975 to 1980.

One of the underlying factors causing profits to lag behind sales growth is escalating overhead and selling expenses (SG & A). Over that same six-year period, the SG & A of those 17 companies rose 70%, outpacing sales growth and cutting profits. Moreover, the analysis did not consider the impact of inflation. Yet inflation must enter into the measurement of profit performance. We will look at two studies that show the impact of inflation. The first is of department stores, the second of food stores.

Impact of Inflation

One of business's key guidelines in assessing the impact of inflation is the Consumer Price Index (CPI). This measures the average change in prices over time for a standard "market basket" of goods and services. The Department Store Inventory Price Index (DSI) represents a weighted measure of goods carried by department stores. The DSI is more specialized and represents but one element of the CPI.

While the DSI helps the retailer account for inflation when assessing sales, the CPI gives a more accurate account of its effect on non-merchandise expenses. This is because the CPI is more representative than the DSI of the cost of new stores, the cost of refurbishing, occupancy escalation clauses, utility cost increases, and the impact of inflation on payroll.

From January 1976 to January 1981, the CPI (representing the expense base) rose 53%. Over the same period, the DSI (representing revenue) rose 26%. Analyzing the same 17 retail companies' net of inflation reveals a sales growth of only 27% when adjusted for the DSI and only 4 1/2% in terms of the CPI. Therefore, instead of the nominal 13% increase in profits, the CPI-adjusted results show a 36% *decline* in profits.

What does this mean? The buying power of the profits generated has actually declined over the six-year period (see Figure 11-1).

The erosion in profits may in part be explained by the performance of the SG & A, which grew far more rapidly than sales, the DSI, and the CPI (see Figure 11-2).

Another Touche Ross study, this one of 35 publicly held food retailers, showed in other ways that historical figures and traditional methods of evaluating performance

Figure 11-1. ADJUSTED PROFITS SHOW A DECLINE IN BUYING POWER

$ MILLIONS

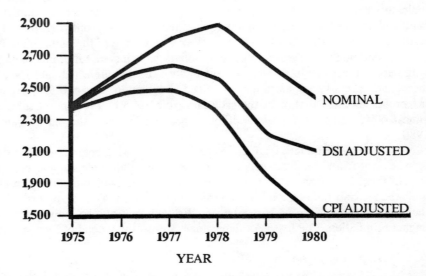

YEAR

are invalid during periods of inflation. To demonstrate the impact of inflation upon traditional financial performance measures, the study analyzed both the inflation-adjusted and historical performance of the 35 companies. Further, in order to evaluate significant findings within the overall sample, the 35 were divided into three groups (Figure 11-3) based upon 1980 return on equity:

1. High ROE—greater than 17.5%
2. Medium ROE—11.5% to 17.5%
3. Low ROE—less than 11.5%

The overall results of the analysis showed that inflation-adjusted return on equity decreased substantially from the historical measurement reported in public financial statements. In fact, 1980 return on equity for the 35 food retailers decreased from 13.2% to - 1.9% after inflation adjustments. Negative net income after inflation adjustments means that insufficient earnings are available for expansion of the business and for paying dividends to stockholders, after providing for the real costs of maintaining the physical operating capacity of the business.

Further, inflation had made it difficult for many food retailers to maintain their business. These difficulties were the result of:

Figure 11-2. EXPENSES HAVE INCREASED FASTER THAN SALES

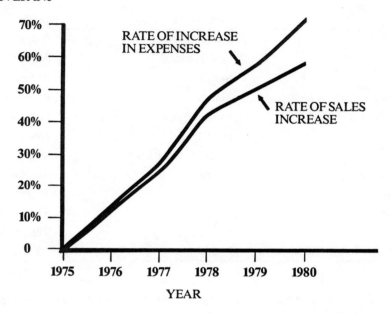

% INCREASE
OVER 1975

- Declining earnings as costs increased more rapidly than prices.
- The income tax penalty associated with higher "effective" tax rates.
- Dividend payout from capital instead of earnings.
- The inability to replace assets when required.

What are the major factors that explain the overall changes between inflation-adjusted and historical performance? Several components of the return-on-equity ratio are impacted by inflation. The factors affecting return are net sales, gross margins, operating expenses, and income taxes. The factors affecting equity are current assets and fixed assets.

Here is the fiscal reality many had been ignoring:

Net sales for the 35 retailers during the 1976–80 period showed little real growth after inflation adjustments. Aggregate sales increased by 47% in historical dollars to approximately $74 billion. However, real growth was less than 2% after adjusting net sales to constant 1980 dollars based upon the CPI. (Other indexes could be utilized,

Figure 11-3. SAMPLE FOOD RETAILERS GROUPED BY 1980 RETURN ON EQUITY

High	Medium	Low
ROE Greater than 17.5%	ROE 11.5 to 17.5%	ROE Less than 11.5%
Albertson's	Dillon	A & P
Big V	First National	Allied Supermarkets
Cullen	Mott's	Bayless
Foodtown	Marsh	Borman's
Giant	National Tea	Fisher Foods
Lucky	Penn Traffic	Foodarama
Schultz Sav-O	Pueblo International	King Kullen
Star Supermarkets	Kroger	Shopwell
Supermarkets General	Ruddick	Thorofare
Thriftimart	Safeway	Victory Markets
Weis	Stop & Shop	Village
Winn-Dixie	Waldbaum	

but the overall trends would be similar.) Further, real growth in net sales was a significant factor in differentiating the high, medium, and low return on equity groups within the sample:

- High ROE companies experienced 21% real growth (approximately 4% per year) over this period.
- Medium ROE companies experienced 5% real growth over this period (approximately 1% per year).
- Low ROE companies experienced a 22% real decline (approximately 4% per year) in net sales over this period.

Gross margins, after inflation adjustments to reflect the current cost of acquiring the goods being sold, showed a mixed trend in relation to increases in net sales. Over the 1976–78 period, inflation adjusted gross margins increased from 19.9% to 21.3%, but they declined to 20.5% over the 1978–80 period as a "gross margin gap" was created when merchandise costs rose faster than prices.

Further, high ROE companies had done a better job managing gross margins than medium and low ROE companies as illustrated by their inflation adjusted 1980 margin of 21.4% versus 20.2% for the medium ROE companies and 20.1% for the low ROE companies.

Operating expenses showed a trend opposite to gross margins on an inflation-adjusted basis. Historical operating expenses were adjusted to reflect the current versus original cost of plant, property, and equipment and depreciation provisions. Over the 1976–78 period, inflation-adjusted operating expenses increased from 19.1% to 20.1%; however, they declined, to 19.9% over the 1978–80 period. The increase of 0.8% over the total period, in an industry with historical net income of about 1%, represented a significant inflation gap created by operating costs rising faster than sales. This was mitigated to some extent by increasing gross margins during the period.

Trends in the size of plant, property, and equipment (PP&E) inflation adjustments implied that some medium and low ROE companies were not keeping their physical plant as up-to-date as high ROE companies.

The cumulative effect of "no growth" sales, declining margins, and increased operating expenses was substantially lower pre-tax income. In fact, 1980 inflation-adjusted pre-tax income for the sample was only $290 million compared to historical reported pre-tax income of $1.2 billion! Decreased pre-tax income increases "effective" income tax rates, thereby causing a "tax on capital."

In addition to taxing capital, lower inflation-adjusted net earnings raised the ratio of dividend payout to income. In effect, for many companies the dividend payout was resulting in insufficient earnings being retained for new investments. Since new capital investments are the source of growth, many companies were restricting their potential for future growth.

Inflation-adjusted *current assets* were higher than historically reported levels because the inventory report was restated to better reflect the current cost of inventory investment. Inflation-adjusted current assets for the overall sample increased by 8% over the period compared to a less than 2% increase in net sales. This indicated a decline in working capital productivity over the 1976–80 period. The high and low ROE groups had the most substantial productivity declines:

- Current assets for high ROE companies increased by 31% while net sales increased only 21%.
- Current assets for medium ROE companies increased by 5% while net sales increased by 5%, resulting in no change in working capital productivity.
- Current assets for low ROE companies decreased by 10% while net sales decreased by 22%.

Fixed assets were substantially higher than reported on a historical basis due to a restatement of PP&E and associated depreciation provisions to reflect current cost versus original purchase costs. As an illustration, inflation-adjusted fixed assets in 1980 were $11.8 billion compared to a historical cost basis of only $7.6 billion!

As a result of the inflation adjustments which increased inventories and fixed assets to better reflect the current costs of these assets, inflation-adjusted equity was substantially higher than "historical" equity. Inflation-adjusted equity provided a clearer picture of the *actual shareholder's investment* in the business.

Impact of Disinflation

By 1982, economic conditions had changed drastically. Recession and fiscal policies had produced a period of disinflation—a sharp drop in the inflation growth rate. Despite this, interest rates remained high. Many companies found themselves burdened with high costs but unable to raise prices high enough to achieve adequate profits.

Retailers had adapted operating and financial strategies to the exigencies of inflation, some doing it better than others. But most had no contingency plans for disinflation.

As price inflation (as measured by the Consumer Price Index) continued to slow, consumer expectations changed accordingly. With operating expenses fixed at high rates because of commitments made with inflationary expectations (labor contracts, leases, debt financing), or continuing to rise faster than prices, companies had more difficulty passing along increases and maintaining current margins.

The change from inflation to disinflation has most affected those companies who can least afford it—the companies experiencing low return on equity. This group was least able to modernize plant and equipment at high current costs because they were unable to pass along these costs by increasing prices.

Fighting Inflation and Disinflation

For disinflation, as for inflation, it is essential to manage the components of ROE. The strategies that will produce the greatest payoffs for most companies are:

- Reducing leverage (debt financing) and strengthening the balance sheet
- Tightening financial and operating control
- Making capital investments conservatively

Persistent inflation saw debt-financed growth and high leverage, with the anticipation of servicing debt later with cheaper dollars. Disinflation – and the possibility of deflation (an actual decline in prices) – turns this assumption on its head. Debt servicing becomes a drain that threatens liquidity and survival. High leverage and high interest will return to haunt some companies during disinflation. However, by reducing leverage and strengthening the balance sheet, a company can produce greater returns for its investors with less risk.

Disinflation and deflation are a time to sacrifice and ride out the recession. Aggressive growth plans should be reconsidered to preserve cash and protect liquidity. Wherever possible, costly short-term debt and floating rate long-term debt should be reduced to alleviate the squeeze of high interest rates in a period of moderating prices. Reducing the ratio of debt to total capitalization will not only improve the balance sheet but also contribute to the bottom line.

Disposition of assets and sale or leaseback of properties can raise needed cash. These techniques are particularly attractive during disinflation because asset values that have risen rapidly during high inflation may have peaked. Smaller changes in stockholders' purchasing power, resulting from smaller changes in the cost of living, provide the opportunity to improve working capital by moderating dividends.

Since price increases can't be used to bail out mistakes, tighter control must be implemented in all key areas. Understanding disinflation's impact on both consumers and competition, and knowing the implication of current financial trends, will help in evolving the best tactics. Three vital steps are (1) cutting costs, (2) improving productivity, and (3) strengthening the company (particularly if it is highly leveraged).

Store-by-store inflation-adjusted analyses should be prepared to compare real growth, ROE, and sales to dollars of investment and contribution. The results will assist in determining whether to continue operating certain stores that consume working capital and capital investment possibilities. In periods of inflation, disappointing operations are sometimes rationalized by increasing property values. Now, however, asset values may be at their peak or shrinking.

The working capital derived from withdrawing from stores and liquidating assets with unacceptable ROE can be used to reduce debt load or finance alternative investments. Although this approach may result in reduced sales volume in the short run, it provides an excellent opportunity for companies to improve cash flow and reduce costly fixed charges in operating expenses.

When prices are rising, companies are not penalized for, and have even profited from, carrying large inventories, since holding gains usually offset carrying costs and produce inventory profits. However, in a period of disinflation coupled with high "real" interest rates, the cost of overstocking is not offset by holding gains. The result is a reduction in operating profits. Improved inventory control will promote leaner inventory levels by improving turnover and reducing carrying costs, all leading to increased operating profits.

Managing margins is one of the key components of ROE. Retailers should use the current state of the economy to obtain more promotions and deals from manufacturers. With money tight and prices falling, inventory turnover is important to them.

Pricing strategies should be reviewed to obtain the highest margins on sales while still remaining competitive. Inventory mix should be managed with emphasis on higher-margin items.

Operating expenses can be controlled by tighter budgeting controls. Ways to increase employee productivity should be investigated and the current economy used as leverage to achieve labor concessions from unions. Compensation programs for nonunion employees and executives should also be reevaluated.

Long-term capital investments, which lock in the cost of doing business in the future, are used as a hedge on the cost side when revenues are expected to rise along with inflation. During disinflation, companies should rethink their growth policies and be aware of the increased need for improving cash flow and liquidity. This is the time to set healthier growth objectives through more conservative capital investment strategies. It is harder to justify projects in the face of moderating product prices, high interest rates, and a slow-growth economy.

Fund high-margin, low-risk projects such as remodeling or expanding existing stores or buying units from a competitor in trouble. Interest-sensitive projects should be delayed since present interest rates may have excessive built-in expectations of future inflation, burdening all except those who can prepay without a penalty.

Financing projects internally is also a key factor in investment decision making. Concentrating growth efforts along a narrow line will enable companies to strengthen their operations and protect their balance sheets.

Disinflation presents the retail industry with benefits as well as problems. The companies best equipped to survive the present and uncertain future will probably have a light debt load, strong cash flow, and the ability to finance expansion internally.

Successful management requires adaptability, as well as an instinct to act decisively in a program to reduce leverage, tighten controls, and improve productivity of resources. All of this assumes the ability to assess all aspects of performance accurately and quickly.

Sales and Profit per Square Foot

While the impact of inflation is an important part of performance measurement, there are other factors that are just as, if not more, important. A critical element in accurately determining performance is sales and profit per square foot. This is especially important because sales growth resulting from additional store locations may be hiding unit-by-unit deterioration. Results from the study of the general merchandise stores mentioned at the beginning of this chapter demonstrate this fact.

An analysis of 13 general merchandise retail companies showed that sales per square foot increased only 25% in nominal dollars (compared to the 60% increase in total sales) and generated a 20% *decline* when measured against the CPI (see Figure 11-4). Pre-tax profits per square foot declined 18% in absolute dollars and declined 53% when measured by the CPI (see Figure 11-5).

This analysis seems to indicate that the expense structures required to support the increased number of stores (including both home office and store expenses) was greater than the gross margin dollars being generated by the increased sales per store. Expenses can rise faster than the gross margin dollars for a number of reasons:

- New stores might take sales away from older stores.
- New stores might fail to reach their volume and profit potential.
- Older stores might experience a decline in sales and/or profitability even without the impact of new stores.

In short, on an average, stores are not generating sufficient profits to cover increased operating expenses to provide an adequate build-up of capital for subsequent growth, maintenance, and refurbishing.

Figure 11-4. ADJUSTED SALES PER SQUARE FOOT SHOW A 3% GAIN (DSI ADJUSTED) OR A 20% LOSS (CPI ADJUSTED)

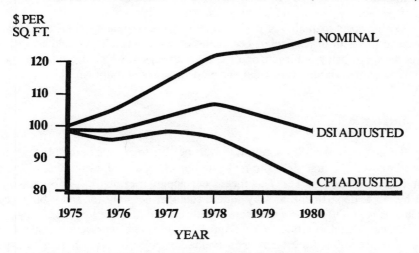

Figure 11-5. PRE-TAX PROFITS HAVE DECLINED

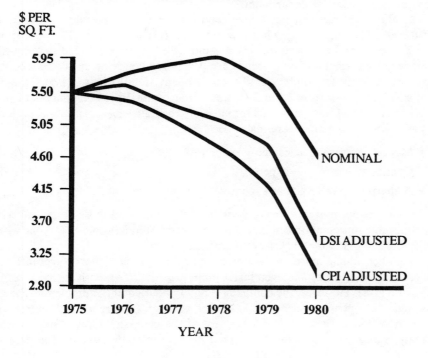

While some SG & A may be considered a function of a number of stores, our analysis indicates that SG & A per square foot increased at a rate equal to or greater than sales per square foot for 15 of the 17 companies in our study.

With respect to quality of performance of these companies, then, and regarding the overhead problem in particular, economies of scale normally associated with sales increases were not being achieved, and SG & A expenses, which are typically considered fixed or semi-variable, were behaving as if they were totally variable.

Strategies

To survive in the 1980's, retailers must be able to reverse both of the conditions mentioned above. The first step is to make an objective, critical evaluation of the company and the markets it serves. This means developing meaningful performance information by store, department, and by square footage, not only for sales, but expenses and profits as well. Often one weak store can severely damage a total company.

Track this information over a number of years and represent it in the form of a graph. The graphic picture helps keep evaluation objective. It is harder to expect a turnaround next season when the trend shows five years of deteriorating performance for a company, location, or department.

Evaluate the marketplace objectively. Who is the competition? Who are our real customers? Has that changed in the past five years, and what are the implications?

Two examples demonstrate why it is important to track detailed store-by-store performance, even when company trends are good. One company in the Touche Ross study showed a fairly favorable overall total company trend (Figure 11-6). However, the company had grown from 15 to 20 stores in four years. Based on analysis of store-by-store performance trends, adjusted for inflation, the following scenario was projected for this company if no action were taken:

- Modest increase in sales and gross margin
- Continued increase in expenses
- A sharp drop in profits as expenses outran gross margin.

Management was not moved to make some hard decisions, and those projections (Figure 11-7) became representative of actual performance. Why? Because everyone wished for a magic wand—and took heart in the sales numbers.

Another much more successful company experienced very favorable sales growth (60% in four years) and even faster profit growth (70%), with a good return on sales (Figure 11-8). However, the company is not without potential problems. One geographic region is a poor performer. It has lower sales, gross margins, and, moreover, a 3% store contribution versus 12% for the rest of the company. Only a store-by-store trend analysis and a plot of weak stores on a map revealed these facts. The data was

Figure 11-6. PROJECTION OF POSSIBLE FUTURE PERFORMANCE

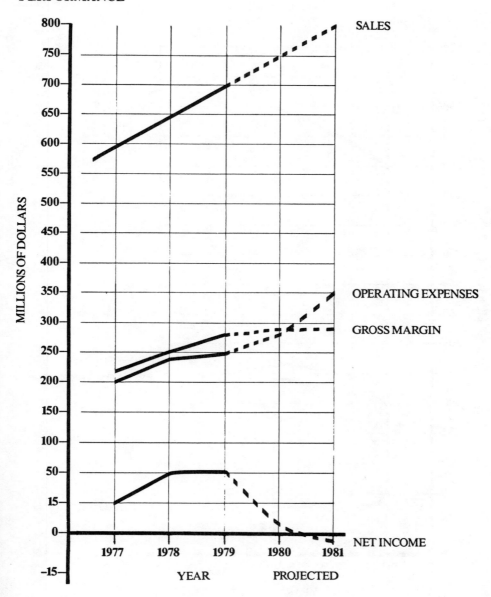

Figure 11-7. PAST PERFORMANCE

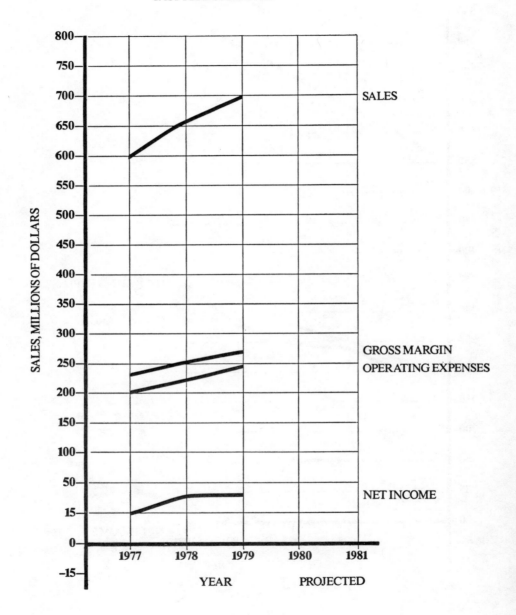

PAST PERFORMANCE

Figure 11-8. STRONG OVERALL GROWTH CONCEALS WEAK PERFORMANCE AT SOME STORES

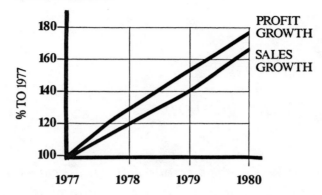

there, but management simply had not looked at it that way. The company is now launching a study of this region to determine how to modify its performance.

Understanding what's behind the total company performance, then, is extremely important. Only when armed with this information can the retailer select the actions and strategies that are right for the company. That information should help answer the following questions:

What should be the major priorities for action and change?

Is the company at or near its practical limit for gross margin improvement? For store staffing reductions?

What other opportunities exist or need to be explored for improved profitability? Organizational restructuring? Reassessment of overhead staff levels? Elimination of less productive stores? Elimination of functions? Change in merchandise mix? Modified store hours?

Are merchants "market" pricing and unconsciously failing to pass on the impact of inflation?

Are there other management decisions that require reassessment?

Is the expense level indicative of an overstored position or of inadequate attention to the overhead budgeting process?

Precise solutions and priorities will vary for each company, by market segment and geographic area. But one thing is clear: the success model for retailers has indeed changed. No longer do sales increases alone indicate success. The new model requires the vision and analytical ability to measure profits and return on investment—and to measure these trends at store level where the action is.

12

Cash Management

OVERVIEW: Cash is a resource and must earn a reasonable return for the company. Through careful planning and control of funds, the company can meet its cash requirements and take advantage of timely business opportunities. By studying the cash cycle, the manager can find opportunities to improve the company's cash position. Six areas for improving the cash position are: cash forecasting; cash gathering; cash disbursing; cash investing; cash concentration, reporting, and control; and banking relations. A short checklist can help in assessing a company's present cash management system and reveal possible areas of improvement. A number of techniques can be applied to implement these improvements.

Although the buy and sell relationship is still the cornerstone of retailing, it is no longer the whole operation. The way a company handles ancillary functions is having a greater and greater effect on profits. One of the most vital of these ancillary functions is cash management. As the cost of money rises, retailers, like other business managers, are looking at cash as an asset, a resource that must be conserved and must earn a reasonable return for the company. With money market instruments offering double-digit annual rates, and with overnight and weekend investing available, the returns on cash can be considerable.

Cash management can be defined as the planning, organizing, and controlling of short-term corporate funds so that the company can:

- Meet its payroll, overhead, cost of merchandise, and other obligations that can be predicted with a fair degree of accuracy.
- Be prepared for unforeseen events requiring quick availability of funds, such as sudden downturns or a major maintenance expenditure.
- Take advantage of business opportunities, such as an attractive short-term investment or a stock acquisition.

To keep the company in a position to meet its obligations, handle emergencies, and seize timely business opportunities, the cash manager tracks and controls the flow of funds through the corporation. His prime objective is to collect receipts as quickly as possible and to delay disbursement as long as possible while meeting obligations on time. In doing this, the company is minimizing working capital and idle bank balances and maximizing the cash that is available for generating the return.

The Cash Cycle

The cash collection and disbursement pattern is naturally affected by the cash cycle. The cash cycle involves the same steps in every company:

1. Raise cash by selling stock, issuing bonds, or taking loans.
2. Invest that cash in assets such as plants and equipment, inventory, and accounts receivable.
3. Use those assets to generate more cash, which can either be reinvested in more assets or result in net income for non-cash charges.
4. Return that newly generated cash to investors in the form of dividends.

A simple graphic view of cash flow emphasizing receipt and disbursements is shown in Figure 12-1.

The collection float refers to the status of funds in the process of collection. It starts at the time the sale is made and ends when your account receives collected funds. This process of collection involves a number of steps and the greater the delay between

Figure 12-1. CASH FLOW PROCESS

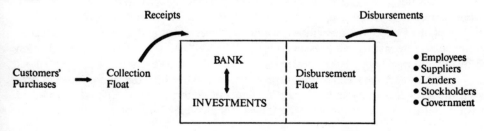

the steps, the longer the float period. The longer the float period, the more cash is tied up in company operations. If your company is slow in preparing and sending an invoice or in handling and depositing the customer's check, then your company is responsible for extending the float period. Add to these internal delays those created by the post office, the customer, and the bank, and the float time is even greater.

Besides collection float, which you wish to keep as short as possible, there is disbursement float. This is the time between your making a purchase and having cash withdrawn from your account. Just as you try to shorten the time of collection float, you make every effort to lengthen disbursement float, without paying additional charges or endangering vendor relationships.

Six Components of Cash Management

Six activities are essential to effective cash management: cash forecasting; cash gathering; cash concentration, reporting, and control; cash disbursing; cash investing; and banking relations.

Cash Forecasting

Will operations fund next year's new equipment program? Are credit lines adequate if we plan to open ten new stores? Can we repay our loan next month? Cash forecasting helps retailers answer these questions.

Cash forecasting is the projection of future cash needs for inventory and personnel expenses, overhead, expansion, and unforeseen events or business opportunities. It is one of the most important elements in business planning.

Cash forecasting requires the preparation of a cash budget. This is usually an annual budget figured on a monthly basis. The cash budget includes expected receipts, expected disbursements, and beginning and ending balance. The anticipated expenses and disbursements can be based on historical experience. For example, with sales of $100,000 in sporting goods last year, the cash manager might expect receipts from that department to be the same, allowing for inflation, next year. Expenses can be similarly estimated.

In preparing the budget, the cash manager must also be guided by overall company plans. For example, if the company plans to open new stores during the year, expenses and receipts connected with this expansion must enter into the budget.

Cash budgets can be completed in varying degrees of detail and for a variety of time periods, depending upon reporting objectives. The forecasts will result in a monthly plan of expected accounting events, such as sales and capital expenditures. Detailed cash forecasting requires an understanding of "real" cash flow due to collection and disbursing cycle lags. Report formats will be daily or weekly.

Once you have defined reporting formats and periods, the major issue in preparing the budget is the accuracy and timeliness of your forecasts. Financial modeling software and the microcomputer make the cash manager's job a lot easier.

Cash budgets are updated on a regular basis to make sure that performance matches plan, just as strategic and six-month merchandise plans are updated periodically. With careful cash budgeting, the company knows just what its operating cash must be and how much cash can be invested for greater return.

Cash Gathering

The amount of cash available for investments depends largely on the speed with which the company can collect its receipts. If customers are slow in paying bills, then the company must tie up more of its money for operations. If the company can collect receipts quickly, it then has greater cash resources for investment. The object of speedy cash collections is to reduce the float.

In retailing, collections are made through cash receipts, checks, and bank and private label credit cards. Each medium has its own processing procedures and float time. To reduce this float time, the accounts receivable procedures must be streamlined and made as efficient as possible. Analyze collection efficiency by reviewing receivables (turnover, aging, uncollectibles) and collection cycle (average time lags and float). Each significant receipt item should be tracked to identify mail location and time, payer's bank, and clearing time.

A number of techniques have been developed to speed the clearing of checks once they have been sent by the customer. Many banks are becoming more cooperative in the use of these techniques. Automated clearinghouse transactions (ACHs) speed collections. Morning deposits with same-day processing and special handling by the bank of large items can be negotiated.

Lockbox service is another technique to speed collections. Lockboxes are centrally located collection post office boxes. Customers will mail their remittances to these lockboxes rather than to the company. The company's bank has authorization to collect mail from the lockboxes several times a day and process the checks. This way the cash is deposited into the company's account much sooner than if the checks were processed at the company's office and forwarded to the bank. A hard copy of names, dates, account numbers, and such is forwarded to the company.

A *preauthorized check* is a signatureless demand deposit instrument that is used to accelerate the collection of fixed payments. The customer signs an authorization agreement with the company that allows checks to be drawn against his account at the specified interval. *Preauthorized debiting* is a system whereby a customer's account is automatically charged funds due on an agreed upon date.

Concentration, Reporting and Control

Concentration banking places the collection function closer to the customer by establishing sales offices at centralized locations for the collection and processing of customer receipts. Concentration banking mobilizes funds from these centralized locations, whether they are banks or company operational facilities, into a central cash pool.

The cash manager must then monitor only a few cash pools to obtain maximum use of funds.

The objective in cash concentration is to speed cash receipts from local operations into a centralized account to minimize idle balances. Once pooled, these funds can then be used to pay vendors or be invested to maximize returns.

To achieve cash concentration objectives, consider concentration accounts, local target balances, a daily sweep of accounts, a balance reporting system, and an incentive system to encourage better local cash control. Timely and accurate reporting allows the retailer to monitor and control collection efficiency and pinpoint bottlenecks. These reports include information on sales, shipments, billings, collections, deposits, and availability of funds.

Cash Disbursing

The objective in regard to payables and disbursements is to achieve two conflicting goals: to maintain good credit standing by paying bills on time and to minimize costs by delaying payment as long as possible. Thus, the key issues are when and how the disbursements are made.

Guidelines for disbursement include:

1. Control payables by the due date so as not to incur additional charges.
2. Take all cash discounts, and mail checks on the last day of the discount period.
3. If discounts are not taken, do not mail checks until the last day of the net payment period.
4. If the discount is not offered, mail the checks on the last day of the net payment period and assume that the period is 30 days when not specified.

While these guidelines may seem obvious, the difficulty lies in controlling disbursements so that these steps are followed all the time. It might be necessary to revise information systems to spot whether or not discounts are taken and to indicate when disbursements are made. This can be done by requiring exception reports that highlight early or late payments. Tracking down the reasons for these exceptions can reveal an improper procedure that is using cash unnecessarily.

As part of a review of all accounts payable procedures, management can monitor vendors by types of terms and by their attentiveness to dates. Those that offer the best terms obviously save your company money. This kind of information should then be relayed to merchandising and upper management. If the same goods can be obtained from the vendors offering better terms, purchases from other vendors should be reduced, thereby reducing the company's cash outflow. This kind of monitoring might also spur buyers to negotiate more aggressively for extended terms.

The company may be better able to take full advantage of extended terms if bank credit lines have been obtained. Having such credit available and using it wisely is another way of controlling disbursements on a sound cash management basis.

In making disbursements, cash can be conserved by using zero-balance accounts. Zero-balance accounts are special disbursement accounts having a zero dollar balance on which checks are written. As checks are presented to this account, funds are automatically transferred from a central control account.

Cash Investing

Investing idle cash and obtaining credit facilities is yet another responsibility of the cash manager. The manager's objective is to maximize yield and minimize risk on investments, and to maximize availability and minimize cost of credit.

Several factors impact your ability to achieve these objectives:

- The quality of your funds/cash forecast(s).
- Your familiarity with investment and credit vehicles.
- Your ability to develop an investment/borrowing portfolio strategy tailored specifically to your requirements.

To identify improvement opportunities, you will need to determine how accurate your cash forecasts have been in predicting your investment and borrowing requirements. Secondly, analyze your credit arrangements and investment portfolio to determine how well these match your requirements. The key is to find the vehicles best suited to your needs.

Banking Relations

Good cash management requires cooperation from a good bank or group of banks. Maintaining good bank relationships is necessary to ensure borrowing availability and to minimize balance requirements, while compensating banks fairly for services performed. The competitiveness in the banking industry makes it beneficial for companies to choose their banks carefully.

A good bank is one that is stable, has the ability to provide adequate financing, has branches close to your location, and meets the cash management needs and changing requirements of your company.

Establishing and maintaining sound banking relations will affect your ability to achieve many of your cash management objectives. Your banker can assist you in implementing some of the improvement techniques identified—lockboxes, concentration accounts, zero balance accounts, and so on. Providing your banker with timely, accurate financial statements and forecasts will be helpful in developing your banker's confidence and understanding of your business. This is particularly important in obtaining necessary credit. Identifying a banker who can satisfy your existing and future service requirements will be important in implementing an effective program.

The cost of service varies from bank to bank. If you are looking for a new banker, ask several bankers to quote cost of unbundled services. Once a banking relationship is established, monitoring bank performance will ensure that service levels are effective and cost-efficient. Your banker should provide a monthly account analysis to assist in your evaluation.

In summary, effective cash management can be achieved by using these tools and techniques:

1. Use cash flow forecasts to plan needs.
2. Speed up cash receipts by effective management of accounts receivable and by reducing float.
3. Manage accounts payable and delay disbursement.
4. Manage bank relations by planning needs accurately, selecting banks carefully, and maintaining a close working relationship with the banking community.
5. Maintain prudent financial policies regarding capital, debt, and dividends.

Specific applications of these techniques will vary from company to company. A technique that conserves cash for a large company might actually be too costly for a smaller one. But by knowing the potential gains available through effective cash management, and evaluating the options in achieving it, management can turn cash into a productive asset.

Identifying Opportunities for Cash Savings

A company seeking to improve its cash management can find out where opportunities for improvement lie by (1) understanding the particular features of the organization relevant to cash management and (2) examining the existing system of cash management.

Your Organization

Four areas deserve special consideration when analyzing your organization: cash collection methods, inventory control, disbursements control, and overall company objectives.

Unless you operate a few stores in a well-defined market area, most of your cash collections are handled by store employees scattered over a wide geographic area, and you use local banks as cash depositories for your store receipts. Your challenge is to achieve cash control and concentration with minimum demands on store employees and at minimum cost. If you have not implemented a cash control system or investigated the cash concentration techniques available, your opportunity for cash management improvement is high.

Another area to examine is your inventory control system. Inventory represents a significant portion of invested capital. If your reporting system does not analyze product movement, profitability, and return on investment, you are probably tying up your cash without sufficient end return. Furthermore, if you have not established the responsibility and incentive for controlling merchandise at the store level, you might be paying for more inventory than necessary. Careful monitoring of stock levels and turns could significantly impact cash flow.

The ability to forecast and monitor disbursements is an important element of any retailer's cash management program. Your payables system should allow you to schedule your vendor payments, forecast future payments, produce paid items report, and evaluate float by vendor. If it doesn't, you may not be receiving the full benefit of disbursement float. Secondly, you need to plan and monitor your capital expenditures. If your credit requirements have been based on outdated information, opportunity may exist for reducing borrowing costs.

Any effective cash management program requires the cooperation of every major function within the organization. Sometimes the goals and objectives of these functions are in conflict with cash management objectives. For example, eliminating idle balances and speeding up collection time from local banks to corporate accounts may be detrimental to local bank relationships. If cash management policies, objectives, and strategies are not established by the top executive and integrated with other objectives, achieving the proper balance between cash management and other operational objectives will be difficult. The degree of home office control and local autonomy also is a top management decision that should enter the cash management policy.

Your System and Procedures

Once you have reviewed the features of your organization outlined above, examine the existing cash management procedures to see if there is room for improvement. Any of the following conditions can be a symptom of poor cash management practices:

- Numerous bank accounts, and a multitiered banking network.
- High average daily idle balances in local and corporate banks.
- Commitment for credit facilities far exceeding projected borrowing requirements.
- Lack of cash forecasting for cash requirements determination, short-term investments, and borrowing decisions.
- No fundamental enhancements in cash management practices in the recent past to address the impact of the 1980 Monetary Control Act, or advances in information and processing technology.

The following cash management checklist can help you evaluate the performance of your cash management system and uncover weak spots that represent possibilities for cash savings.

Your Cash Management Rating

How well are you managing your cash function? What specific areas need improvement? Completing the checklist below can help answer these questions.

	Yes	No	Don't Know
1. Are you monitoring the time it takes to bill your receivables?	___	___	___
2. Do you produce account receivable aging reports and monitor the collection period for each account?	___	___	___
3. Have you evaluated the time it takes to receive account payment after it has been placed in the mail?	___	___	___
4. Do you know how long it takes to convert bank deposits into available funds?	___	___	___
5. Are you informed daily of your balance levels, deposits, and availability of deposits on all your major bank accounts?	___	___	___
6. Are you satisfied that you have a system that achieves the proper balance between cash and inventory controls, and store operations?	___	___	___
7. Is your cash pooled daily in central account(s) facilitating investment of idle balances, when appropriate?	___	___	___
8. Are your account balances equal to or less than your compensating balance requirements?	___	___	___
9. Are you satisfied that increasing the flow of funds from multiple collection points to a centralized account would not have cash benefits, or is inappropriate?	___	___	___
10. Have you evaluated the cost/benefit of using anticipatory Automated clearinghouse (ACHs) to move cash from local banks to a central account?	___	___	___
11. Are your large dollar volume receipts immediately available for corporate use?	___	___	___
12. Does your existing payables system allow you to: Schedule disbursements to ensure no early payments?	___	___	___
Take advantage of discounts offered?	___	___	___

Monitor discounts available and discounts taken? ___ ___ ___

13. Are you satisfied that you are receiving all vendor rebates that are due, and that their collection is timely? ___ ___ ___

14. Have you evaluated the impact of your existing inventory levels on your cash requirements and evaluated methods of reducing inventory while retaining service levels? ___ ___ ___

15. Do you receive and review the following monthly:
    Account analysis? ___ ___ ___
    Bank statements? ___ ___ ___

16. Do you perform the following at least monthly:
    Account reconciliation? ___ ___ ___
    Comparison of estimated to actual charges? ___ ___ ___

17. Can you do a reasonably accurate cash forecast for:
    5 days? ___ ___ ___
    30 days? ___ ___ ___
    90 days? ___ ___ ___

18. Can you forecast your funds flow and requirements
    Monthly? ___ ___ ___
    Annually? ___ ___ ___

19. Have you evaluated the cost of compensating balances versus a fee arrangement to pay for bank services and credit lines? ___ ___ ___

20. Do you monitor your bank's performance regarding?
    Balance or fee requirements? ___ ___ ___
    Earnings credit factor? ___ ___ ___
    Processing and/or availability float? ___ ___ ___
    Service pricing? ___ ___ ___
    Balance calculation? ___ ___ ___

Rate your organization by counting one point for each "yes" response. Then evaluate your score on the following scale:

Points	Rating
26–31	You're doing a good job
20–25	There's room for improvement
20	You have significant improvement opportunity

To help you determine which elements of your cash management program need strengthening, the questions are grouped by area of function:

Questions 1–6: Cash gathering

Questions 7–1: Cash concentration, reporting, and control

Questions 12–4: Cash disbursements

Questions 15–8: Cash forecasting

Questions 19–0: Bank performance monitoring

If there is room for improvement in your cash management function, you have already taken the first step toward making it—you have highlighted the areas to be improved. The next step is to develop your cash objectives and a plan to achieve them. A review of each of the components given at the beginning of this chapter can prepare you in that effort.

When the questionnaire has identified an area for improvement, examine it more closely to understand the key issues affecting your ability to achieve results. Select sample transactions and documents, and perform detailed analysis. For example, when reviewing collections you will want to know mail location and time, payor's bank, and clearing time for major customer receipts. Once you have identified problem areas, then you can define appropriate management tools and techniques.

Identifying the Payback

Having identified opportunities for improvement in your cash management, the next step is to define high payback areas by quantifying costs and benefits. You will need to estimate the opportunity costs of current processing methods, benefits of improvement opportunities, and costs to implement improvements. In addition, you should document organizational impacts and other considerations.

This is important to establish proper focus for further analyses and to set program implementation priorities. In addition, you can determine how cash management improvements measure up to other investment project opportunities.

Once you have assessed paybacks, you can develop an implementation strategy that:

- Accomplishes activities with immediate payback and low relative costs.
- Pays for more detailed requirements study from established cash flow streams.
- Implements more costly activities later to achieve additional cash flow benefits.

Consensus and Commitment

If the senior executive is also the company's cash manager, then obtaining consensus from other operations executives and a commitment to proceed with improvements will not be difficult. However, proceeding with improvements can be a problem for the middle management cash manager. Generally, this problem can be partially overcome if the senior executive has been involved in establishing cash management program objectives and goals. Secondly, the cash manager must develop an implementation plan that communicates urgency and creates impetus to move the program forward. This can be accomplished by identifying high payback projects that will have a recurring and significant impact on the bottom line.

Getting the Job Done

Why is it that high payback opportunities often don't get implemented? A failure to implement may indicate a need to complement internal resources with external talent who:

- Have technical know-how and understand the cash management technology and regulatory environment.
- Have experience implementing change and can be an effective interface between functions.
- Can reduce executive and staff time required for the intense but short-term effort of identifying and implementing improvements.

A management consultant experienced in cash management can supplement your resources in achieving your program objectives. Your banker can also be of assistance in implementing specific cash management techniques.

Once you have identified the resources, you are ready to begin implementing your improvement opportunities. You will want to perform a more detailed review of high opportunity areas to confirm preliminary findings and re-examine costs and benefits. Once your improvement opportunities are in place, you must continue to assess the results of your program. Also consider performing a comprehensive preliminary review once every one to two years to ensure that you remain current with technology and regulatory changes. Your payoff for a sound cash management program will be improved profits.

13

Inventory Shortage

OVERVIEW: Inventory shortages cause the retailing industry to lose great sums of money each year. A number of points in the retail cycle have been identified as the main sources of shortage. Improving the procedures and controls in these areas can reduce shortage significantly. A study of companies with low shortage reveals that they all have well-planned and well-executed shortage control programs, all with a common set of features. POS systems are one of the most successful methods of identifying problem areas to be investigated by management.

Inventory shortage squeezes the bottom line very tightly. More than 2% of sales is lost to shortage. That means retailers are losing more than $10 million a day. Approximately 15% of the price of any item in a retail store goes to combat or compensate for the costs of dishonesty or error in inventory control. Yet the entire cost cannot be passed on to the customer, so shortage cuts into a company's net profit, sometimes very dramatically.

While shortage is a complex and universal problem and will never be eliminated, it can be contained. Experience shows that the keener the management, the lower the shortage.

Stock shortage can be defined as all unexplained shrinkages in the value of merchandise available for sale. These shortages are reflected as discrepancies between the value of merchandise in the book inventory and that in the physical inventory. Specifically, a shortage results when the book figure is higher than the physical; when the book inventory is lower, an *overage* occurs.

For example, a buyer purchases five picture frames at a total cost of $15, with a retail value of $25. Three frames are sold. The inventory should show two units remaining, at a cost value of $6, and a retail value of $10. Any discrepancy in those closing figures—the number of units, cost, or retail value—would represent an overage or shortage.

Causes of Shortage

Shortage is caused chiefly by physical loss of goods and by clerical errors. Goods can be physically lost through a number of means:

1. Theft, which accounts for about half of all shortage, committed by professional thieves, by customers, by employees, and by those in the store on business.
2. Unreported breakage, damage, or disappearance.
3. Inaccurate measuring (for example, a customer pays for 25 feet of cable and receives 30 feet).

The most common clerical errors accounting for shortage are these:

1. Incorrect price marking (for example, a $15 item inadvertently marked at $5 will result in a shortage of $10).
2. Failure to report a price change. (This results in a discrepancy between book and physical value.)
3. Charging purchases to the wrong department. (This creates a shortage in one department and an overage in another.)

Trouble Spots

Dishonesty and error are therefore the primary causes of shortage. The areas with the greatest potential for shortage are warehouse operations, store operations, and the accounting system.

In the warehouse, shortage can result from receiving the wrong or damaged goods, incorrect counting, improper marking, careless storing that ends in loss, and shipping or transferring goods to the wrong location.

In addition to errors, theft and pilferage in warehouse operations can be a major problem. Collusion between warehouse employees and truckers is one means by which goods purchased are never received by the store. Individual or group thievery from the storage or shipping area is another.

In store operations, goods received at the store may be counted incorrectly, left on the truck, misdirected to an employee's car, or removed with the trash. Employees in the stockroom or on the selling floor may "pocket" items. Clerical errors at the register also add to shortage.

Professional thieves, needy customers, or others seeking the thrill of "beating the system" constitute a major source of retail shortage. Storerooms and unattended counters are prime areas for shoplifting. Other people who are in the store on business (*e.g.*, on a construction job) sometimes contribute to shortage by loading their tool boxes or coat pockets with unpaid-for goods.

Because of the volume of transactions in a retailing business and the number of people involved, it is no wonder that the accounting system is another major trouble spot with respect to shortage. Four main areas to attend to are:

1. *Document control.* Controlling the flow of documents in a retail business is absolutely necessary if shortage is to be contained. Paperwork on the receiving docks must be completed with care to reduce shortage there. Those papers must then be forwarded and processed accurately so that book inventory will match physical inventory. Claims against and returns to vendors can be a critical source of shortage if the paperwork does not account for discrepancies. Customer returns, transfers, and price changes are other operations that must be recorded accurately or else shortage will result.

2. *Separation of functions.* Related functions in an overall process are often separated or assigned to different individuals to achieve accuracy and to reduce the possibility of thievery or fraud through a system of checks and cross references. In the accounts payable department, all input must be reviewed and balanced against cash receipts, cash disbursements, and correspondence. In the accounting department, cash disbursements must be reconciled with bank records. All sales, whether cash, check, or charge, must be audited.

3. *Inventory reconciliation.* Physical inventory is obviously a critical element in determining valid shortage figures. Procedures for taking inventory must be reviewed and updated, thoroughly taught, and monitored closely to ensure accuracy. Physical inventory time is not the time to cut corners or attempt to reduce paperwork. Book and physical adjustments must be made, incorporating into the final tallies unfilled saleschecks, CODs, merchandise in transit, returns to vendors, repairs, and unrecorded paperwork.

4. *Financial control.* Financial control is weak when sales and inventory data are inaccurate. Accounts payable must be reconcilable against the stock ledger, cash, and accounts receivable matched with sales.

All shortage affects profits, even "book" shortage or bookkeeping errors. Book shortage can conceal merchandise and store profitability, cash shortages, theft, fraud, and lack of control. It can also create an atmosphere that can leave the company vulnerable to theft and fraud.

Controlling Shortage

In one- and two-store operations, "eye-ball" control and personal contact by management can limit shortage. Small organizations also foster greater feelings of "family" and loyalty, which reduce shortage. But as companies grow, that personal touch is impossible to maintain. Yesterday's methods of control are no match for today's potential for shortage.

Touche Ross & Co. recently conducted an Inventory Shortage Reduction Study for the National Retail Merchants Association. The object of the study was to determine the specific systems and controls that effectively limit shortage. The study indicated that a number of retail chains have gotten the upper hand of shortage. Interviews with executives from these companies reveal that successful programs contain a set of common elements. Let us examine the features in these successful programs.

Management Commitment

Primary among the features of a successful shortage control program is top management commitment to the war on shortage. When members of management's inner circle (CEO, CFO, and president) participate actively on a company shortage committee, shortage gains visibility as a company problem. Employees realize the importance of proper control and that the company is not about to "accept" shortage.

Widespread Involvement

Key representatives from merchandising, store operations, finance, and personnel should join top management on the shortage committee. They should be able to provide input into the problem from their own perspective and also be in a position to make decisions that make things happen. In other words, the people on the shortage committee should represent all phases of the business, be decision makers, and have sufficient clout to get people to change their ways.

One firm reported that it once had a position called "Vice President of Shortage Control." The position was eliminated because it became a target—shortage was looked on as his fault and his problem. The company recognized that shortage originates in many areas. To reach the many sources of the problem, then, everyone—from sales clerks and receiving dock hands up to the CEO—has to be responsible and be a part of the solution.

Shortage Goals

Another important component of shortage programs is a set of clear, realistic goals. Rather than being one big number in the firm, the goals should be translated to the stores, merchandise departments, and, when possible, classifications. With specific goals, people are less able to divorce themselves from shortage. If the company goal is to reduce shortage by half a percent, a department head might not take much notice.

However, if the department goal is to reduce shortage by half a percent, the department head has to take notice because he or she is in the spotlight.

Goal setting requires effective measurement tools to determine if goals are reached. In addition, the organization must be structured to allow people with the proper skills and authority to perform tasks needed in shortage control. The security director, for example, should not be responsible for taking physical inventory. That's the task of the control department, which can do it more effectively.

Compensation

By setting realistic goals and measuring achievement with accurate tools, management is in a position to add incentive to the shortage program. In one company that incentive took the form of compensation. The company created a compensation formula for everyone from store manager level to vice-chairman. The formula is composed of quantifiably measurable factors, one of which is shortage. In this way, performance on the shortage goals directly affects individuals' compensation. At store level, perhaps 10% of the store manager's salary might be affected; for the vice-chairman it might be 5%; for people in inventory control, as much as 25% of their salaries might be affected.

Identification of Tasks

To achieve shortage goals, everyone in the firm must perform specific relevant tasks. Management or the shortage committee must identify potential trouble spots and offer procedures for dealing with them. For example, one firm interviewed in the study has buyers review their purchase journals every month with shortage auditors from the control group. Reports of this review are given to merchandise managers as another control, to ensure that company policy is followed, and to emphasize that buyers are responsible for their own paperwork.

Discipline and Diligence

Shortage control requires discipline and diligence. People must spend the time to see that the controls written into the shortage program are applied consistently. It is not enough, for example, to have a control log. There must be follow-up to make sure the logs are completed on a timely basis and that someone actually confirms log entries.

Recordkeeping

Respondents to the shortage reduction study said that internal theft, external theft, and recordkeeping were about equally responsible for shortage. In the companies with good shortage results, however, recordkeeping was viewed as a more serious source of trouble. These companies allocated resources accordingly, putting greater emphasis on controlling paper at all points in the merchandise cycle. Theft was not disregarded as a source of shortage, but these retailers saw shortage totals drop as they focused attention on recordkeeping.

Paperwork problems can be responsible for shortage at any one of these points:

Purchase order	Sales reporting
Receiving and marking	Wrap and pack
Checking	Delivery
Distribution	Accounts payable
Transfers	Statistical (recording of data)
Vendor returns	Physical inventory procedures
Price changes	

As part of the task-setting step, management identifies who does what at each point and how the task must be done. Controls that comply with company policy are then built into the flow of paper accompanying purchases, shipments, and sales. Who monitors the flow and enforces the controls is also written into the program.

The successful firms interviewed have the recordkeeping aspect down firmly in their programs. They constantly audit procedures and see that documents are filled out accurately. Systems and procedures have been designed accordingly and are reviewed periodically. Management sees to it that systems are not short-circuited by people who, even in the interest of increased productivity, decide to "streamline" their operation. Shortage often results from the well-intentioned but misguided effort to save time.

Training

To alert employees to all of the implications of their actions, the low shortage companies stress training. One firm has its employees attend a seminar in which they learn how their job interacts with merchandise control, security, and loss prevention. They see how an error or omission at one point can result in shortage someplace else.

Besides raising the level of consciousness, these training programs also try to elicit suggestions for combating shortage. When people are directly responsible and accountable for their own shortage, they tend to develop their own shortage reduction strategies. In a high shortage department, for example, management can ask the people in the department for suggestions to reduce the shortage.

One company conducts a value awareness program. Cashiers are taken on a tour of the store and shown new merchandise. This gives them a sense of prices. If cashiers catch a price switch at the register, they are rewarded. Another training program teaches cashiers where to look for concealed merchandise—for example, inside thermos bottles, under caps of aerosol cans, in pockets of garments. Individuals who spot errors or attempts at theft are publicly recognized and rewarded. Awareness and incentive are increased even further by peer recognition programs.

Security Program

Security is a critical element in each of the successful shortage programs studied. In each case, individuals involved in store security leadership were members of the firm's management team. Career paths were created for security people so they could rise within the firm outside of the security department. They received greater respect and cooperation and performed with a broader view of the company's mission and shortage strategy.

In the firms interviewed, loss prevention was emphasized over apprehension. Employees recognize this emphasis and understand that lectures on shortage are not veiled accusations. Apprehension, of course, is a part of any good security program and is reinforced with rewards and compensation reflecting one's record.

POS and Shortage

Many companies have made their POS systems a potent weapon in the war on shortage. POS can help control shortage, whether it be accidental or intentional. POS can provide insight into many areas of potential exposure: cash shortages, fraudulent post voids, illegitimate customer returns, employee discount abuse, intentional undercharging, supplier or vendor theft, and price changes, markdowns, and underrings.

POS helps fight shortage by collecting performance data. This can be done by control point—by department, register, or employee. Data can also be collected by exposure type—cash overage/shortage, post voids, refunds, credits, employee discounts, and undercharging. Data can be summarized for each exposure type by control point, giving number of instances and items and dollar amount. Data can be summarized daily, weekly, month-to-date, or year-to-date.

POS also helps management develop performance standards. Specifically, management can analyze historical activity, establish seasonal norms, set performance goals, and monitor current performance against historical and current goals. With data collected from POS, management can compare daily, weekly, or monthly activity against standards. Management can specify threshold criteria for identifying high-risk performance patterns. For example, 20% above standard for post voids or 10% above standard for frequency of shortages would be cut-off points indicating exposure candidates.

In identifying high-risk candidates, POS can be helpful in interfacing with the sales audit system and in developing an internal exposure audit system. This exposure audit system can help to establish performance standards, compare activity to standards, identify high-risk performance patterns, and generate exception reports that flag potential perpetrators.

The purpose of these POS-generated exception reports is to identify departments, registers, and employees requiring investigation. The reports single out only those departments, registers, or individuals whose activity exceeds the performance standard threshold. The report can display the actual activity against the standard for numbers of instances and items, dollar amount, and other figures. POS, then, does the statistical detective work that an army of on-the-spot sleuths could not. It provides constant and comprehensive coverage of these critical areas and enables management to employ human control in the most strategic places and situations.

Part Four

PLANNING FOR SUCCESS

14

Three Retailing Failures

OVERVIEW: Studying the successes and failures of other retailers is always illuminating because it can help point out opportunities and weak spots in one's own operation. In particular, examining the road to ruin that some companies have traveled can provide a set of danger points to avoid. The closer one looks at retailing failures, the more one realizes how similar they were in their approaches, repeating the same kind of mistakes. This chapter reviews three major retailing failures: W.T. Grant, Robert Hall, and Neisner Brothers. Analysis reveals the common threads in these and other failures, and points the way to a formula for success.

The Variety Store: W. T. Grant's

On February 11, 1976, one of the great traditions in retailing died when a committee of creditors voted for the liquidation of W. T. Grant's. Despite efforts to revive the ailing giant, Grant's was consumed by its own excesses.

Liquidation brought an end to a business that had grown from a single store into the third largest variety store chain in America. At its peak, Grant conducted business in more than 1200 stores in 43 states, and employed over 82,000 people. In 1972, only three years before liquidation, Grant's total sales eclipsed $1.6 billion, generating $33 million in profits. The following year, though sales increased, profits dipped to only $8 million. Twelve months later, closing figures showed a loss of $177 million.

History

W. T. Grant left school at the age of fifteen in order to find work and help support his mother. At his first job he worked as a messenger in a store. Soon after, Grant bought an interest in the store and later, with borrowed money, he bought out his partners. This became the first W. T. Grant's, a small variety store in the corner of the YMCA building in Lynn, Massachusetts.

From that inauspicious beginning in 1906, Grant opened other local stores and gradually but steadily expanded his domain. When American business and industry boomed after World War II, Grant's grew to become the third largest variety chain, just behind F. W. Woolworth Company and Kresge's.

Following the conservative policies of Mr. Grant, his stores prospered by selling basic goods such as hosiery, underwear, notions, children's clothes, and low-cost women's apparel.

When Grant retired as chairman of the board of directors in 1966, his successor initiated a more aggressive policy of store expansion and merchandise diversity. For a few years profits continued to rise. Then fortune turned.

Crisis

How could Grant's, the country's 17th largest retailer and 3rd largest variety store chain in 1972, plunge from its lofty position to liquidation in 1976? Some observers shake their heads in wonder. Others, however, say the signs of erosion had been evident years before the demise. Rapid expansion, a confusing multiplicity of store images, frequent changes in merchandising strategies, a revolving door in the executive office, and a general lack of judgment and control flashed clear signs of trouble long before the end.

Expansion. Between 1969 and 1973 Grant's opened 369 stores. In one month, October 1969, they cut the grand opening ribbons on 28 stores, 15 on a single day. This rapid expansion triggered a domino-like reaction on management, merchandise control, internal communications, and financial operations. The expansion was too broad and came too swiftly for it to be controllable.

Site selection was often poor and terms were exorbitant. In 1973, for instance, Grant's paid $85 million in leases. Later, when the closings began, many of the stores could not be subleased, and the high rents proved to be a drain on cash.

Image and Inventory. Another problem created by the rapid expansion was that instead of seeming to be a coherent family of stores working under one policy, each store seemed to offer a different kind of Grant's. After building its reputation as a small town and downtown variety store, Grant's took on a new image—in fact, a number of them. In the mid-sixties, Grant's ventured into larger towns and opened stores of 90,000 square feet. At the same time Grant's opened big new stores of 150,000 square feet or more in large malls, co-anchoring some of these with Sears and Ward. Yet the original small stores in small towns were not forsaken, and still more of these were opened. In 1973 Grant City appeared on the scene, presenting full line, family center stores.

Grant's changed not only the physical image of its stores, but also its merchandise mix. For some 60 years, Grant's had catered to the budget-minded shopper. Suddenly Grant's was up-grading its apparel and it was making a push for big ticket items like TV sets, furniture, air conditioners, and washing machines. Yet Grant's was not offering the low price of a discounter or the service of a Sears. And the use of private labels on these large items backfired. Instead of increasing margins, these labels only inhibited sales. Shoppers were reluctant to buy Bradford color television sets at brand name prices.

The buying public seemed to be confused by the many faces of Grant's. Not only were the stores different sizes, they all carried different merchandise. Customers no longer knew what to expect from Grant's.

The decision to trade up lacked consistency and a natural progression. Besides confusing shoppers, this broadening of the merchandise mix caused other problems. Inventories bulged, and dollars could not be freed up to buy new goods. New stores were trying to sell stale merchandise. Yet the company did not want to balance inventory through markdowns that would reduce margins.

Communication and Control. The inventory problem was intensified by inefficient management, another result of overexpansion. A strain was placed on managers at every level and training could not keep pace with expansion. With this lack of central controls, inadequately trained store managers operated their stores almost independently. Grant's permitted store managers to order up to 80% of their merchandise on their own, price it, and send invoices to New York for payment. It was not unusual for three Grant's stores within a 10-mile radius to charge three different prices for the same item. Because the company frowned on markdowns, store managers took markdowns on their own initiative and covered them by not reporting brisk sellers. They would order goods and hold up invoices, thus increasing their own budgets and understating the cost of purchases.

Inventory control was further complicated by the lack of a sales classification system. Buyers who were already stretched thin had to rely on inaccurate store figures as their only guidance for promoting certain items. Book inventories were inaccurate, and even spot physical inventories were impossible because the company had too few internal auditors.

Credit. This inability to control inventory was matched by an inability to control credit. Until 1974, there was no central management of credit. Each of the 1200 stores kept its own credit information, and payments were made directly to the stores. Terms in many stores were extremely generous. On only the strength of a signature a customer could buy anything, and be given 36 months to pay — at a minimum of $1.00 a month. From 1969 to 1974, accounts receivable ballooned 86% to $602 million. Credit losses accounted for 62% of the firm's deficit.

Statistics. During the period of its greatest expansion, 1968 to 1972, sales went up 50% but earnings remained constant (Figure 14-1). Sales per square foot dropped from $35.13 to $32.50, a level which was less than half that of Grant's major compet-

Figure 14-1. THE RISE AND FALL OF W. T. GRANT'S

Year	Sales (Millions)	Profits (Thousands)	Number of Stores
1960	$ 512.6	$ 9,198	864
1969	1,210.9	41,809	1,095
1970	1,254.1	39,577	1,116
1971	1,374.8	35,212	1,168
1972	1,644.6	33,787	1,208
1973	1,849.8	8,429	1,189
1974	1,762.0	−177,340	1,053

itors. These numbers, which should have been read as danger signs, eventually resulted in huge increases in the company's long-term debt. The debt continued to grow from that point on as many suppliers began insisting on COD shipments. While the debt swelled to $700 million, suppliers were given liens on Grant's inventories as a guarantee they would be paid.

Leadership. Throughout the expansion and collapse, a number of individuals served as company leaders. W. T. Grant's brother-in-law, Edward Staley, had served as president from 1952 to 1959, and was chairman of the board during the expansion. His president was Richard C. Mayer. When the expansion program ran into trouble, Mayer was replaced by Harry Pierson at the end of 1974. As things worsened, company veteran James G. Kendrich was summoned from Grant's Canadian subsidiary to save the sinking ship. Kendrich closed stores and tried to return Grant's to the "basics" merchandise strategy of earlier years. But when the company began borrowing heavily, lending bankers exerted greater influence in the running of the company and replaced Kendrich with Robert Anderson, a former vice-president of Sears.

Chapter XI. On October 2, 1975, with liabilities over $1 billion, which exceeded assets, Grant's filed for a voluntary Chapter XI proceeding under the Bankruptcy Act. With more bank money pumped into the firm, hopes were high that the reorganized Grant's could stay afloat. Using information gathered from numerous studies of Grant's merchandising strengths and weaknesses, Anderson outlined a program of efficiency and revised merchandising strategies to justify those hopes.

Anderson planned to reduce selling space in 125 of the stores that remained open, thereby reducing the number of salespeople and department managers and hence the payroll of each store. Despite these reductions, Anderson expected that sales volume would remain the same, and that sales per square foot would increase.

Anderson also hoped to increase efficiency by requiring monthly profit- and loss reviews for each store. Advertising would be centralized and focused on major markets. Through this media buying efficiency, advertising costs would decline.

On the merchandising side, Anderson called for an emphasis on everyday items, particularly aimed at young families with a yearly income between $12,000 and $17,000. More than half of this merchandise would be in wearables, and much of that in children's wear. Notions would comprise 10% to 12% of the merchandise budget. About 21% of selling space would be reserved for soft home furnishings including domestics, curtains, drapes, linens, and towels. Accompanying this tightly defined market would be a switch to more brand name merchandise.

But the chaos of the previous years could not be undone quickly enough. Tightening and centralizing credit operations, cutting payrolls, closing 60% of their stores, reducing the size of the others, redirecting the merchandise approach, and changing leadership could not save the company.

Sales reports were still conflicting and inaccurate. When the 1975 sales report was revised downward, the banks called in consultants to prepare a budget for 1976. Their budget projected a loss of $50 million, calling for an additional loan of $200 million to replenish inventories. When the consultants estimated that six to eight years would be needed to determine if Grant's could survive, the committee of secured creditors voted for liquidation.

Conclusions

The collapse of Grant's was caused by a number of interrelating factors, all of which are ultimately attributable to poor management.

1. *Expansion was the principal cause of failure.* Poor sites were selected and the objectives of expansion were unclear. Too little analysis of the number, location, size, and nature of the stores went into the planning for expansion.

2. *Provisions for training were inadequate* to meet the needs of expansion. Management resources were stretched thin, and untrained people were thrust into critical positions.

3. *The organizational structure proved inefficient* for 1200 stores of different sizes and personalities, though it had been adequate for 800 small variety stores. The result was a greater dependence on individual store managers, many of whom were ill-prepared for the job even under the best of circumstances.

4. *A lack of credit control* allowed runaway accounts receivable to go unchecked until they drove the company into an irreversible situation.

5. *A weak system of communication* between stores and the central office caused the lack of inventory and credit control. This poor communication was also partly responsible for the poor marketing and merchandising decisions that helped bring Grant's down.

6. *An inability to read the significance of the statistics* allowed a bad situation to deteriorate beyond a point of return. The number of store openings, of square feet, even of sales should not have distracted alert management from the meaning of declines in earnings and sales per square foot.

Once set in motion, these factors interacted to create an uncontrollable monster. The ultimate control rested with management to plan, organize, coordinate, and measure all activities. Because Grant's management did not exercise that control, the monster—once a great name in retailing—destroyed itself.

The Specialty Store: Robert Hall

Robert Hall this season
will show you the reason
low overhead, low overhead

Responding to this popular jingle, budget-minded shoppers flocked to Robert Hall for their clothes in the 1940s, 50s and 60s. Store after store opened until there were more than 400, making Robert Hall the third largest clothing chain in the country.

Yet Robert Hall was only a subsidiary of an equally successful parent, United Merchants and Manufacturers. Besides the clothing outlets, U.M.M. operated 40 full-line shopping centers, 61 textile plants in 11 countries, and a profitable finance company, employing a total of 32,000 people.

U.M.M. grew slowly and built its fortunes on the success of all its operations, but it was almost crippled by the failure of just one of them. That failure was Robert Hall.

History

The business that grew to be the diversified United Merchants and Manufacturers, the third biggest publicly owned textile company in the nation, began in 1912 as Cohn-Hall-Marx, a converter of textiles. As a converter, Cohn-Hall-Marx bought unfinished fabric from weaving and knitting mills, prepared color and pattern designs for it, arranged for a finishing plant to dye or print the fabric, and then sold the finished goods to apparel manufacturers and retail stores. Seeing the potential for higher profits by doing their own spinning, weaving, and finishing, Cohn-Hall-Marx merged with several manufacturing plants in 1928 to form U.M.M.

In 1934 U.M.M. established a textile plant in Argentina. Gradually this overseas venture spread to ten countries, mostly in South America, and at one point in the 1970's accounted for much of U.M.M.'s profit.

Successful in that endeavor, U.M.M. created United Factors in 1935. This was a factoring business which provided credit services for textile, apparel, and retail companies. Showing good judgment in its selection of clients, United Factors built its annual volume to $1.4 billion.

Then in 1940, seeking to increase profits by selling its own clothes in its own outlets, U.M.M. opened the first Robert Hall store. The simple name reflected the conservative styles of featured merchandise and the no-frills atmosphere, which were as much the store's trademark as the private labels on the clothes. The low-budget family, clothes-hungry but still frugal after the difficult years of the Great Depression and World War II, welcomed the low cost and good quality of Robert Hall's tailored clothes. As newspaper and radio ads repeated the message of values going "up, up, up," and prices going "down, down, down," Robert Hall outlets sprang up one after the other in freestanding buildings on highways throughout the country.

Sales and profits soared through the fifties and early sixties. In 1969, pretax profits hit an all time high of $14 million. In 1971, sales of $244 million accounted for one-third of U.M.M.'s total volume. In 1972, to meet the challenge of fast-growing discount stores, Robert Hall opened a number of large, full-line stores called Robert Hall Villages. In these, Robert Hall operated the soft goods departments and leased the others. By 1975, 400 Robert Hall stores had opened, making it one of the largest chains of men's, women's, and children's apparel in the country.

By opening the Robert Hall Villages, the chain was acknowledging the success of the shopping center concept, popularized by other chains at least ten years earlier. Opening the Villages was also an admission that the Robert Hall success formula was weakening. Sales had stagnated, profits had dropped. In 1975, Robert Hall showed losses of $21.6 million; the next year losses almost doubled to $41.8 million.

U.M.M. came to the rescue of its subsidiary by picking up its losses, but could do that for only so long. In June 1977, to keep itself afloat, U.M.M. closed Robert Hall's doors, and the clothing chain filed for bankruptcy under Chapter XI. Shortly after, the parent company was forced to do the same.

The austerity of the Robert Hall stores was typical of the entire U.M.M. organization, a family-run business. There were no plush offices, company planes, or even expense accounts for executives. Yet most executives (many of whom were related), as well as hundreds of other employees, made U.M.M. their careers.

The long years under leadership which did not make needed changes are seen as one of the major reasons for Robert Hall's collapse.

Crisis

U.M.M. had problems in a number of its operations, but Robert Hall was the biggest and most serious. Though the parent organization can be accused of over-diversification, Robert Hall must be cited for its stagnation.

Sticking with a winning formula is wise when all of the variables remain the same. But when the times, the people, and buying habits change, the formula for success must also change. Robert Hall did not change its formula until it was too late and that intransigence brought the chain down.

Location. During the rise, Robert Hall stores were mostly freestanding structures located on islands off highways in or near urban areas. The stores were strategically situated away from other similar outlets that might compete for the same broad customer market. Yet the appeal of Robert Hall's low-priced clothing was strong enough to draw people to these less convenient locations.

In the sixties, communities began to grow outside of urban areas, and suburban shopping centers and malls comprised of a variety of stores also grew in popularity. They made shopping easier and brought it closer to suburbanites. Facilitated by easy access and plentiful parking spaces, the idea of near-by one-stop shopping caught on— except with Robert Hall.

Not until the prime sites and the best terms were swept up by more foresighted retailers did Robert Hall see the logic of abandoning its freestanding islands. But by the time Robert Hall finally decided to follow the crowds, it was too late.

Image and Inventory. The image of Robert Hall had already been firmly implanted in shoppers' minds when the first Robert Hall Village was conceived in 1972. That image included stores that looked like white rectangular boxes, bare and bland inside and out. The image also contained pipe racks crammed with tailored clothes, all of which looked the same, regardless of size, style, or year. And the image was a valid one.

The Robert Hall merchandise remained the same, even in the Villages, because management's concept of the budget-minded shopper remained the same. Management failed to take into account that the Robert Hall shopper of the late sixties and early seventies had more money and wanted a share of the "good life." This consumer attitude was reflected in the demand for less conservative clothing, for sportswear, and for more stylish merchandise. The blue serge suit and felt hat that Robert Hall once sold to both father and son would no longer satisfy either of them. Former Robert Hall customers now shopped where they could buy cute and colorful infants' and children's wear, the latest teen fashions, and casual clothes for the modern adult.

But Robert Hall management remained firm in the belief that there would be a return of tastes to the formal fare of the fifties. Rather than take markdowns to unload the inventory, management stored the goods in warehouses. When the return to conservative styles did not materialize, Robert Hall could not get rid of its stale merchandise nor scrape up the capital to replace it with new goods.

Statistics. Misreading changes in society and merchandise preferences was compounded by Robert Hall's and U.M.M.'s failure to interpret their own statistics. Despite inflationary prices, population growth, and an overall increase in consumer buying, Robert Hall's sales figures remained constant. In 1975, Robert Hall lost $21 million on sales of $237 million. The following year, sales increased to $259 million, but losses shot up to $41 million.

Dun and Bradstreet's reclassified Robert Hall's credit line to a $100,000 limit. The parent organization, U.M.M., began backing Robert Hall's credit. But despite pretax profits of $30 million from three of its major business lines, U.M.M. suffered an overall loss of $19 million for the year ending June 30, 1976. To cover the losses, U.M.M. sold its successful United Factors subsidiary, surrendering its most viable source of cash.

U.M.M.'s return on investment from 1969 to 1974 was averaging less than 5%, while that for all other manufacturing companies was more than 11%. Though the book

Figure 14-2. ROBERT HALL SALES AND CONTRIBUTIONS

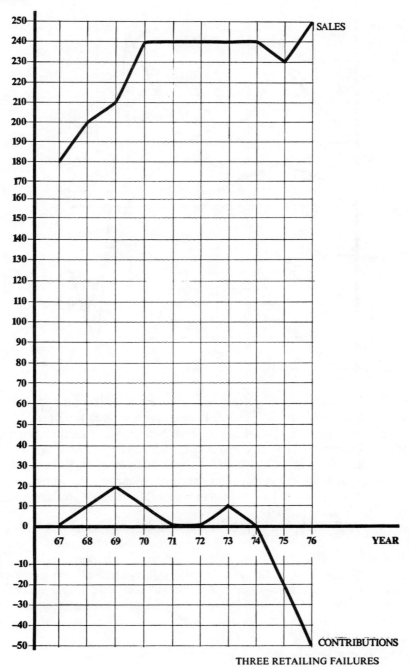

Figure 14-3. U.M.M. INCOME AND ROBERT HALL CONTRIBUTIONS

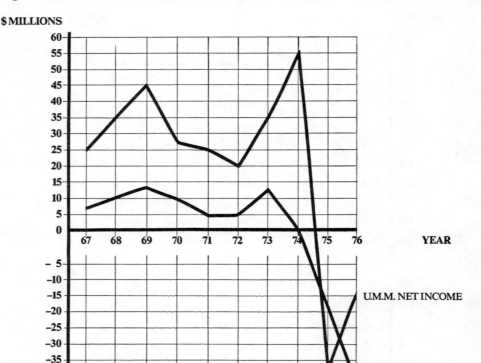

value of U.M.M. common stock was $50 a share, it was selling for $12. U.M.M. sales in fiscal 1974 were $963 million, and in 1975 dropped to $925 million.

Leadership. U.M.M. and Robert Hall had grown as family companies. Jack Schwab and Lawrence Marx, cofounders of U.M.M., were cousins. Marx ran the company until 1938. Schwab was its president from 1939 to 1959. Schwab's son Martin grew up in the business and eventually became president in 1968. Harold Rosner, one of the cofounders of Robert Hall, served as the clothing chain's president until the late 1960s.

Martin Schwab seemed to have recognized that an aging and inbred management can lead to stagnation. In 1971, he created a policy of mandatory retirement at age 68. The policy did, however, provide for numerous exceptions.

In 1975, Schwab brought in an outsider, George L. Staff, to make some sweeping managerial changes. In one year, six of twelve executive and senior vice presidents were new. Gordon F. Heaton was brought from Sears to become president at Robert Hall.

Figure 14-4. ROBERT HALL SALES PER SQUARE FOOT

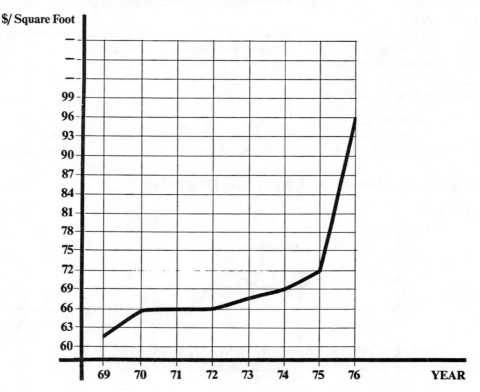

Remedies. Heaton outlined plans to save the chain, labeling merchandise mix as its most serious problem. Under Heaton, the emphasis would shift from tailored suits and coats to leisure clothes and infants' and children's wear. Merchandise quality controls would be established, guaranteeing consistency in sizes and colors. Regional distribution centers would speed deliveries to stores as needed. And a markdown policy was written.

A number of stores would be closed, particularly those in freestanding locations. Robert Hall Villages were to be scaled down to about 70,000 square feet. And all Robert Hall stores would be remodeled inside and out to reflect the new "with it" image. Girls' and boys' departments would be clearly distinguishable from ladies' and men's. Manuals, complete with photographs, were sent from the central office to all store managers detailing suggestions for merchandise displays.

Organizational structure was revamped. There would be five distribution managers: one for each of three geographic regions, one for malls, and one for the Villages. Each manager would report to the national fashion distribution manager, creating a smoother flow of goods in and out of stores.

To publicize the new Robert Hall, the advertising budget, which had been slashed from over $10 million to $1.5 million a year, would be beefed up. And a new jingle would be created.

But time and money ran out before Heaton's plans could be fully implemented and tested. To save the parent company and continue its textile business, U.M.M. decided to close all Robert Hall stores and sell the factoring business. Thus, in June 1977, Robert Hall filed under Chapter XI. Soon after, because the overall debt had grown too large, U.M.M. also filed for bankruptcy.

Conclusions

Stagnation was the principal cause of Robert Hall's failure. Robert Hall's complacency in staying with its people, policies, procedures, and merchandise image in the

Figure 14-5. ROBERT HALL PROFITS PER SQUARE FOOT

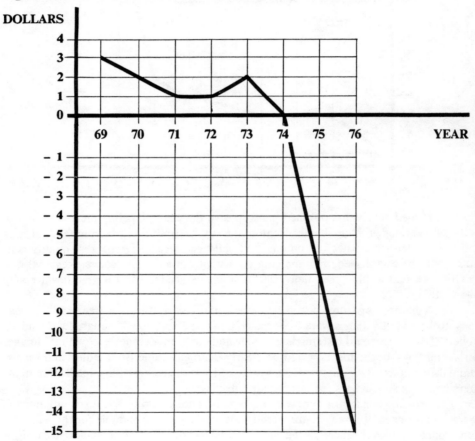

face of major changes in the retailing industry and in society at large turned profit to deficits. This stagnation is evident in a number of phases of Robert Hall's operation, each of which contributed to the bankruptcy.

1. *The leadership at Robert Hall was old, familiar, and in-bred.* Having led the chain to its success, management continued to work a well long after it had been drained. Age, family ties, and internal promotions will not necessarily cause stagnation, but the Robert Hall management team seemed unable to read the signs of change and decay. Insulated from outside voices that could have expressed these signs, management made a number of unwise decisions.

2. *The decision to locate in freestanding buildings and to reject the malls and shopping centers* proved to be unwise. When Robert Hall finally recognized this, it was too late.

3. *The inability to perceive changes* in society and in budget shoppers, and to anticipate the effect of these changes on apparel retailing, drove customers away from Robert Hall.

4. *The refusal to take markdowns*, which would have enabled Robert Hall to make its merchandise changes sooner, compounded that blunder.

5. *The inability to read the significance of statistics*, particularly static yearly sales figures, contributed to management's poor vision.

These factors put Robert Hall in the red. U.M.M.'s approach to recovery seemed unwise. Changes were made too late, and by selling United Factors, U.M.M. lost its most profitable arm.

The Discount Store: Neisner Brothers

Like W.T. Grant's, Neisner Brothers opened new stores at a pace that outran its ability to control and finance operations. Like Robert Hall, Neisner Brothers suffered from a tired image that had lost its hold on the buying public. Added to these factors were increased competition, poor merchandising strategies, a top-heavy management structure, and two crippling storms. The net result was the demise of a 66-year-old retailing company that at one point had close to 200 stores and generated more than $150 million in sales.

Like Grant's and Robert Hall, Neisner Brothers realized the error of its ways and took decisive measures to change the operation and the bottom line. Those measures seemed to turn things around. After two straight years in the red, Neisner Brothers showed a net profit in 1977. But operating losses led to credit problems and vendors panicked, insisting on COD shipments. Though hopes were bright, cash on hand was insufficient to meet those vendor demands. The strong medicine seemed to be working, but Neisner Brothers had run out of time.

Figure 14-6. NEISNER BROTHERS' VITAL STATISTICS

Year	Sales	Profits	Stores
1960	$ 75,492,000	$ 115,000	170
1961	76,289,000	278,000	173
1962	76,883,000	−184,000	182
1963	75,250,000	100,000	181
1964	81,000,000	328,000	180
1965	84,751,000	700,000	185
1966	85,973,000	443,000	191
1967	94,216,000	676,000	193
1968	101,734,000	492,000	187
1969	119,644,000	1,023,000	176
1970	132,441,000	1,088,000	175
1971	136,915,000	1,142,000	170
1972	141,000,000	210,000	166
1973	148,165,000	525,000	159
1974	150,654,000	−505,000	n/a
1975	152,304,000	−10,600,000	132
1976	147,630,000	1,164,000	120
1977	136,985,000	−2,390,000	86

Source: *Chain Store Age*, Variety Edition, May 1973, p. 76.

History

Abraham and Joseph Neisner formed a partnership in 1911 and founded a business that was to bear their name until 1978. They began with a small five-and-ten-cent store, which led to other stores and other ventures, including a realty company and sporting goods supply companies.

Neisner Brothers developed a solid reputation and following in the five-and-ten, variety store business. One successful store spawned another until the Neisner Brothers' name was seen on stores in 19 states and the District of Columbia.

In 1961, Neisner Brothers acquired Myrtle Mills Discount Store in Unionville, Connecticut. As the discount craze spread during the 1960's, Neisner's Big N Discount Stores grew in volume and increased in number until there were more than 40 Big N's in Neisner Brothers' chain of over 190 stores, with sales volume peaking at $150 million.

As discounting grew, the five-and-tens lost their appeal. Neisner Brothers tried changing these to junior department stores and later to convenient discount stores. But the variety store concept held on, tainting Neisner's discount image.

Neisner Brothers continued its expansion though its profits and competition warranted a halt. When that realization eventually reached management, it was too late. In 1977, Neisner Brothers filed for protection under Chapter XI of the Bankruptcy Act. A year later, the chain which had been whittled down to 55 stores was acquired by Ames Department Stores.

Crisis

Neisner Brothers' growth was strictly numerical. Stores increased in number but internally the organization did not mature. As discount competition became more sophisticated and intense, Neisner Brothers could no longer hold its share of the market, and the weight of its rapid expansion caused the cave-in.

Expansion. Like other discounters, Neisner Brothers grew with the industry. But Neisner did not have the foresight to plan for a leveling off. Despite fluctuating profits through the sixties, Neisner Brothers continued opening new stores. Showing unabashed optimism, the chain took lengthy leases on properties, some for up to 99 years. Many of these were small stores in strip centers on the edge of small towns. Some were in poor locations that turned out to be unprofitable. When they could not be sold or sublet, Neisner Brothers found itself paying over $1 million a year for shuttered property, draining away $5 million during its last three years in business.

As the number of units increased, the organization grew until it was split into two distinct divisions, one for the Big N Stores, and one for the convenient discount stores. This structure change added people and positions to the corporate staff, particularly at the high-salary levels. Now there were two merchandise coordinators, two inventory control managers, and two directors of store operations. The data processing department also expanded and went beyond the needs of the company. Fred Silverstein, named CEO in 1974, later said that Neisner Brothers had the data processing capabilities needed by a company doing four times Neisner's volume. Like the rent for the shuttered stores, the additional money being spent on DP brought in no return.

Even as new units were being opened, there was not enough money available to stock them. It was common for merchandise to be taken from an existing store and placed on the shelves of a new store. The result was that many stores, old and new, were under-inventoried.

Image and Inventory. Though a good portion of Neisner's sales was generated in its Big N discount stores, its lengthy heritage as a variety store hung on. Even after the junior department stores were transformed into convenient discount stores, the public did not perceive these as full-fledged discount markets.

While the variety store heritage was partly responsible for Neisner's double image, poor merchandising strategy added to it. Customers were not sure what they would find in any Neisner store. Product assortments varied greatly because store managers ordered only what they wanted.

In effect, Neisner's was trying to be all things to all people, especially in its smaller stores. In fashion apparel, for instance, these stores might have had a couple of feet of dresses, and a few feet of skirts and uniforms, all in junior, misses, and half sizes. But there was no real selection in any one assortment.

Even after the conversion to the convenient discount stores, inventories still included variety store items such as coin purses, knick-knacks, and low- priced giftware. Such merchandising strategies confused the public and hampered sales. At the same time, large inventories at great cost were required, with the distribution center stocking more than 19,000 SKUs.

Competition. While Neisner's confusing image and poorly stocked stores were driving customers away, many competitors were opening stores to receive them. Perhaps realizing Neisner's vulnerability, retailers who were not saddled with an old-fashioned image, who were more in tune with the modern shopper, and who were better versed in discount merchandising, invaded Neisner's territory. Over the 18-month stretch just before Neisner entered Chapter XI proceedings, competitors nudged their way into Neisner's market at the rate of one store a week.

Natural Calamities. Though competition added to the headaches Neisner was making for itself, nature saw fit to exacerbate the situation. In 1972, Hurricane Agnes ripped through much of Florida, leaving floods and destruction in her wake. With more than 40 stores in the state, Neisner suffered flood damage and losses totaling over $1 million. Though sales that year increased by $5 million over the previous year, profits dipped from $1.1 million to $210,000.

Then in the winter of 1977, after sweeping changes were made in Neisner's operations and the company was showing signs of averting failure, a severe snowstorm hit the northeastern United States, the location of Neisner's distribution center and of its heaviest network of stores. With residents literally snowed-in for days, Neisner lost 1,000 store hours in its key New York State market. Even those stores not closed by snow were unable to receive merchandise from the distribution center in Rochester. When roads finally became passable, Neisner spent more than $300,000 in overtime pay to expedite merchandise shipments.

Remedies. After profits dipped almost $1 million between 1971 and 1972, management took steps to turn things around. Fred R. Silverstein was hired as president to improve the bottom line figures as he had at Uncle Bill's Discount Stores.

Silverstein saw that the Neisner Brothers stores had not changed sufficiently to meet the needs of shoppers in the 1970s. He worked to create a new, clear image of a discount chain. Both the larger and smaller stores would carry the same basic assortment of merchandise, and the price gap between them would be narrowed, thus capitalizing on Neisner's mass-merchandising potential.

The largest stores were reduced in size, so that eventually there were six grades of Neisner stores ranging from 15,000 square feet to 50,000 square feet. Most stores were targeted for a face-lifting and redecorating.

Unprofitable stores were closed, consolidated, sublet, or sold so that eventually only 55 stores remained in the chain that had numbered 193 only ten years earlier. Staff was reduced and a minimum man hour scheduling policy was instituted. In 1975, Silverstein consolidated the convenient discount and larger discount areas into one division, eliminating several high-salaried positions. The total payroll reduction that resulted from these changes and from store closings amounted to $35 million. Data processing was trimmed, adding to savings.

Major changes were also enacted in merchandising policies. Eliminated from the inventory were fashion apparel, furniture, major appliances, and all variety store merchandise. Basic tops and bottoms, soft home furnishings, and housewares were beefed up. Assortments were expanded in better-margin softlines and minimized in low-margin, promotional areas. Working under the theory that consumers were now buying less but more often, the new Neisner's wanted to satisfy the daily needs of customers rather than to stock up on items which were purchased only on special shopping trips.

Overall inventory was therefore pared down. Stores now had 6,000 to 7,000 fewer SKUs in their inventory, and SKUs at the distribution center were cut from 19,000 to 11,000. Inventory expenses were cut further by tying assortments to store and department volume, resulting in a turn of 12 times a year at the distribution center. Besides providing greater flexibility to meet the needs of specific markets, this procedure ensured the overall consistency within markets that would help overcome customer confusion about what they would find in a Neisner Brothers store.

The new image was publicized through an advertising budget that was 4% of sales. Tabloids increased by 40%. Radio and television were used for the first time in 1976 in the attempt to tell consumers, particularly the young shopper and young marrieds, that Neisner's convenient discount stores and Big N stores both wore coats cut from the same mass-merchandising cloth.

Impact

When Silverstein assumed leadership of Neisner Brothers in late 1974, the company had a meager inventory, no payables, and no cash. The chain almost went under after suffering deficits of $505,000 in 1974 and $1.6 million in 1975. But the company staved off bankruptcy with timely credit agreements. After two years of sweeping changes, Silverstein seemed to have the ship afloat again when 1976 figures showed earnings of $1.1 million, despite an operating loss of $814,000. By the third quarter of 1977, losses were cut 40% from the previous year. There was $43 million in inventory, and $1.5 million in the bank.

But in September 1977, a credit bureau recommendation put Neisner on revision, citing lack of confidence in the chain's takeover of its leased hardware, paint, and auto departments. Though the bureau recalled its recommendation three days later, vendors had heard the alarm and became nervous. On October 25, the credit line was pulled again, after the operating loss of $475,000 for the quarter was discovered.

The death knell had been sounded. In December, Neisner filed for protection under Chapter XI of the Bankruptcy Act, claiming assets of $59.9 million, liabilities of $46 million, and a creditor list that ran for 200 pages. Vendors refused orders and Neisner was virtually out of stock for Christmas.

The following December, the remaining Neisner stores, 21 Big N and 34 convenient discount units, were acquired by Ames Department Stores of Connecticut.

Silverstein had led his organization in a gallant effort to save the company, but he came up short. After 66 years, Neisner Brothers had run out of time.

Conclusions

A multiplicity of factors caused the failure of Neisner Brothers. Its collapse is a reminder that retailing is a volatile business and that unless management is ever-vigilant, success can soon turn to failure.

Neisner Brothers did not watch its finances, its inventory, its customers, and its competition carefully enough. The company grew in number but failed to change in stature. These contradictory elements are evident in the specific causes of collapse.

1. *Expansion was a principal cause of failure.* Poor sites were selected and burdensome leases were negotiated. Many stores were only half stocked with merchandise.

2. *The change in corporate structure put a strain on finances and adversely affected inventory control.* The creation of two separate divisions, with additional positions and payroll, was not warranted. The growth of the data processing department was out of proportion with the needs of the company and resulted in greater waste.

3. *The variety store image impeded Neisner's success as a discounter.* The image was partly the result of heritage and partly the result of the company's variety store merchandise and its inability to inform the public of the kind of store Neisner was.

4. *The inability to stock its shelves with the proper inventory mix drove customers away.* Taking inventory from old stores to new stores, trying to carry too broad an inventory, and being understocked in the goods that sell in discount stores drove profits down and customers away.

5. *Competition entered Neisner's markets and took customers away.* Because of its poor merchandising strategies, Neisner was unable to defend its territory.

6. *Two storms hurt operations severely.* Though these storms were more damaging than normal, hurricanes in Florida and snow in Rochester have to be expected. Locating the distribution center in such a vulnerable area was not a sound decision.

Common Factors in Retail Failures

The bankruptcies of W. T. Grant's, Robert Hall, and Neisner Brothers are dramatic examples of the fact that past success has no bearing on continued success in retailing. These and other instances of failure demonstrate that the volatile nature of retailing requires continuous planning, consistent performance, and constant vigilance. To act without careful thought, to become slipshod in operation, to overestimate the company's stature, or to lose sight of the customer can bring even the retailing giants to their knees.

Figure 14-7. RETAILERS FILING UNDER CHAPTERS X OR XI

Company	Sales on Date of Filing
Arlan's	$ 206,000,000
Unishops	140,000,000
Parkview Gem	145,000,000
Mangel Stores	99,000,000
Interstate Stores	306,000,000
Mammoth Mart	143,000,000
National Bella Hess	172,000,000
Daylin	308,000,000
W. T. Grant	1,850,000,000
Abercrombie & Fitch	23,800,000
United Merchants	1,029,000,000
Neisner	150,000,000

These stories reveal a set of common factors that are present in most retailing failures. These factors resulted from ignoring the basics of retailing. Those basics have to be taken out and reviewed or they can become lost in our sophistication, our complacency, or our carelessness. These factors are the signs that retailers must look for to avoid the fate of Grant, Robert Hall, Neisner Brothers, and a host of others (see Figure 14-7). Understanding these factors of failure can help the retailer to:

- Determine the effectiveness of management information and process
- Improve this process
- React more decisively

When the word "react" is brought up, we think of the reactions of Grant, Robert Hall, and Neisner to their problems. Each did react, and each was making decisions that seemed to be turning things around. But each ran out of time.

"If only there had been more time." This lament is heard around almost every retailing failure. Time often seems more precious than money. Management, bankers, and creditors often try to help a company "buy" time by adjusting lending and credit agreements and by extending additional spot credit. But, once eroded, a company's credibility with its vendors and customers is almost impossible to restore. Cash pumped into the company is applied to past deliveries, but stores continually need new merchandise. Vendors, as the case studies show, will ship goods only COD, and even then reluctantly. Customers quickly switch allegiance after realizing a store does not have the merchandise they want.

Given enough time, retailers in trouble can right themselves, eventually pay their creditors, and even generate profit. But vendors cannot wait that long. Once problems have surfaced, time cannot be bought. The secret of success—of avoiding failure—is to buy time *before* the problems surface, by identifying shifts in the company's performance early.

Such shifts start occurring 12 to 18 months or more before financial difficulties become obvious and public. In Grant's failure, for instance, profits began to drop four years before the company filed under ChapterXI. Robert Hall's sales figure remained constant for a number of years before losses began to show on the bottom line. Declining profits were part of the Neisner picture as early as1972, two years before its substantial loss and five years before Chapter XI.

In other words, a company in trouble doesn't get that way over night. So those who moan "if only there had been more time" do not realize there will never be enough time if management waits until it is knee-deep in red ink before it suspects there might be a problem.

Some companies begin to worry about their situation only after they find themselves in a tight cash position, unable to take discounts, unable to make timely deposits of payroll taxes, having to subordinate loans to banks and creditors, and reluctant to set up sufficient reserves.

But these are not causes or even symptoms of trouble. These are *effects*. By the time these effects have surfaced, the causes of trouble have long been at work, eating away the heart and soul of a successful business. The companies that look at these effects as causes of failure are the ones that soon after moan, "If only there had been more time."

The idea then is to look for *true* signs of trouble, the early symptoms of problems. Once these are spotted, the company can work from them to the underlying causes. Only when the *causes* of trouble are identified and eliminated will the weakened company become strong again. Identifying these causes early is the only way by which the company will have the time to react decisively.

Early Warning Signs of Failure

Physical or operational problems manifest themselves as financial difficulties. A retailing company needs cash to replenish merchandise and pay its operating expenses. Without that cash, the company will not be able to stay in business. So the retailer must monitor the cash flow, keeping a watchful eye out for traces of these elements which drain liquidity.

Consider a company's liquidity as a tank of cash (Figure 14-8). Numerous elements can drain that tank. Some of those draining elements will appear on the profit and loss sheet and some will be found on the balance sheet. They are, therefore, readily available to the manager who can recognize them as early warning signs of trouble.

Figure 14-8. ELEMENTS THAT ERODE LIQUIDITY

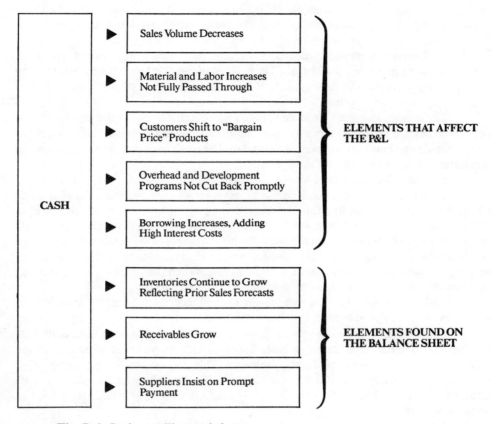

The P & L sheet will reveal that:

1. *Sales volume is decreasing*, either in actual dollars, or in units or sales per square foot. This fact in itself naturally reduces the cash flow into the company, though the amount going out remains the same.

2. *Gross margin is dropping.* This can occur as a result of the decrease in volume or the company's inability to adequately build material and wage increases into the pricing structure. W.T. Grant's sales rose continually though gross margin slipped. If these increases in cost of goods and wages have to be absorbed by the cash from a stable or reduced sales volume, gross margin will obviously drop.

In addition, customers often shift from higher- to lower-priced products, particularly during a downturn in the economy. This results in a different sales mix. If provisions are not made in the pricing or expense structures, gross margin can suffer, reducing available cash.

3. *Overhead and development programs are not being cut back promptly.* When business is in a decline, these programs become out of line with business needs, further reducing cash and profits. Neisner Brothers, for example, drained more cash than necessary with its two-division organizational structure and overly large data processing department.

4. *Borrowing increases.* Because of the conditions already mentioned, loans must be taken to generate needed cash. These loans increase interest payments, thereby placing an additional drain on liquidity. Borrowing from Peter to pay Paul creates a continuously worsening cycle.

These trouble signs should be visible upon careful study of the profit and loss sheet, and they are the indicators management looks for to avert serious difficulty. Signs of liquidity drains can also be seen on the balance sheet. These can have an even more devastating effect than those on the P & L.

Elements found on the balance sheet are:

1. *Growth of inventories.* Essentially, inventories grow because of a slow reaction to sales decline, a lag in adjusting the open-to-buy, or an imbalance created by a shift in customer demand. When Robert Hall continued stocking its stores with clothes that had gone out of fashion, it was faced with this burdensome inventory which reduced cash liquidity. Rather than take markdowns, Robert Hall decided to hold onto its inventory, hoping public taste and customers would return. When that decision proved wrong, the huge inventory problem was compounded by the carryover.

Although some organizations would take higher than normal markdowns to reduce inventories, the net result is still a lower cash position.

2. *Growth of receivables.* As customers struggle through a downturn, they limit their purchases to conserve their own cash. Management often tries to counter this type of sales problem by easing credit requirements. This means accepting greater risks. Very often this backfires, as it did in the case of W.T. Grant's, where credit problems accounted for more than 60% of the company's deficit. Not only is cash not added to the liquidity tank, but inventory is also lost.

3. *Vendors' insistence on prompt payment.* Suppliers, sensing the company's problems, become nervous and insist on prompt payment, further depleting cash. This was a problem for each of the companies studied and for just about every failing retailer. Once this insistence on COD begins, things worsen as the cycle of cash liquidity drain repeats itself with greater furor and a more drastic drain on cash.

These signs, which should appear on the financial statements of any retail company that is experiencing trouble, ought to flash red lights of warning to management. Too often, however, overly optimistic managers or shortsighted ones look at only sales volume growth, extension of market share, the progress of a few hot items, or the number of new locations, and do not consider the impact on liquidity. Grant's is a prime example of a company that was misled by such statistics. Grant's failed to take a look at other data on its financial documents that would have been more reliable indicators of its real posture. Increased sales were read as a sign of strength. Decreasing gross margin and swelling inventories, however, should have been seen as foreboding signs of failure.

Understanding this liquidity drain cycle enables management to determine its susceptibility to these financial traps. Managers who are successful over the long haul generally understand the cycle, insist on sound planning, and, equally importantly, measure performance against plan. If dangerous trends such as sales decline, creeping inventory and receivable levels, profit erosion, and cash drains appear, alert management recognizes immediately their significance and takes decisive action.

The profit and loss and the balance sheets therefore provide the early warning signals of failure. Management must watch for and detect them.

Causes of Retail Failure

Spotting the early signs of trouble on the company's financial statements is the first step in avoiding business failure. These signs tell you that you have a problem. The next step is to find out what is causing the problem. The final step is to solve it successfully.

Usually there is no single cause of company failure but rather a combination of causes. These causes, however, can be reduced to two general categories: errors and growth and errors of stagnation.

Errors of growth are those mistakes that accompany rapid expansion. Generally these errors are:

1. Management resources are stretched too thin and become inadequate.
2. Organization structures are not changed to correspond with new growth.
3. Systems of communication and control are not sufficiently modified to accommodate new growth.
4. Ineffective marketing/merchandising decisions are made in site and merchandise selection.
5. An inability to sustain cost-effective operations results from geographic dispersion, inefficiencies, and lack of control.

Errors of stagnation are those mistakes that stem from a company's reluctance or inability to change. Generally these errors are:

1. Lack of new blood or thinking in management.
2. A stunted system of communication and control.
3. Constant sales volume with escalating costs.
4. Marketing/merchandising decisions that fail to recognize changes in customer base.
5. Operating factors that are no longer productive.
6. An inability to spot declining profitability.

Errors of growth are treacherous and common. They come about when past success and ambition feed each other and cloud otherwise sound judgment. It is the hearty optimism of early expansion success that causes companies such as Grant's and Neisner Brothers to step up the pace beyond their capacity to control the growth.

How do these errors of growth drive a successful company to failure? Let us review each.

1. *Management resources are stretched too thin and become inadequate.* Because the company grows too fast, a shortage of qualified personnel in management positions results, both in the corporate office and in the stores. As was seen in the case of Grant's, this shortage generally leads to accelerated training and a lowering of standards to meet needs. A two-year training course is compacted into six or eight weeks so that managers can be spun out in time for new store openings. The criteria for management selection, which once were knowledge, experience, intelligence, and desire, now become speed and convenience.

When Grant expanded too rapidly, it found itself short on management talent. Stores were managed by people who were ill-equipped and poorly trained. People with similar inadequacies were manning positions in the corporate offices. Therefore, more responsibility was given to people who were less able to handle it.

Stores do not operate themselves, merchandise does not miraculously appear on the loading dock, and cash is not automatically collected and disbursed. Even in organizations with tight controls, someone must run the store, and no retailing system can be "people-proof." At the corporate level, planning and control cannot be devised and improved by a management staff that is overburdened.

People—good, well-trained people—are needed. The point seems obvious, yet it is so often forgotten during management's infatuation with expansion. The need for well-trained personnel is a basic fundamental of retailing, which, when overlooked, becomes an error of growth and can lead to failure.

2. *Organization structures are not changed to correspond to new growth.* Unbridled growth often results in a failure to modify the buy/sell relationship that has been traditional in the company. For instance, companies may begin as a series of leased departments, then grow into self-operating units. Or the same person in the home office is still responsible for sales floor scheduling and profits of his department, but instead of having one or two stores he now has 60 or 100.

Another condition, the opposite of an overburdened structure, often results from rapid growth. Overstructuring occurs, and empires are built where they are not necessary. In trying to emulate the giants of the industry, a 50-store company will take on the structure of a 500-store company, without scaling down that structure. Payrolls swell, and duplication, waste, and general inefficiency spread. Neisner Brothers made this overstructuring error when it split into two divisions, one each for its large and small discount stores, only to revert to the original unified structure two years later. Neisner's overzealous leap into data processing resulted in a system that was much too large for its needs, thereby creating another huge expense which was unprofitable and unnecessary.

3. *Systems of communication and control are not modified sufficiently to accommodate new growth.* As the company grows, stores march further and further away from the home base. Communication often breaks down and control is lost. No longer is there accurate performance reporting by store and department, and inventory management systems falter. At Grant's, individual store managers would take markdowns on their own initiative and cover these by not reporting brisk sellers. Some of these managers would order goods and hold up invoices, thus increasing their own budgets and understating the cost of purchases.

Another area over which the home office can lose control during expansion is credit management. Here again Grant's is a prime example. Because of the flurry of store openings and the stretching of central office personnel, communication with and control of the stores was not what it should have been. Store managers were too often left to their own devices. When the push for sales came, store managers relaxed credit requirements to ridiculous levels. By the time the central office was able to detect and change credit procedures, accounts receivable had skyrocketed 86% to $602 million. This lack of control over credit may have been the most serious of Grant's mistakes, since 62% of the firm's deficit in 1974 was attributed to credit losses.

A third area that suffers from unfettered expansion is that of shortage control. When a company has insufficient time to train managers adequately, it has even less time to provide effective shortage control programs. Yet this is another of those basics that when ignored can peck away at profits.

Another basic, in-service programs to update the skills and rekindle the spirit of all management personnel, also becomes a thing of the past in a company that is on a course of breakaway expansion.

4. *Ineffective marketing/merchandising decisions are made in site and merchandise selection.* When companies grow too quickly, stores are often opened on sites that prove to be undesirable and unprofitable. Not enough study goes into site selection, either because of a lack of time or because of an arrogant optimism that says "We can't miss."

With more time or caution, the company might conduct demographic studies that could reveal that the population in a particular area is declining, or that, while the number of people remains constant, the average income is dropping. Traffic flow studies might reveal that a new highway is planned in the area and could easily draw your customers to competitors. Or investigation may show that the congestion caused by narrow streets and lack of parking will discourage the public from driving to the store.

Robert Hall, a case in point, found that its strip center stores were hurt by the attractive malls. With changes in energy costs, mall sites may not be as appealing as they were in the 1960s. So each area and each time period is different. Thus, there is need for such studies.

Another factor that hasty expansionists overlook is the permanence of major industries in an area. If the business that employs a large number of people in your market (whether they be residents of the area or workers whose jobs bring them into your market) decides to shut down, or move, or suffers a long strike or layoff, a prime retailing site could become a poor one.

Companies that are successful in one state or region may not find the same kind of customer acceptance in another. A regional chain that grew on the customer loyalty it developed in its small local stores cannot expect to find that loyalty in another state or region where its name is relatively unknown.

Similarly, a company trying to change its image must consider the impact of that change on its customers. Robert Hall could not shake its image of the no-frills, one-style clothing store, and Neisner Brothers' reputation as a variety store impeded its growth as a discounter. Ways of reading the mind of the public have to be established before such changes can be made.

The same is even more true when a company attempts to diversify or to expand into an unfamiliar industry segment. A discount chain, for example, that wants to add a complete food line to its merchandise has to realize there are many types of problems and needs in food retailing different from the problems and needs with which they are familiar.

Overconfident retailers who lack vision think they can move from one region to another, or change from one industry segment to another, or shift from one image to another with ease. But sets of variables in site selection, customer acceptance, and the company's own capabilities must be considered before making serious commitments in those directions.

5. *An inability to sustain cost-effective operations results from geographic dispersion, inefficiencies, and lack of control.* As geographic expansion occurs, the lines of communication lengthen, making it more difficult for management to become aware of problems and to react to them quickly. It becomes necessary for management to rely on others to control and display merchandise. Without adequate controls, inventory can build or markdowns can become excessive. If the appropriate systems have not been put in place, inefficiencies and poor controls may result. In addition, timely information from remote locations may be difficult to obtain without computer support or costly courier services.

Continued expansion increases paperwork at the central office, placing a strain on staff or requiring an increase in the staff and budget. The strain is especially great during periods of rapid expansion when outmoded systems begin to crumble. Very often the necessary controls are forgotten or eliminated in an effort to reduce costs, causing further problems and losses.

When a company expands over a large geographic area, the physical distance from store to merchandise and from store to central office can be a problem, and one whose cost must be considered. Will the company be able to operate with the same cost-effectiveness if the radius from the distribution center to the most remote location is doubled? How will shipping costs and timeliness be affected? Will other distribution centers have to be built? Will inventory for the new stores be decentralized and, if so, how will that impact cost-effectiveness?

The location of Neisner Brothers' distribution center in Rochester became a problem when snow closed much of that area to vehicular traffic. Stores out of the area, whose customers *could* get out to shop, had to suffer the same lack of merchandise shipments as those that had been snowed in. This illustrates the importance of the location of distribution centers and of their proximity to stores. If new stores are going to be located far away from existing units, will the cost of stocking those stores be any more costly than stocking existing stores?

Operations can also be adversely affected by expansion when management is so far removed from stores that meaningful contact—including that all-important personal contact—is reduced or practically eliminated.

Another factor related to cost-effectiveness and growth is that of detection. Expansion and resultant sales growth can often hide inefficiencies. Buoyed by high sales, management may not realize that the additional volume is being generated at too great a cost. The new stores have not only added merchandise costs and personal expenses, but they have also created situations in merchandising, in distribution, and in communications which are inefficient and wasteful, yet can go undetected for a good length of time.

Cost-effectiveness can be influenced by the higher wages demanded by quality personnel in a particular area. If a company moves to a region and then discovers that the wage standards there are higher than what it is used to paying, whether these be for positions in management or the stock room, profit projections will be noticeably affected. A related factor would be the complete lack of adequate personnel in the area. Hiring incompetent people at any wage will cost the company dearly.

These errors of growth, then, are some of the primary causes of retail collapse. They stem from expansion which progresses without ample time, thought, and planning.

Rapid growth can create many problems for the retailer, often serious enough to lead to bankruptcy. At the other extreme, but equally as dangerous, is company stagnation. Stagnation is the danger of going out of style, of becoming complacent, of seeing once-popular sites succumbing to urban decay or shifts in demographics.

Companies often become the victims of stagnation when they erroneously label their lack of forward movement as "stability." Aware of the perils of growth, these companies try to keep their heads by remaining stable. Unfortunately for some, this stability leads to a hardening of the business arteries, to corporate stagnation.

Let us take a look at the main causes of corporate stagnation:

1. *Lack of new blood or thinking in management resources and organization.* Just as the expanding company suffers from an inability to develop new managerial talent fast enough, the stagnant company suffers from the absence of new people and thought in the management pipeline. Management positions are held by the same people for years and years. There is little cross-fertilization of ideas with those outside the

company. New talent is not recruited seriously, and in-service programs for the staff are redundant or nonexistent.

In such companies it is common to find individuals spending excessive time at the same grade level, thus reducing the motivation to grow and the opportunity to change. Do such people add years of experience to their backgrounds, or do they merely repeat the same experience over and over? Generally, it's the latter.

The "recently syndrome" is also characteristic of these stagnant situations. Should an outsider or an occasional newcomer suggest a different way of doing anything, the response generally is, "We tried that recently, and it didn't work." "Recently" in these organizations may mean five or ten years ago.

The biggest problem with a stagnant management is that it is too tightly oriented to "what used to be." Attitudes toward everything from cash management to merchandise assortment are tied to the past and are slow, if not impossible, to change. Winning formulas are cast in concrete in such companies and management will not toy with them. Something very drastic must happen before that formula will be altered, and usually that something comes in the form of a sharp drop in profits and the knock of bankruptcy on the door.

Robert Hall embodied the company whose management team saw little change over the years. This management team clung to its concept of customer, merchandise, and strip center locations too long. By the time new people were brought in to effect change, Robert Hall had already sealed its tomb.

2. *A stunted system of communications and control.* At one time retailers felt that the best control over their business was loyal employees. "Develop loyalty in your employees and that will prove far superior to any system of checks and balances." This may have worked at one time, but with the expanded size of retailing companies and with the profile of today's work force, such loyalty is almost impossible to develop on a widespread basis.

Retail chains have too many stores and employees to expect the kind of loyalty they used to nurture in cozier settings and patterns. In addition, many workers today do not seem to have the same attitude their parents did toward their jobs and their companies. Turnover is much greater, perhaps reflecting the "me-first" mentality. Yet companies that have relied upon loyalty in the past, often continue to do so or fail to come up with viable alternatives.

In the area of communication, these stagnant companies tend to feel that the old ways are ample. They seem to ignore the fact that the competition is using increasingly more sophisticated communication and information systems.

Management that once could "see for itself" what was going on in the stores and warehouses just cannot do that in the multi-store chains. Yet some companies try, usually with poor results.

3. *No "real" growth in financial performance.* Some companies watch their sales volume as the major indicator of their health. If sales increase or remain constant, or if they parallel the trend in the industry, these companies feel safe because in the

past these numbers have yielded satisfactory profits. What such companies do not realize is that by standing still they are falling behind. And not only behind their competitors, but also behind their past performance.

There is no real sales growth unless it is in real dollars, because sales dollars may not keep pace with inflation. Inflationary increases tend to hide transaction declines. If the operating budget is tied to sales dollars, the company runs the risk of building the expense structure far higher than it can carry, especially if the structure is built on inflated sales dollars.

In addition, it may be difficult to generate cash for refurbishing if, even though sales are growing, money is continually being reinvested in increasingly more costly goods.

In other words, financially speaking, the company that is stable during an inflationary period is actually declining. Note that the sales volume at W.T. Grant's continued to grow, almost until the end.

4. *Marketing/merchandising decisions fail to recognize changes in the customer base.* Complacent management may not keep track of its customer base to determine its makeup and breadth. Robert Hall, for instance, built its success on a customer interested in economy first. As public attitudes shifted and general affluence grew, Robert Hall maintained its no-frills, low-priced merchandise. Robert Hall's customer base eroded without the company's being aware of it until it was too late.

Studies to understand the changes in customers must be conducted periodically to react with suitable changes in strategy. Some companies, however, seem to feel that consumers are as static as they are.

Part of that customer profile is composed of age. Customers and buyers seem to mirror one another. When the buying staff becomes old, it tends to buy for an older customer. Too much of this can label a store and make it off-limits to other segments of the buying public.

Ten to fifteen years ago there were many marketing areas where only one store dominated. With the rapid expansion of the 60s and 70s, this scene has changed, and retailers must change accordingly.

5. *Operating factors are no longer productive.* Continuing "what used to be" may be an unprofitable practice. For example, services such as free alterations, gift wrapping, and check cashing may no longer be productive. The cost of these services may far outweigh the return, yet the company that just maintains the *status quo* may not recognize that.

The age and longevity of the sales force may no longer be right to attract the customer base a company hopes for. Unless management is aware of this possibility, the discordant relationship between sales staff and customer can prove costly.

6. *An inability to spot declining profitability.* Sales may increase, but if they do not increase as rapidly as the consumer price index or the local sales trend, that sales increase will be erased. If the gross margin increases, but the corporate expenses increase faster, then earnings will actually decline.

Overhead, which is often considered a fixed expense, is not really fixed, but rises and squeezes out profit points. Oil to heat stores and gasoline to run trucks, for instance, tend to cost more and more each year, so management must not be guided by the overhead figures of previous years.

Taking Preventive Action

If these errors of growth and errors of stagnation are the common factors of retail failure, a valid question is "What can you do to identify them?" Obviously, this is a diverse group of indicators, so there is no single answer, but management can protect against the creeping effects of these excesses with a little attention to certain basic management techniques. These techniques fall into three categories: (1) profit measures, (2) quality of performance, and (3) periodic studies.

Let us briefly review each of these categories.

Profit measures. These include sales, gross margin, and contribution, and should be available by merchandise department, by store, and by region. This sounds very basic, but retailers must honestly ask themselves whether or not they have these measures available. Are they available in a useful fashion? Do they show trends? Retailers must look realistically at these performance measures and not just be blinded by numbers that might look good for today.

Quality of performance. In measuring the quality of the company's performance, a number of indicators must be assessed.

1. Sales per square foot. How often is this important measure of productivity checked? Is it checked on a trended basis?

2. Inventory aging. Is the reporting on inventory accurate? Does it reveal what is turning and what is just sitting?

3. Accounts receivable. Do the reports reveal their age? The repeaters?

4. Credit management policies and techniques. When sales are down, does the company push sales at the expense of credit risks and cash flow?

5. Vendor correspondence. This is a key indicator of efficiency, of the ordering, receiving, and accounts payable functions. What is your vendor correspondence revealing about your quality of performance?

6. Inflation-adjusted financials. Is growth real or not when the impact of inflation is removed?

Periodic studies should be made of a number of key segments of the business. These studies should cover customer profile, management profile, personnel profile, appropriateness of corporate objectives, and expansion programs. These studies are recommended every three to five years, depending on the area, size, and needs of the company. But they should be made on a regular basis and should impact the strategies of the company.

Critical Questions

In order to implement the management techniques described above, a number of critical questions must be asked. Only when these questions can be answered is management in a position to successfully measure, control, and direct its business. These critical questions are:

1. Do we have meaningful performance measures? Can we measure performance by store, by department, by classification, by SKU? If we cannot, how do we go about equipping ourselves to do so?

2. Do we trend our data to provide a clear picture of subtle shifts in number and volume of sales, in buying patterns?

3. Do we know who our customers are? When was the last time we drew a profile of our customers? (These profiles are needed often, not only after a dramatic change in the "neighborhood.")

4. What do we know about our personnel? What is the age, experience, rate of turnover, ambition of our staff?

5. Have operations outgrown internal controls? Is ours a well-thought out system or is it just a patchwork built randomly over the years?

Conclusion

Is there any magic in this approach to avoiding failure? No, it is just good common, business sense. Success lies in continuing to apply these management techniques, to make appropriate appraisals of the complete organization, to interpret the results, and to take creative, effective action when that is indicated. Not magical, but not easy either, as W.T. Grant, Robert Hall, and Neisner Brothers can attest to.

15

Strategic Planning

OVERVIEW: As retailing moves forward in an era of increasing change and economic uncertainty, good planning is more important than ever. The vagaries of inflation, high interest, consumer restraint, layoffs, and many other factors affecting the economy make it very dangerous for retailers to sail along on the status quo. Because of the choppy waters, retailers have to exert more control over their businesses. And control requires planning. The successful retailers are those who make good plans for all phases of their business—merchandising, operations, information systems, finance. In addition to developing good plans, the successful retailer sees to it that these plans are implemented.

The sobering analyses of the failures of W.T. Grant's, Robert Hall, and Neisner Brothers provide ample motivation for continuous assessment of performance and reformulation of strategic plans.

Strategic planning—isn't that one of those textbook terms no real company actually gets involved in? That boards of directors keep bringing up only to be superseded by more pressing practical matters? That may be the case in some companies. But the leading retailers today consider strategic planning to be a critical step in the business process.

Stated simply, strategic planning sets performance objectives for the company and determines the means for achieving those objectives. It is a very thorough process that examines every aspect of the business and involves all levels of management. It is this thoroughness that is the most significant contribution of strategic planning. It forces all levels of management to think through their reasons for working on a particular project and establishes the ground rules for everyone's performance. Planning also provides for alternative scenarios so that when faced with falling sales and profits, decisive steps can be taken in time to turn the situation around.

A Five-Year Itinerary

Strategic planning is much more than a six-month merchandise plan. It is a five-year itinerary that determines:

Where the company stands today

Where the company would like to be for each of the next five years

How the company is going to get there

What resources are required in getting there

What the risks are in trying to get there.

In assessing the company's present status and future ambitions, strategic planning helps in the immediate handling of day-to-day concerns. Strategic, long-range planning assists management in organizing, directing, and controlling the business on a daily basis. It helps to identify and prioritize key issues facing the organization, issues that might otherwise be ignored or put on a back burner. Long-range planning increases management's awareness of how the company functions and how performance can be influenced. It increases communication among the company's top management group and provides a uniform set of goals and objectives for the entire organization. At the same time, strategic planning provides a frame of reference for the annual budgeting process.

Elements of a Corporate Strategic Plan

Although all formal business plans vary somewhat depending on the individual company's style and particular needs, there are several basic elements of a corporate strategic plan.

The first element is a statement of the *corporate mission*, which describes the nature of the company. The corporate mission answers questions such as what business are we in? Who is our customer? Where is our market? What are our products?

The second element in a strategic plan lists the *corporate objectives*, the results the company wants to achieve and what it wants to become. Objectives would specify where the company wants to be within the industry in terms of sales, market share, total units, store size. For example, a corporate objective might call for sales increase of 15% a year so that sales volume doubles to $100 million by a certain year. Profitability in terms of gross margin, operating income, net earnings, stockturn, and return on investment would be targeted. Productivity would be charted, with reference to staffing, space utilization, promotion, and automation. And diversification objectives including those bearing on merchandise mix, product lines, mergers and acquisitions would be identified.

After setting corporate objectives, the company would *review the marketplace* to examine the competition, the industry, the condition of the economy, and the regional changes within the markets in which the company operates. This review of the economic, demographic, and industry trends helps evaluate the feasibility of the corporate objectives. The hard data coming from such a review can tell the company early on that its objective of doubling sales in five years is either unrealistic or too conservative.

Also assisting the company in evaluating its potential to reach its objectives is the fourth element of strategic planning, the *assessment of the company's strengths and weaknesses*. This calls for an honest appraisal of company performance in terms of such factors as image and reputation; expertise in the functional areas of merchandising, operations, finance, personnel, and promotion; quality of employees; level of financial and merchandise control; the company's financial position; and the responsiveness of the all-important information system.

This kind of thorough assessment not only evaluates a company's potential for long-term growth, it also highlights those areas that are slipping and need attention. Management can make adjustments where necessary before a major overhaul is needed.

At this point, knowing who the company is, where it wants to go, the potential for getting there, and the conditions that will allow it to, the company can then go to step five in strategic planning, establishment of *corporate strategies*. These would detail the programs needed to achieve the objectives and estimate the benefit or contribution each program will make. A growth strategy, for example, might determine that expansion plans concentrate only on existing markets to capitalize on advertising and distribution advantages. A diversification strategy might limit diversification to vertical integration to reduce the company's operating expenses by eliminating charges paid to other companies. Operating strategies might include a new purchase order system to speed ordering and improve control.

Preliminary tactical plans are then drawn up for each department in the company. These tactical plans identify the mission and responsibilities of each department in terms of what it must do to satisfy corporate objectives. The merchandising department, for instance, may determine that, to meet the corporate objective of financial planning, it must know well in advance what resources it will need to purchase merchandise. Therefore, one tactical plan of the merchandise department might be to develop a procedure for six-month merchandise planning, and to provide training for this.

Secondary plans on new business ventures and acquisitions are formally explored as part of the strategic planning process. The type of business, its objectives and promise, and the reasons for merging it to the existing company are examined.

Much of the coordination of the strategic plan is done at a *planning conference.* All individuals involved in strategic planning are brought together for this single purpose. The total management group discusses the plans, so that each manager knows more about the operation of the individual components of the company and about their roles in the corporate scheme. All of the elements listed above, from corporate mission through secondary planning, are discussed by the entire management group.

The conference encourages an exchange of views on the various plans and elements of them, so that they can then be modified where necessary. The give and take among department leaders that results benefits not only the long-range plans but all of the everyday operations of the organization.

After plans are modified, the final element of strategic planning is set. This is the *budgeting and monitoring* process. The key to successfully implementing a business plan is to set up the mechanism to monitor actual performance against the plan on an ongoing basis. A plan is dynamic and can only be effective if it is continually revised to reflect the most current performance and characteristics of the business. This can be achieved by monitoring the plan and reacting to exceptions of performance by first identifying the reasons for falling short of expectations and then by taking corrective action.

The monitoring tools required to maintain effective control over the performance against plan include the accounting, inventory, merchandising, and sales systems.

Factors Affecting Plans

Strategic plans can be more effective if the following guidelines are followed. First, they should be guided by the CEO. These plans have the most far-reaching effect of any of the company's plans and must therefore fall under the direction of the CEO. The CEO should not work in a vacuum, however; instead, all levels of management should have input into these plans.

Because of the scope of strategic plans, they can only be developed over a period of time and with a great deal of care. They should be put in writing and include quantitative and qualitative objectives and performance measures. Strategic plans, while long-range, are not permanent documents. They are only effective if updated periodically and rewritten every five years.

Strategic, long-range planning is a major undertaking. But it is the cornerstone of successful companies.

Implementing the Plan

The critical step in successful implementation is the creation of the plan itself. A poorly conceived or unrealistic plan has little chance of being implemented. But when a plan is based on realistic expectations and is understood and accepted by all of the people it affects, implementation is then a more natural second step.

A good plan, regardless of the area of business, should have several key elements:

- Strategic goals and objectives established by senior management
- A bottom-up perspective
- A commitment from the people it affects
- A basis in historical information
- A recognition of changing conditions
- Specific and measurable objectives and actions
- A realistic timeframe with intermediary target dates

Goals and objectives. Senior management is clearly in the best position to establish strategic goals and objectives for the retail company. These goals and objectives could address such things as new types of retail outlets, new consumers to be reached, or geographic expansion. With these goals and objectives clearly defined, each retail operating function is in a position to prepare its operating plan in support of the overall strategic direction.

One retailer who became lackadaisical about developing the company's strategic goals and plans saw the negative impact on sales rather quickly as things began to get out of hand. Buyers, for example, were making purchases more on individual assessment of who the company's customers were than on policy or on updated information. Without a clear directive from the top, these buyers were almost forced into this kind of freelance position. It didn't take long for this disorder to impact sales negatively.

Bottom-up perspective generates commitment. Two other elements of the successful plan are committed people and bottom-up development. These two elements really support one another. By having functional management and its staff develop the detailed operating plan, the plan becomes *their* plan, as opposed to someone else's plan. They are, therefore, committed to it because they have had a role in developing it. However, that does not mean that top management should not review the operating plan to ensure that it is in conformance with the strategic direction, or that it is adequately aggressive or conservative as required.

One of the reasons for Japan's high productivity is the commitment of employees. Japanese management strives to get its workers involved, to give them a voice that will be listened to. This involvement, more than anything else, seems to motivate people to care more and to do their best to make plans a reality.

Historical information and changing conditions. Through EDP, POS, and other sophisticated systems retailers today can generate a wealth of useful information about performance. This information should be brought into the planning process since it is the recorded past and present on which the future of the business is based.

While historical information can be very useful in providing a foundation on which to base future plans, it can be no more than a foundation. Today, retailers are faced with rapidly changing economic conditions, new customer demands for convenience, a myriad of new products, and increasing competition. Therefore, the judgment and experience of the operating people must be applied to the historical information to ensure that the plan addresses today's reality. In addition, for measuring performance and progress against the plan, plan data must be compared to current information. The traditional report of merchandise and sales information against last year's comparable periods and status is useful, but it does not give sufficient measure of where a company stands today against where it *planned* to be today. In other words, the plan has to be flexible. The retailer has to modify it as the current situation dictates. Plans can be based, in part, on the past, but must be measured against today's actual figures.

Measurable objectives and goals. For any plan to serve as a useful aid, objectives and goals must be measurable. Without specific information in these areas, it is impossible to know whether the plans are being turned into reality or not. Probably the most critical element of successful implementation, whether it is merchandise planning, POS implementation, or something else, is specific targets against which progress and achievement can be measured.

If the first step to turning plans into reality is a good plan, then the second step is managing to the plan. In managing to the plan, reporting measures must exist that track progress against the plan and highlight variances on a regular basis, normally monthly for annual operating plans. If conditions are changing rapidly, the report frequency should be shortened to minimize the time to report variances from the plan. For example, as the six-month merchandise plans call for sales at a certain level and margins at a corresponding level to achieve profit goals, the merchandise reporting system must report on a monthly basis against those figures. If, however, we find that there is a shift in the economy or a critical sales month is coming up, the reporting interval should be shortened to every two weeks or, in some cases, every week. By doing this, lower sales can quickly be recognized and planned purchases and inventory levels reduced accordingly. This action can help eliminate markdowns or reduce the size of markdowns that otherwise would have to be taken.

Likewise, if you have a POS implementation plan that calls for POS benefits to result from a 10% reduction in inventory with the same service level to customers, then you must put a mechanism in place to measure the inventory level before and after the implementation. In addition, if you find you are achieving that target, management should review the target and see if a new one can be developed to increase profits even further. The key, then, is to set specific targets, measure progress against those targets, and revise as appropriate.

Timeframe and target dates. The final step in turning plans into reality is to recognize that a plan is not a static document. The plan should not be changed frequently or on a whim. But as the conditions that established the original assumptions change, then the plan must be modified to reflect those changes. Typically, a quarterly report on an annual basis is called for, with annual updates to the company's five-year planning cycle and creation of the new annual operating plan. The results of this year's plan become the historical information to form the basis for the next year's plan.

To be useful, then, plans must be well conceived and well implemented. They require imagination, attention to detail, and consideration of the basic principles of people-management. With careful creation and execution, though, plans for success become realities.

Market Research

One important element in planning a retail future is market research. Market research has been around a long time. Evidence of market research dates back to the 14th century when textile manufacturer Johann Fugger established a market research network by having strategically placed relatives exchange detailed letters on trade conditions and finance throughout Europe. In this way Fugger, operating from Augsburg, could make accurate trading decisions based on current knowledge of the supply and demand for money and goods throughout the continent.

It is from these early roots that the premise of marketing research was developed. That is, business executives learned how to organize data objectively and to use it in making better decisions.

Today's expertise and advanced technology has brought market research to a sophisticated science. Yet market research in the retail industry is still in the Dark Ages, except for the most progressive companies. While these industry leaders support a wide variety of decisions with information drawn through up-to-date research techniques, the majority of retailers still rely on little more than a blend of alchemy and intuition.

Excuses for not using research range from "I already know my customers" to "I am too busy" to "research is too theoretical or complicated." These arguments are weak reeds in today's competitive business environment. Only with a systematic gathering and analysis of market data can the modern retailer expect to develop reliable answers consistently. Marketing research helps reduce the risk in decision-making, and as competition intensifies, it will become increasingly important for retailers to base decisions on fact rather than on market instincts.

Market research can be an integral part of choosing a good location for a new store, spotting merchandising opportunities, measuring the effects of store promotions, improving distribution decisions, improving the retailers' promotional strategy, determining consumer behavior, reaching appropriate pricing decisions, and assessing the consumers' image of your stores.

Determining the Effects of Store Promotions

To illustrate the use of research in practical decision making, let us look at store promotions, a significant and consistent expenditure in the retailer's budget. It is

Figure 15-1. OIL FILTER PURCHASE FACTORS

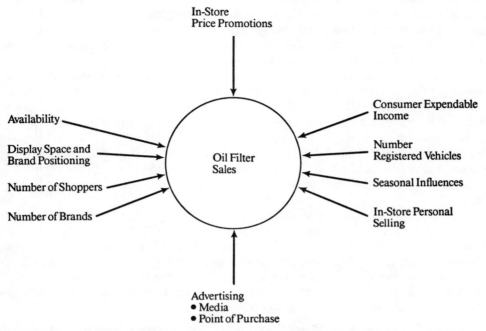

assumed that through promotions you spend some money to make more money. Unfortunately, most retailers only guess whether their promotion dollars are being well spent.

There are, however, several ways to test promotion effectiveness. If the goal is to test qualitative factors such as consumers' attitudes or reactions to store promotional activities, personal interviews or mail questionnaires could tell you how charismatic your promotional dollars have been.

Generally, most retailers are more interested in measuring the incremental sales dollars that result from promotions. How can you measure the change in sales volume? Audits of the firm's records or reports generated from POS equipment are probably the least costly way of measuring the changes in sales volume. Sales levels are typically measured at three time periods of equal length, before, during, and after promotions.

Measuring variations in sales volumes, however, is only effective when the change in sales can be directly related to the change in promotion expenditures. The difficulty in isolating the direct relationship of promotional expenditures to incremental sales is that very frequently the changes in sales are the result of many factors, not just promotional activities. Other items that can affect the change in sales include price changes, availability, changes in consumer expendable income, display space, and position on the shelf.

To normalize these and other factors, many market researchers use controlled experiments. This technique is frequently used by researchers in scientific analysis. The basis for the approach is to use several similar stores in the experiment, and conduct a specific in-store promotion for one group while the other group is exposed to a different promotion or no promotion at all. Measuring the change in sales for all groups, and comparing results for the "controlled" store to those of the others, the retailer is able to measure the incremental sales effect of the promotion.

Let's take an example. Assume that you wanted to test the effect of a price promotion for oil filters in three stores (Store A, Store B, Store C). The first step would be to attempt to make all the stores equivalent in all ways except for the different price of the oil filter (i.e., same product signs, same number of competing brands, same availability, equal display space, same media advertising, etc.). This step is of critical importance to assure validity of the test. Uncontrollable factors such as differences in consumer expendable income from one test site to another and the number of registered vehicles in each store trading area should be taken into account when analyzing test results.

After the stores are normalized, you are ready for the test. In this hypothetical case, the price of oil filters should be increased in Store A by 34% and decreased in Store B by 34%, and the price in Store C should remain the same. Price measurement should be conducted during equal time periods before, during, and after the promotion, and sales measurements should be taken for each time period. In this way you would be able to isolate the effects of the price promotion and determine its effectiveness, as shown by the following hypothetical test table:

| | Before Promotion | | | Promotion | | |
	Price	Units Sold	Revenue	Price (% Change)	Units Sold (% Change)	Revenue (% Change)
Store A	$2.98	100	$298.00	$3.98 (+34%)	90 (−10%)	$358.20 (+20%)
Store B	2.98	90	268.20	1.98 (−34%)	126 (+40%)	249.48 (−7%)
Store C	2.98	110	327.80	2.98 (0%)	110 (0%)	327.80 (0%)

The results show, in concrete figures, that buyers did in fact respond to the price promotion. In Store A where the price was increased by 34%, unit sales fell off by only 10%, giving a net increase in revenues of 20%. The 34% price reduction in Store B resulted in a 40% net unit increase, which led to a 7% decline in revenue. Sales in Store C remained constant. The conclusion that could be drawn from this hypothetical test is that consumers were not overly sensitive to price increases. The tack to decrease price and make up for it with increased unit volume did not pay out, as some retailers are apt to assume or conclude from looking only at units sold.

This is only one simplified example of how market research can quantify the effects of decisions—past or future. The same kind of logical procedure can be used in gathering information for decisions on many things from the price of toothpaste to the acquisition of a paper mill.

16

Site Selection

OVERVIEW: Its stores and warehouses or distribution centers are important in any retail organization. Of primary concern is the location of these facilities. The stores, of course, must be accessible to large numbers of the kind of consumer the retailer hopes to sell to. The warehouse or distribution center must be close enough to all outlets to provide them with the merchandise they need when they need it. The wise retailer takes advantage of a number of research tools and information sources to improve site selection for his stores.

Buildings solidly constructed on a strong foundation generally last longer than those propped on stilts. The solidity of construction reduces structure shifts, minimizes cracking, and eliminates costly repair work and the need to move or build anew. Spending some time and money wisely in the initial stages of construction almost always pays plenty of long-term dividends.

The same principle applies in selecting a site for a retail store. Whether the store is a first or the one hundredth in a chain, among the most critical elements in that store's "foundation" is its location. Some retailers open shop in a location simply because it is the only vacant space within a stone's throw from home or from the home office. Others may take a walk around the block before signing the lease. Both would seem to be just sticking their stilts in sand.

Knowledgable retailers make a thorough examination of possible locations before investing their money and dreams. They know the investment will be large, and they want as reasonable a prediction of success as possible before making a commitment.

New and Old

Site selection for a new store is a standard problem but retailers must also concern themselves with the locations of established stores. Neighborhoods change and populations shift. Urban renewal programs, highway construction, and mass transit improvements can reduce once bustling commercial activity to an uneasy stillness. Big profits can dwindle into serious deficits.

Rather than waiting for the water to reach the bridge, retailers with vision periodically re-examine the viability of their existing locations in terms of the future. Long before the expiration of a lease or before an area's decline is a well known fact, the successful retailer examines his current location just as he would a new one. Here we will outline site selection for a new store, but the process is the same and just as important for evaluating the location of an established store.

Company Profile

How does a retail organization go about selecting a location for a store? The first step is to determine *who you are*. That is, what kind of store are you planning? What kinds of merchandise do you plan to sell, at what price levels, and to whom? Knowing who you are ensures that any evaluation you make about an area will be made in terms of your purposes.

The introspective review should first include an evaluation of the company's competitive strengths and abilities.

What are the company's financial capabilities? Can the expansion be successfully underwritten? To determine the answers, review the cash position, contingent liabilities, unsecured assets, royalty agreements, goodwill and profits, and other financial commitments.

Next, does the organization have the managerial resources needed to direct the expansion and operate the new outlets? There are many famous examples of successful retail chains such as W.T. Grant's that brought about their own demise partly by spreading their managerial talent too thin.

Satisfied that the financial and managerial resources are sufficient to expand, the next important factor to consider is the company's *image*. What is the company offering customers—price, service, convenience? Understanding your own stylistic constraints can be very helpful in limiting the number of site choices. That is, by knowing who you are, you can better focus on only those sites that are consistent with your store's image. This saves time and reduces the risk of a poor location choice.

Location Philosophy

Next examine preferences for general locations. Do you have any geographical limitations? Are you zeroing in on a specific area? Do you plan to expand your existing distribution networks? Would you prefer a city to a suburban location? A highway location? Do you want a shopping center, a mall, a neighborhood row of stores? Would you do better away from any other stores?

An important issue is proximity to your other stores. There are several advantages to locating stores in the same region—advertising economics, inventory balancing, savings in shipping. Yet you may conclude that the real opportunities for growth lie outside the region you are now in.

Proximity to the competition is another factor. If an area is known for a type of service or product, you may want to locate your store there despite the competition present. Certain areas have developed reputations as the place to go for carpeting or diamonds or electronics. You may want to compete directly with other retailers like yourself, knowing the "district" will draw customers to your store.

These preferences may be the result of past experience, good or bad, or of preliminary studies. Before selecting one general location, however, further study must be done to answer as reasonably as possible the big question: Will your store in this location make money?

Demographics

The analysis of potential store locations can get technical and *should* get technical if the organization is serious about thoroughly evaluating areas. The most significant criterion is the population density. How many people are there in proximity to the location? An even more important question is how many of these people would buy the kinds of merchandise you sell and at your prices?

To refine the population study even further, one must find out the percentage and number of singles, newlyweds, young families, and senior citizens in the area. What is the breakdown of age, education, race, and nationality? What are the typical income distributions? What are the disposable income levels and on what items are they expended? What are the community psychographics or life styles? Is the population stable, growing, or declining? What has the trend been over the last ten years and is that trend expected to continue?

A location surrounded with retirement communities would probably not be best for a store catering to children's furniture. A store heavy in garden equipment and outdoor furniture is not likely to do well in an area of high rise apartment buildings.

Income statistics about the population can indicate how much people in the area can spend, and for what kinds of merchandise. Lower income levels tend to buy more necessity items; upper income levels buy these as well as a larger number of luxury items. What is the income level of the people in the area under consideration and what do you sell?

In the same context it is important to note that income is clearly associated to education and occupation. While it is difficult to say whether a person buys an item because of education or because of income, it is reasonable to predict that persons of similar income but differing educational backgrounds would form separate market segments for many products.

This information, when matched against the store's merchandise plans, can give a reasonable estimate of potential sales volume—the solid rock of a good foundation.

For example, an area with declining population may project a low estimate of sales, and flash a warning light as a location to be avoided. If, however, recent figures show a turn-around in population, and these numbers plus other tangible signs of growth suggest a rebirth of an area, perhaps this would be a good location. Settling in before the peak of the rebirth could enable an organization to reap the benefits of lower initial costs and a number of very good years before the competition jumps on the bandwagon.

On the other hand, if a growing area has begun to level off and is saturated with stores of competitors, a retailer with foresight may choose to avoid that location.

Knowing your merchandise, then, leads to knowing your customer. Through an analysis of population characteristics, an organization can determine how many potential customers are in the area.

Modified Gravity Model

But just how big is the trading area? For example, could a store consider every resident of a state in its trading area?

A method for estimating the number of potential customers in an area can be provided in a *modified gravity model*. This model draws a correlation between the population density and the ease of accessibility to the store. The model identifies as the "primary opportunity market" the area that is within six-minute driving time from the proposed store locations. The secondary market includes areas within a 20-minute drive from the store.

Therefore, after you have identified your customer profile as having features x, y, and z, you can calculate your aggregate opportunity market by finding out how many x, y, and z people can drive to the location in six minutes, and how many in 20 minutes. Then determine if that opportunity market would give you the sales needed to generate your required operating profits.

Driving time is a constant that can be used in evaluating any type of location. In a downtown location, driving may be slow, but greater numbers of people are generally concentrated in such an area. Suburban shopping malls are often further away from the largest number of people, but because auto traffic moves more freely to those areas than to downtown, the speed offsets the distance. The better the roads, the broader the area in this formula. The store situated at the junction of two major six-lane highways, one traveling north and south, the other east and west, increases its area and potential customer base. The fine highway network makes the store accessible in 20 minutes to people who may be many miles away.

When the potential opportunity market is dependent on people driving to the location, parking becomes a necessity. Will the location provide ample parking for the numbers of cars you expect to be transporting customers to the store?

Another factor is mass transportation. Whether the store is in town or on the highway, the customer base can be expanded by people who can take a train or bus to the location. Larger numbers of senior citizens, for example, are bused regularly to certain shopping locations. Would the proposed store be able to capitalize on this kind of traffic?

Other Factors

Population characteristics and site accessibility are two primary criteria in selecting a retail site but other factors must also be considered. When "buying" into an area, a retail organization not only gets the area's people, it also gets its local government, laws, and tax structure; its schools, culture, and recreational facilities; its industries, pollution, and layoffs. In short, the store will be affected, directly and indirectly, by the entire political, social, economic, and cultural atmosphere of the area.

Directly, the store's costs will reflect local taxes, licenses, zoning laws, building codes, Sunday closings, and parking regulations. The quality of the schools will impact the caliber of a large portion of the store's staff. The kinds of industry in an area not only affect the kind of consumer, but also the consistency of purchasing power. A local industry with frequent shutdowns, layoffs, and strikes can seriously reduce your customer base for periods of time. A community with a single major industry is subject to becoming a ghost town if that industry moves, taking your customers with it.

Will the area be able to provide enough of the kind of workers you need? Are the support services here? Will you have trouble getting professional accounting and advertising services? Will deliveries of merchandise be reliable and affordable?

Indirectly, your store will be affected by the progessivism of the community or the lack of it, by the kinds of residents and industries that will be lured to or driven from the area by the political, social, cultural, and economic conditions. The retailer, then, must realize that he buys more than a plot of land when he breaks ground for a store. And in looking at the total community he buys into, he must look not only at the community as it is today, but also as it is expected to be in years to come.

Satisfied that the future bodes well for the community and for the store in it, the retailer then considers cost. How much will it cost to build or lease in this location? What will renovations, preparations, equipment, and maintenance cost? After figuring these long-term and immediate costs, will the sales volume be great enough to generate a satisfactory profit?

Availability of Sites

If by the above analysis you ascertain that the area is a good one for your store, the search for the specific site begins. Is there an available site in the location desired? The best laid plans of even the most analytical retailer often go astray when he finds that there is no empty land to build on or vacant stores to buy or lease. When this happens, plans may have to be put on a shelf until a site is available.

Perhaps the only available site is surrounded by competitors. The question then is whether the customer base is large enough to support another store. If it is not, then it's back to the drawing board to look for another location.

Performing a *competition analysis* is crucial in many retail decisions, particularly in site selection. A new store is likely to be in direct competition with some establishments and compete only indirectly with others. In analyzing competition, a discounter, for example, may have to look at stores such as drug stores and supermarkets, as well as at other discount stores. In addition, it is important to be aware that competition can be less of a factor in a growing market than in a stable or contracting market.

The essence of competitive analysis is measuring the degree of store saturation. When a trading area does not have enough stores to provide satisfactory consumer service, it is said to be understored, and when there are too many stores to yield a fair return on investment, it is overstored. Conditions that indicate an area is understored include:

- Sales per square foot in existing stores are unusually high.
- Many people have to travel farther than they want to travel to shop.
- There are few or no vacant buildings.
- Population per a particular type of retail store is low.

Note that the above factors do not measure the *quality* of the local competition. Yet that quality is an important consideration. Though an area appears to be overstored, there may still be an opportunity for a new store if the quality of the present competition is low.

Research Tools

Planners can use a number of research tools and methods in selecting retail locations. Some of the best sources of information are U.S. Census Reports. These reports can answer questions such as these: How many persons or families live in a particular area? How has this number changed over time? How old are these people and where do they work? What is their income? How many own their homes and how many rent? How long have they lived here? What is the value of their homes and the monthly rental payments? How many cars, air conditioners, refrigerators, and other appliances do they own?

Census of Business Reports on Retail Trade provide figures on the number of retail establishments by major lines of trade in a given area. They offer the number of retail sales, the number of paid employees, and the total payroll by business.

Since consumer census reports are completed every ten years, reports used toward the end of a decade show dated figures that may have to be adjusted. A useful volume that fills in the gaps between census years is *Survey of Buying Power*. Published yearly by Sales Management, Incorporated, this book gives much of the same information as the census reports.

Chambers of Commerce, local trade associations, and other retailers are other sources of helpful information. State agencies can provide you with information such as traffic statistics and road construction plans.

The information is available and can be obtained, with a little digging. The successful retailer has found that it is better to dig for information before selecting a site or before the decline starts. If not, he might have to dig out from beneath the rubble of his own crumbling organization.

17

Allocating Space for Profit

OVERVIEW: Because space is a valuable and costly asset for retailers, they have learned sophisticated techniques to make the most profitable use of selling space in their stores. Types of floor patterns, location of merchandise and departments, and the amount of space given to departments are considered carefully. Space use formulas enable retailers to compare one department's use of space in producing profit to another's. Planograms are diagrams specifying the exact location and placement of every item sold. These diagrams are developed after careful consideration of many factors such as size and bulk, customer demand, and profitability of each item.

With the cost of real estate escalating along with the number of items retailers must display for sale, the successful merchant is the one making the most profitable use of every square foot of space in the store and warehouse. Misuse of space can be as detrimental to profits as poor buying or careless hiring.

Effective space utilization works on a number of basic retailing principles plus modern-day statistical analysis. By following a basic formula, the retailer can measure earnings of departments by the square foot, and then reallocate space accordingly.

When an architect sits down to draw up plans for a new store, he is concerned with preparing a blueprint for a facility that will be pleasing to customers and will help make money for the owners. The plan will vary from store to store depending on the image management wants to project. Architects will design the store in consultation with management whose input will reflect their merchandising expertise, including their knowledge of layout and display. In utilizing space in existing structures, management must look carefully at layout and the effects on profit.

Layout

Some stores with a wealth of available space are not achieving their potential in profit. Yet other stores, though smaller, are reaping greater profits. The difference might be intelligent layout. Layout in retailing includes four elements:

1. The overall arrangement or pattern of the store
2. Classification of merchandise
3. Assignment of departments to locations
4. Allocation of space to each department

The first type of layout is the *gridiron*, which is a rectangular arrangement, most often seen in supermarkets. In the gridiron pattern, merchandise is displayed in straight, parallel lines, with secondary aisles at right angles to these. The other pattern consists of curving or circular aisles, creating a less rigid effect. This is called the *free-flow* pattern. The free-flow pattern cannot display as much merchandise as the gridiron, but it can present more merchandise to the customer at one time, and can increase impulse buying by leading the customer past more merchandise.

Though the free-flow pattern appears more casual, it is not haphazard, and, as in the gridiron, merchandise is assigned by *classification*. A single department will contain merchandise of a related nature—*e.g.*, picture frames, hooks and wire for hanging, nonglare glass. Another approach to classification would be to group together all merchandise to be used by a particular type customer—men, women, boys, girls. Some stores classify their merchandise according to their requirements for stocking and display. Many stores use all three approaches to classification in planning layout. The successful retailers know the reasons behind their using these approaches.

A third element of layout is *department locations*, or situating departments within the store. Traditionally those departments with the highest earning power are placed in the most valuable, highly trafficked areas of the store. In the large department stores, this is generally between the entrance and the escalator on the main floor. "Demand goods" departments are housed in more remote areas on the theory that people are most willing to walk a distance for goods they absolutely need, such as houseware items and work clothes. In getting to these departments in the well-planned store, shoppers must pass luxury, high margin item departments, and thereby be tempted to buy goods not on their shopping lists.

Unfinished furniture, refrigerators, and other items requiring large floor space occupy areas in the deepest recesses of the store. Walls will be used to hang merchandise that can be displayed well in that fashion. At the entrances, customers will find convenience goods and other items for which they would not make a special trip but can always use.

Merchandise, then, is classified and placed in a store for the convenience of the customer and of management, with the effect on profit being the ultimate concern. With these factors in mind, the retailer considers the fourth element of layout, *allocation* of space to departments. The retailer allocates space not only according to the type of material and displays needed, but also according to its profitability. In other words, is it profitable to use so many square feet of main floor space to generate so many dollars?

Model Stock

To determine the size of a department's selling area, which includes clerk and customer aisles, stock areas, registers, and displays, the *model stock* method is used. This method requires using the merchandise plan to estimate the amount of planned stock. Consider how much of this stock is to be displayed, how it can best be displayed, and how much space will be needed. Add whatever space will be required for registers and work areas, and you have the total space needed for the department.

What happens if the total exceeds the space available? Some stores will make the merchandise fit by squeezing everything in, but often such overcrowding does not do justice to merchandise, and sales drop. When space is limited, reducing the assortment is often a more profitable alternative.

Here, as in almost every aspect of retailing, profitability becomes the deciding criterion. How can you tell which departments are most profitable? The space use formula can help answer that question.

Space Use Formula

To determine whether a department can "afford" the space it occupies, the profitability per square foot of that department is measured. Big-ticket items, naturally, ring up greater sales than lower-priced items, yet the ratio of *profit to square feet* may be better for the high-priced item.

There are three calculations involved in figuring space utilization profitability.

1. $\dfrac{\text{Total sales}}{\text{Total square feet}} = \text{Sales per square foot}$

2. $\dfrac{\text{Cost of merchandise sold}}{\text{Total square feet}} = \text{Cost of merchandise sold per square foot}$

3. Sales per square foot − Cost per square foot = Gross margin per square foot

Using the gross margin per square foot, departments of varying sizes selling different types of goods can be compared. Gross margin per square foot can tell which departments are doing well, which are not, which might improve if expanded, and which can be reduced in space allotment.

After using this formula you may find that your departments rank just as you had expected they would, and therefore do not need to reallocate your space. But now you will know that your "feel" for things is supported by the statistical data.

If the figures show a need for adjustment, you have the experience and analytic tools to reapportion your departments and measure the effect.

Profit Improvement Through Planogramming

The concepts of layout, department locations, model stock, and space use formulas come to life in the form of the planogram. A planogram essentially is a diagram of how merchandise is to be displayed in a store. It specifies location on a shelf, number of facings, and all other factors relevant to display. The diagram tries to make the most of what is known about item profitability as well as the psychology of buying habits and selling inducements.

Most retailers want to optimize margin. Therefore, those merchandise classifications that contribute the greatest margin are given prominent display positions, like the end caps, while lower margin classifications are placed in the center of lower traffic aisles. This strategy is usually carried forward from a broad class to subclass to an item's position in the display.

Once a general position is found, height is considered. Eye level and slightly below are considered the prime positions for attracting shoppers' attention.

The retailer must decide, however, if it is best to put the higher-margin assortments and items at eye level. Would it be more profitable to place the better-selling but lower-margin items in the prime positions? Some recommend that the higher markup items be given the greater consideration. Others prefer optimizing sales on the theory that retailers should respond to the greatest customer demand.

Now for the next decision. How much? How many facings? Too little and the retailer runs out of stock and gives poor "in stock" service to the customers. Too much and the inventory costs go up and, perhaps more importantly, valuable space that could be used for other items and assortments for incremental sales is wasted.

The display quantity depends on some important factors: lead time, expected demand, pack size. The planogram considers the amount of a particular item that will be needed to satisfy customer demand. Lead time—the period of time between ordering an item and receiving it at the store—is an ingredient in the replenishment process and also considered in planograming. Pack size, too, enters into the quantity displayed. The number of items in the pack is considered in the planogram to prevent, where possible, displaying half a pack and storing the other half.

Figure 17-1. SAMPLE PORTION OF A PLANOGRAM.

SUB CLASS PAIN RELIEF, ANTI ACIDS, EYE CARE, SKIN CARE, FIRST AID

SECTION 3

1. 123 Sominex Tabs (3 Facings)
2. 456 Dramimine (2 Facings)
3. 789 Titralac 100's (2 Facings)
4. 101 Bisodol Mts. (2 Facings)
5. 112 Alka 2 30's (2 Facings)
6. 131 Alka 2 85's (2 Facings)
7. 415 Alka-Seltzer 36's (6 Facings)
8. 161 Gelusil Liquid 12 oz. (3 Facings)
9. 718 Di-gel Liquid Mts. 12 oz. (3 Facings)
10. 192 Sinutab 30's (2 Facings)
11. 021 Sinutab II 30's (1 Facing)
12. 222 Sine Aid (2 Facings)
13. 324 Sine Rest (2 Facings)
14. 373 Chooz 20's (2 Facings)
15. 252 Gelusil 100's (2 Facings)
16. 627 Bufferin 100's (6 Facings)
17. 282 Midol 30's (2 Facings)
18. 930 Rolaids 75's (2 Facings)

SECTION 4

19. 313 Rolaids 150's (2 Facings)
20. 233 Bufferin 225's (3 Facings)
21. 343 Alka-Seltzer 25's (5 Facings)
22. 536 St. Josephs Aspirin 100's (2 Facings)
23. 373 St. Joseph's Aspirin 200's (2 Facings)
24. 839 Alka-Seltzer 75's (4 Facings)
25. 404 Regular Phillips Milk of Magnesia 12 oz. (4 Facings)

Preparing the Planogram

To draw up a planogram, you need store floor plans, data on item and department performance, and input from merchandisers on trends, patterns, plans, and expectations.

On a floor plan, a scale diagram of the store is laid out department by department, and divided into sections. Counters, display cases, and walk space are drawn into the diagram and numbered. Each section is set aside for a subclassification of items within the department.

Working from a complete list of items within the subclass, a precise space allocation for each item is drawn into the diagram. This is the point at which judgment and item performance must enter the picture. The height and width of space given a particular item, the number of facings it receives, the shelf or case in which it is placed, and its position at end or center must be decided upon.

Many questions must be answered. Should fast sellers or slow sellers be placed in the most optimum (for example, eye-level) spots? Because of an item's bulk, should it be given more space? Is the number of facings decided by size, by performance, or by design?

Past performance, expectations, and judgment enter into these decisions. Once they have been made, however, the space allocation for each item is written into the diagram.

In making the diagram complete, every aspect of display must be entered—fencing, baskets, snap rails, peg hooks, manufacturers' racks, or any special fixturing.

To facilitate preparation, the diagrams can be drawn on large sheets of paper, and names of departments and items can be neatly typed in and numbered. Then these sheets can be reduced in size and reproduced for distribution to the stores. Particularly crowded sections of small items can be drawn to a larger scale.

But before the planogram is finalized, it is tested. That is, the items are actually placed on the shelves at a layout site. Any problems with the design can be worked out here, so that the planograms that go out to the stores are actually workable.

In addition, photos are taken of these displays to give store personnel an even clearer guide in stocking their shelves.

The stores, then, will receive a set of plan sheets for each department. Each sheet would include: (1) the department number and name, and its subclassifications, (2) a complete list of every item in those subclasses, each bearing an identifying number and the number of facings it is to receive, and (3) a detailed diagram of the department's space, divided by sections according to subclass, with outlines for displays, and the names and identifying number of each item inserted in the proper space.

Included along with the plan sheets are photos of what each section should look like when completed to plan and labels for each item to be placed on the appropriate shelves. These would designate clearly that the space between labels is to be stocked with the items printed on the label to the left.

The store manager then has a vehicle that will enable his least-experienced employee to maintain the shelves properly. Individual input and judgment is still required of store managers, buyers, and department heads because the planogram is subject to change. Portions of it will change when seasonal items are replaced. The entire plan should be revised each year, as a reaction to the new sales and profit data. At that point, the "human" information of individuals at various levels should enter into the formulation of the new plan.

Planograming enables a large chain to put into each of its stores the benefits of its research. While some modifications may be made from store to store, planograming provides a uniformity throughout the chain that makes customers more comfortable. The planogram is based on quantifiable data and maximizes the use of space by minimizing the opportunity for human error or neglect in merchandise display.

In chains where the size of stores varies, a planogram is made for each prototype. In this way five or six planograms may be required, but they will be sufficient to control the orderly and profitable layout of hundreds of stores.

More sophisticated companies have used their computers to do much of the tedious arithmetic required to weigh profitability of one item against another, and to take ten feet from Department 1 and divide that between Departments 9 and 16.

Benefits

Why should a retailer go through the bother of planograming? What will a planogram do that other layout or display plans will not do?

First, the planogram will increase sales. The planogram uses historical data of sales and profit to display merchandise, telling what space is producing the greatest sales and profit. By learning the locations of greatest productivity, and by allocating space accordingly, one should increase sales. Tied to the allocation of space by sales and profit is the placement of related items. Place allied merchandise near the best sellers to increase impulse buying.

Sales will also be increased when, through the use of historical data and the planogram, the store makes a better balanced use of display space for fast sellers and slow sellers.

The planogram will designate a precise location for each item. A staple item, placed in its specific location, can be easily found by the customer. This "permanent" location also makes it easier for store personnel to keep track of such items for reordering.

The planogram is prepared with much forethought and makes for the most orderly and appealing displays, thus increasing the potential for sales.

Another benefit of the planogram is its capacity to reduce inventory investment while improving stockturn. The planogram reduces the possibility of a retailer's allocating a great deal of space, requiring a large investment, for merchandise which sells poorly. The planogram enables the retailer to allocate knowingly some of that space for faster sellers, and at the same time to reduce the amount of money invested in inventory that does not sell.

In addition, the planogram provides for at least a "pack" space for each item, so that it can all be on sale, counted, and reordered more easily.

This provision for a "pack" leads to a third significant effect of the planogram, namely reduction in shrinkage. By placing the entire pack on the shelf, partial packs no longer have to be taken back to the stockroom, where mishandling often leads to shrinkage. The planogram takes into account the susceptibility to pilferage, and places high risk items in more secure locations and displays.

Better arrangement through planograming enables the retailer to identify more easily those seasonal items that will not be reordered, and allows sufficient time to take whatever action is necessary to sell these at the best possible price.

Operating expenses can also be reduced by using the planogram. If items in the ordering book follow the sequence of the planogram, much time will be saved when ordering. Similarly, once locations are fixed and shelves labeled, time can be saved in filling and maintaining shelves.

The final and most significant effect of planograming is an increase in net profit. By increasing sales and stockturn while reducing inventory and labor expenses, profits will improve dramatically. The company can continuously reap greater profits from the one-time creation of a sound planogram.

Those companies that have gone to planograms have found the results to be quite impressive. Inventory investments have been cut by as much as 25%. Labor costs have been reduced by 15%. And in the all-important profit category, gross margin dollars have been known to increase by 15%.

In an age when retailers are seeking all kinds of ways to improve profit, they are coming to rely on what would seem to be a common-sense and basic technique— the store organized and displayed for profit.

18

Distribution Facilities Planning

OVERVIEW: Warehouse and distribution facilities must be planned in coordination with the company's expansion plans to minimize delivery costs and delays and to ensure adequate facilities to meet the warehouse and distribution needs of the growing company. Location, size, heating, and lighting are primary factors to consider when planning an efficient, economical support facility.

Retailers traditionally have devoted more time and resources to planning what merchandise they will carry than to the issue of how to get the merchandise to the stores. The warehousing and distribution functions were assumed to be in place and working, unless inadequate service levels demonstrated otherwise. As a result, modifications to the warehouse and distribution facilities were usually achieved in reaction to need rather than planned and implemented in anticipation of need.

Lately, however, more and more retailers are recognizing the need to expand their planning efforts to include the entire logistics function. But the person most commonly assigned this planning process is the present distribution manager. While he may be an excellent operations manager, he may not always have the necessary skills or background to plan and design new facilities. And if he truly is the operations manager of the distributions facility, he probably will not have the time necessary to do the planning and design for new facilities. Most retailers who have attempted in-house designs will agree that the task is better left to those with the time and necessary skills, aided by appropriate input from the operations people.

Developing a Plan

Planning a warehouse or distribution facility today requires some rethinking of traditional approaches and priorities. Of high priority is the long-range business plan. The retailer should develop a growth plan that addresses some basic issues such as:

Who are we? What segment of the industry are we in?

In which direction is the business growing?

Where will future stores be opening?

What new distribution requirements will result?

A sound business plan is the starting point for taking a more sophisticated approach in the actual planning and design of new distribution facilities. This new emphasis also borrows technology from the manufacturing industries to do a better job of planning future requirements and to utilize the latest state-of-the-art technology. Specifically the approach focuses on four prime concerns of warehouse and distribution facilities: location, size, heating, and lighting.

Location

As the cost of fuel climbs, the cost of transporting merchandise from the warehouse to the stores takes on higher priority in the management of operations. The location of the warehouse with respect to present and future store locations becomes a more important influence on the cost of operations and bottom-line profits.

In selecting the location for a new or additional warehouse, the planner should be aware of some powerful analytical techniques. Computer programs are now available that, when provided the necessary input data, will perform a "center of gravity" analysis to identify the location and route optimization. This will result in the lowest cost of transportation to the stores. In general, this approach considers such factors as cost per mile for trucks, location of existing stores, probable locations of new stores, location of vendors, and potential for backhaul.

This approach discourages some more traditional priorities such as combining general offices with warehouse, having buyers tour the warehouse daily, placing the warehouse near a prototype store, and combining soft goods distribution with hard goods warehousing and distribution.

Site selection is another important consideration in planning new facilities. Because of the high cost of new construction and financing, most new warehouses are built for current and short-term future needs. But the building can be designed for modular growth through adjoining additions as may be required in the future. Site selection should consider this approach. The specific location of the first module on the site should take into consideration the most likely growth pattern requiring future additions.

Size

The most important parameters in determining the size of the warehouse are obviously inventory storage requirements and mode of order selection. Most retailers normally experience seasonal variation in inventory to one degree or another. The maximum required inventory for all departments at any one time will generally indicate warehouse size. However, this seasonal peaking should be examined by the buying departments to determine what, if anything, can be done to smooth the peaking, particularly for very bulky, high-volume items. Often, splitting of large orders into smaller releases is possible. To the extent the peak inventory cannot be reduced, management should try to accommodate it in outside warehouses for the short term. Renting a certain amount of flexible capacity is generally less costly than buying the additional capacity and having it underutilized most of the year.

A relatively new technique for inventory and facilities planning is *distribution requirements planning* (DRP). This is a fairly sophisticated computer system with roots in the manufacturer's *material requirements planning* (MRP) system. For the manufacturer, MRP basically plans specific time-phased inventory requirements by product, based on known demand or very accurate forecasts. The DRP system extends this logic to planning inventory levels at each of the distribution centers, based not on traditional inventory replenishment systems but rather on planned demand requirements.

The DRP system can be applied to retailers, but the benefits may be less dramatic than in manufacturing. The demand for the item (retail sales) must be forecast with a high degree of accuracy to minimize inventories. Furthermore, supply of the item from the vendor must be available continuously with reasonable lead times. This rules out application in the fashion soft-goods area, where purchase commitments must be made once for the season. Certain hard goods lines, where demand is fairly constant and therefore capable of being forecast, are potential candidates for DRP. While this appears to be a useful new tool, the cost-effectiveness of the system in terms of inventory reductions must be looked at very carefully.

In addition to total inventory, another determinant of warehouse size is mode of operation and utilization of cube. The latest trend in maximizing available space is the floating bin system. This system assigns backup stock to the first available appropriate location and thereby does not reserve space unnecessarily for items not in house. The declining cost of mini-computers has made the task of tracking product addresses and available space feasible for even smaller retailers. These mini-systems operate on-line to capture location assignments and changes through the day and then transfer the information to the main computer to generate stock movements and picking lists.

Warehouse size will also be affected by picking mode. The trend recently has been to separate products by picking mode even if the same item is picked in more than one mode. For instance, all full-case picking should be done in one area separate from break pack picking, which should be done in a different area. To combine these in one area reduces the picking efficiency of both modes. The racking and handling requirements for these modes are very different. The increased space required is easily offset by savings in picking labor.

Heating

The dramatic increase in energy costs has focused attention on all fuel users, and the warehouse must be included among these. The very design features that make a warehouse operationally efficient (large volume, high ceilings) make it difficult to heat. The numerous large openings required for trucks also make the building susceptible to significant heat loss.

Since hot air tends to rise, most of a warehouse's heating dollars end up warming the upper half of the building. To direct the warm air to lower levels, many warehouses are using large, slow speed, ceiling fans to push the warm air downward. It's an old concept that really works.

Dock seals are another possible deterrent to heat loss. The cost of really effective dock seals is easily justified when considered against the cost of heat escaping through open loading doors. In fact, many new warehouse designs for the colder areas are including indoor truck parking with a double set of doors.

With the steadily increasing cost of fuel and the uncertainty of long- term supplies, many new warehouse and distribution plans are considering dual fuel (gas/oil), hot water space heating systems. This not only provides obvious flexibility in fuel selection but also offers the possibility of using solar collectors to reduce fuel requirements. The large, flat roof of a warehouse is an ideal location to install solar collectors.

Lighting

Warehouse lighting is usually one of the last things with which the retailer concerns himself. But in areas where electricity is relatively expensive, new warehouse designs should consider the latest high-efficiency lights. Their higher initial cost is easily returned, even in single shift operations.

Existing warehouses should also consider conversion to high-efficiency lights, although the payback period will be somewhat longer because the initial expense usually includes a more difficult installation over existing equipment and the removal of the old lights. However, the cost will most likely be justifiable where more light is required, where cost of electricity is high and increasing rapidly, and where lights are needed for more than one shift.

In addition, adequate lighting levels provide benefits far beyond efficiency and cosmetic appearance. Many retailers have found that improvements in lighting can result in improved order selection accuracy, improved order selection productivity, and generally improved worker morale.

The warehousing and distribution functions are critical to any retail organization. In order to maximize the service level provided, the facilities and operating systems should be thoughtfully planned and developed. Since substantial dollars are involved, it only makes sense that this phase of the business receives the proper allocation of resources and management attention needed to ensure a wise investment.

Part Five

RETAILING IS PEOPLE

19

Improving Employee Productivity

OVERVIEW: Employee payroll comprises 50 to 60% of total retail operating costs. While markdowns may salvage something from a poor purchase, there is no way to regain any hour of wasted employee time. And that time will continue to cost more as inflation forces higher wage demands and as competition for full- and part-time workers makes employers meet those demands. High employee productivity requires effective procedures in interviewing and hiring candidates and for evaluating performance, developing sound training programs, and nurturing supervisors skilled in managing people, time, and language.

Hiring Good Candidates

Employee productivity begins at the employment interview, when management decides if candidates are qualified to fill open jobs. Though this interview is often done in a casual, intuitive fashion, it really is a specialized task requiring specialized knowledge and skills.

Before and During the Interview

The objectives of the interview can be phrased as questions the employer should ask before and during the interview. These lead to more detailed questioning that will supply the data for decision making.

1. *Can the applicant do the job?* The interviewer must understand the knowledge and skills needed to perform the job, must thoroughly review the resume or the

employment application before the interview, and must honestly decide whether the position can accommodate an applicant who does not meet all of the job requirements but has the potential to develop through training.

2. *Will the job motivate the applicant?* First be sure that the applicant understands all aspects of the job and not just the obvious positive features. Then explore an applicant's job goals, interests, the rewards being sought, and attitude toward previous jobs and supervisors.

3. *Will the work environment permit the applicant to perform the job effectively?* An applicant does not automatically adapt to an environment, but compatibility should be evident. By identifying the applicant's previous work environment(s), the interviewer can assess how the applicant reacts to job pressures or stress, how the applicant gets along with others, and what qualities, such as leadership style, the applicant displays.

The responsibility for a productive interview session rests for the most part with the interviewer. The interviewer must establish the tone, set the pace, and close the interview when his or her goals have been attained.

The opening of the interview is extremely important, as it usually results in lasting first impressions. The interview should be held in a private, nonthreatening setting. The interviewer can create a relaxed atmosphere through a pleasant greeting and some small talk before the more serious questioning begins. During this state the interviewer should note the applicant's appearance, manner, self-expression, and responsiveness.

The next segment of the interview calls for the gathering of information. An error many interviewers make is spending too much time talking and not enough time listening. A guideline to follow is to allot 25% of the interview time for interviewer questions and comments, and 75% for applicant responses.

The interviewer should not impede the information-gathering process by structuring questions that call for only "yes," "no," or abbreviated answers. Indirect or open-ended questions are more appropriate, as they encourage fuller responses. With such questions the interviewer requires the applicant to answer in statement form, generating opportunities for follow-up questions and answers. Some examples are: Why are you interested in leaving your current employer? How do you schedule your time and priorities? What was the most difficult selling assignment ever experienced and why?

The interviewer can then explore and observe several key dimensions of the applicant's abilities.

Energy—The ability to be a self-starter and to achieve a high activity level. Sample questions to develop the energy issue are: When do you do your best work? How many tasks do you like to tackle at one time?

Communications Ability—Proficiency in verbal and written communications and ability to organize thoughts. Sample questions in this area are: Have you ever done any public or group speaking? Have you been required to prepare reports? What was the reaction to them?

Motivation—The importance of work in personal satisfaction and the desire to achieve at work. Sample questions include: What motivates you? Comment on how your work goals and life goals sometimes conflict.

Salesmanship—The ability to organize and present material in a convincing manner. During the interview process itself, how well is the applicant selling himself/ herself or his/her ideas? Sample questions to ask are: What do you like about selling? What don't you like? What do you think of the statement "the customer is always right"?

Flexibility—The ability to modify behavioral style and approach to reach a goal. A sample question would be: When would you feel justified deviating from company policy?

Initiative—Active efforts to influence events rather than passive acceptance. A sample question: In your opinion, what would be the best ways for you to demonstrate initiative in your job?

Planning and Organizing—Effectiveness of planning and organizing own activities and those of a group. A sample question: What is your procedure for keeping track of matters?

Judgment—The ability to reach logical conclusions based on the evidence at hand. The interviewer should ask questions about information on the resume and on responses to previous questions.

Taboo Topics

The interviewer should avoid certain subjects, however, because they are not relevant to the interview. Any discussion of them could be interpreted as an attempt to discriminate in the recruitment process. The subjects include:

Marital and family status (although it is acceptable for the interviewer to determine whether the applicant can meet necessary work schedule, travel, and other requirements).

Age, sex, race, color.

Birthplace and citizenship (the interviewer may ask the applicant for proof of the ability to become lawfully employed).

Military discharge (but the interviewer may relate experience achieved in the service to the job experience requirements).

Religion (employers must make reasonable efforts to accommodate the religious practices of employees and prospective employees).

Giving Information

Once the interviewer has received answers to all the appropriate questions, he or she should answer the applicant's questions, review the specific job and career opportunities (sell if warranted), and advise the applicant as to when he or she can expect to hear from the organization. Candidates sometimes wait weeks and even months for a letter or a telephone call. If the candidate is ultimately turned down, he or she is not likely to retain positive thoughts about the organization, a situation retailers want to avoid if possible.

Obstacles to Effective Interviewing

With few exceptions, interviewers approach an interview with the best of intentions. Knowingly or unknowingly, however, the interviewer can raise obstacles that can undermine the selection process. Several of these are:

Personal biases of the interviewer—allowing one's biases to influence the interview.

Lack of defined standards for the job—finding an acceptable candidate is difficult if the job itself has not been clearly defined.

Making early decisions—making a decision within the first ten minutes and spending the rest of the interview justifying the decision.

Halo effect—rating an applicant based on one positive or negative characteristic.

Central tendency—rating all candidates in the average range.

Leniency effects—rating all candidates above average.

Overreacting to unfavorable or irrelevant information—overemphasizing particular information while ignoring everything else.

Failure to listen to the applicant.

Jumping to conclusions—listening to only half of a statement, assuming the remaining half is obvious; not thoroughly exploring a statement, circumstance, or situation.

Using stress techniques designed to trap or fluster the applicant—subjecting the applicant to three-on-one interviewing or asking accusatory questions to see how the applicant reacts.

Comparing the applicant's past life to the interviewer's—comparing childhoods, schools, first jobs, vacation preferences.

Failing to control or direct the interview—letting a candidate with a strong personality turn the tables on the interviewer, with the candidate asking most of the questions and the interviewer providing the answers.

Conducting an effective interview is an art. To master it requires a thorough understanding of basic principles, sound training, and constant involvement in interviewing situations. This is the price for good interviewing and productive hires.

Employee Evaluation

Once candidates are hired, a system for evaluating employee performance is necessary in any organization, regardless of its size, for a number of reasons:

- Performance evaluation permits the employee and the supervisor to agree on an understanding of the organization's goals and to identify together how the employee can assist in achieving the goals.
- It allows the supervisor to provide job-related feedback to the employee as a means to improving performance.
- It identifies outstanding performers who should be considered for development, promotional opportunities, and additional merit increases. It provides a mechanism to document salary increase decisions.
- It is a means of displaying the organization's commitment to equal employment opportunity/affirmative action, and helps the organization establish a reputation as a fair and concerned employer.
- It ensures that a supervisor will meet with an employee at a specifically designated time or times each year for the sole purpose of discussing the employee's performance.

Performance evaluation is already well-established and working effectively in many organizations. The more comprehensive the program, usually the more concerned an employer is with the long-term professional well-being of employees.

Popular techniques of evaluation in use today are described below:

Ranking Method. This approach permits the supervisor to rank an employee in comparison to every other employee under his or her direction. The supervisor is not so much concerned with how successfully the employee achieves predetermined goals and objectives, but rather how the employee's performance compares with the performance of other employees. This method is *not* recommended because too much emphasis is placed on comparing one employee to another. Supervisor biases can enter the picture and distort the objectivity. An employee's performance should be judged according to the employee's ability to accomplish job-related goals and objectives.

Narrative/Descriptive Review. In this program the supervisor normally writes a description of the employee's performance, without using any prescribed form. The description could be an essay citing the performance in general. It could involve comments on critical incidents only. The supervisor in reality can structure the evaluation documentation any way he or she deems worthwhile. If such a program is used, it is recommended as a supplement to a program that is more precise in identifying desired job performance characteristics. Without these as guidelines, the supervisor can easily stray from the intended purposes of the job evaluation exercise.

Checklist Method. Using checklists of characteristics related to job performance is one of the more effective ways of judging performance. Some systems involve listing job characteristics and traits. The supervisor checks off boxes indicating that the employee's performance "does not meet expectations," "meets expectations," or "exceeds expectations". More sophisticated programs attach a weight to each of these, resulting in a numerical score. The checklist method works well if the job-related characteristics are carefully selected. The supervisor and the employee must agree on how each characteristic is defined and what constitutes the supervisor's level of expectation. When this is done, the employee will not be confused by ratings for each performance characteristic.

Management by Objectives. This process allows the employee and the supervisor to agree on goals and objectives the employee should accomplish prior to the next performance evaluation. At this session they also review the degree of success in achieving the goals and objectives established at the previous session. The employee thus gains management acceptance of performance standards before he or she attempts to perform the job requirements. The employee and the supervisor must be realistic in the choice of goals and objectives. Agreeing on untenable goals and objectives is unproductive and can damage the reputation of the employee.

A program combining elements of the checklist and management by objectives methods would be most productive for a retail environment. Management should establish a series of job performance characteristics relevant to its own organization and the jobs performed. These factors can be referenced when reviewing the employee's performance. The supervisor/employee discussion of goals and objectives to be achieved then can be incorporated into the process.

The success of performance evaluation is determined by the commitment management makes to it. The program must be selected according to the needs of the organization. Supervisors must be trained in conducting the evaluation. And the program must be adequately publicized to all employees.

The performance evaluation process should first be discussed during the applicant interview cycle. It should then be repeated as part of new employee orientation, and referenced in any employee handbook or information made available to new and existing employees.

The organization must have a formal policy on when performance evaluations are to be conducted. It is suggested that one policy be developed for new employees and one for existing employees. For new employees, a performance review after three months, a performance and salary review after six months, and a performance and salary review at each anniversary date is recommended. For existing employees, a performance and salary review at each anniversary date is called for, and if the salary range of the employee's job is adjusted upward, a performance review should be conducted to determine if that employee's performance warrants an automatic increase.

The supervisor should be sure he or she thoroughly understands the scope and meaning of each of the performance factors to be used. A rating for each factor would be based on specific job behaviors. A summary appraisal is then determined by weighing each factor according to its relative importance to the job performed. Possible performance factors and job behaviors an organization can use are:

Job knowledge	Initiative
Accuracy	Problem solving/decision making
Human relations	Supervision
Work production	Financial responsibility

The performance interview itself is exceedingly important, and the supervisor can make it a valuable exercise if he or she remains aware of several factors. First, the interview should be conducted in a nonthreatening environment. The supervisor should explain the evaluation process, including the criteria to be used in measuring performance, how performance will be measured, what input the employee can give during the evaluation process, and the rewards that can be available for above average performance.

The supervisor must remain objective. A rating of excellent or unsatisfactory on one factor should not prompt the supervisor to give the same rating on all factors. The supervisor should avoid being too lenient or too strict in the overall rating.

The ratings should not be influenced by a supervisor's need to be accepted by the employee. The supervisor must overcome the natural inclination to avoid "offending" the employee. A performance evaluation is useful only if the supervisor discusses the good and not-so-good aspects of performance.

The employee should have an opportunity to react to each element of the rating process. The supervisor must be receptive to the employee's comments. Where there are differences of opinion, the supervisor should note such on the evaluation form.

The supervisor must discuss new goals and objectives with the employee so there is no misunderstanding on what is expected.

The employee should sign the evaluation form at the conclusion of the interview. If the employee disagrees with some of the content, the disagreement should be noted on the form. By signing the form, the employee acknowledges that the evaluation took place. If he refuses to sign, have someone, perhaps from personnel, be a witness to that fact.

Prior to closing the interview, the supervisor should advise the employee if a compensation adjustment is warranted, and what growth opportunities exist for the employee.

All employees want to know that good performance is recognized and rewarded. By following these principles, your organization can structure a performance evaluation program as a positive, productive management tool.

Counseling and Training

A necessary part of improving employee performance is training. While training is an expense, it pays handsome dividends when done well. First, an improvement in employee skill results in lower wage costs per sales dollar because more sales are made, and shrinkage and waste are reduced. Secondly, the skillful, more productive workers feel happier about their jobs. They feel management that provides training has an interest in them and this reduces supervisory problems. Morale, then, is better, and the company benefits from a more stable work force, with fewer problems, less absenteeism, and lower recruiting costs. Well-trained and happy employees approach their jobs with greater enthusiasm, which means greater productivity. The enthusiasm of store employees can be picked up by customers and converted into sales. The net result is increased profits.

In addition, training keeps employees up to par with the new equipment and processes that are continually entering the industry.

If store training is to achieve these objectives, five critical success factors are required: management support, sound programs, evaluation, a superior training administrator, and good instructors.

Management Support

The first component in effective training must be the open support of top management. Employees must realize that top management places great importance on training. Executives can issue memos to this effect; encourage participation with awards, rewards, and certificates; even make appearances at and take part in training sessions. This kind of open support tells employees that the people who run the business know the importance of every job to the smooth running of the operation. Therefore, they are spending time and money to see that each job is staffed by trained people.

If top management support is lacking, employees might approach training like reluctant schoolboys. Those in charge of funding and preparing programs may not go "all out" to develop the best programs possible. But if they know that it is the CEO's "baby," training becomes a high priority for everyone.

Management also has the responsibility of reviewing the general content of programs periodically, to be sure they are up-to-date with company philosophies, policies, planning, goals, and procedures.

Sound Programs

The content of every training session should be valued information, and its content must be tailored specifically to the needs of the group, be they register or stock clerks, salespersons, security guards, telephone operators, buyers, or programmers. The content of advanced training should not be a re-hash of initial training courses, but rather material that takes the employee from where he or she is now to a few steps beyond.

Sound programs make participants feel that what they are learning is useful to them on the job. This implies that the program developer knows intimately the job being discussed. Talking with experienced cashiers, for example, prior to developing a course for cashiers, can shed much light on the practical necessities and concerns of people doing that job. At the same time, supervisors should also be consulted so their concerns about cashiering are incorporated into the course. Too often, however, training sessions are strictly academic, reflecting little insight into the day-to-day realities of the job. This is an easy way to turn off employees and make management view training as a waste of time.

Good programs are well organized. That is, they show a logical sequence in the material treated, as well as a sense of balance. Provisions are made so that participants have ample opportunity to ask questions, make comments, exchange concerns and strategies, and engage in hands-on applications or simulation activities.

Above all, each training session should work toward specific, tangible objectives. "To improve register performance," for example, is too vague an objective. A more specific objective for such a session would be: "Each participant will reduce his/her time for a standard register transaction by 15%." This objective defines observable and measurable behavior—something participants will *do* at the end of the session.

"To combat pilferage by customers" should be defined in terms that specify actions for the participants. For example: "Each participant will recognize the warning signs of potential pilfering and take appropriate action."

Objectives break areas of learning into smaller more definable units. They give direction to the training activity and keep instructors and participants on task.

Evaluation

Objectives also lead to another critical success factor—evaluation. Unless one knows the specific objective of a training session, evaluating its success is impossible. Where appropriate, pre-tests and post-tests might be used to measure the success of a training program, particularly one in which information such as merchandise knowledge is the subject. Where less objective issues such as "attitude" are the matter of the particular training, interviews with supervisors and customers can determine the success of the program. Where "selling" is the subject, sales figures can be used in measurement.

In other words, evaluate the effects of training. Measurement will give added significance to the training, help strengthen programs, and convince management that training brings results.

Feedback is one major element in evaluation. During and at the conclusion of the training session, participants can be asked to comment on the appropriateness, usefulness, and effectiveness of the program. This generally can be done through a questionnaire.

Training personnel can also conduct a follow-up with the participants and their supervisors, to determine the on-the-job effects of the training. After certain sessions, customer intercept surveys can provide useful information on the need for or the result of training. All of this feedback can then lead to modification of the program, or complete revision, for the next group.

The Training Administrator

The driving force in every good training program is the training administrator. This person is responsible for coordinating all training activities, including developing programs, assigning instructors, scheduling workshops and participants. The training administrator is also the liaison to store managers, staff, and management.

It is important that the training administrator keep close contact with top management and know what its expectations of training are. In some cases, the training administrator may have to build up a case to get management to throw more support to the training effort. This can be done by showing the positive results of training sessions. If the bottom-line impact of training can be documented, these results should be presented. For example, if sales in personal computers increase substantially after salespeople attend a "product knowledge" workshop, top management should be made to see the correlation. If accidents on the loading dock decrease after a course in safety, the training administrator should present these facts to management and thereby enlist its support for training.

The training administrator, therefore, must be a versatile individual. He or she must know retailing well enough to coordinate effective programs in a wide variety of areas, must be able to communicate with top management, and must understand thoroughly the teaching/learning process.

Instructors

The people giving instruction in training sessions should be good teachers. That is, they should not only know their subject matter well, but they should also be able to communicate it to each person in the class. The good teacher gains some information about each student beforehand, and plans the instruction accordingly. For some students this might mean preparing more films and graphics and less lecture; for some, more simulation games; for others, more roundtable discussion; for still others, more practice activities. The good teacher varies approaches, remembering the adage that "the mind can absorb only as much as the seat can endure."

The instructors must have a flexibility to adapt to different kinds of students. In a typical store, remember, there are employees of varying abilities, motivation, background, and personality, yet the instructor must succeed with each one.

Most importantly, the instructor must have a contagious enthusiasm for retailing, and convey the importance of each phase of it in the overall scheme of things. Just as the stage director convinces every actor that "there are no small parts in the theater," the good training instructor convinces employees that every job in a retail store is important.

When employees feel their job is important, and that they are important, and when they are trained to do their jobs well, retailers make the most of their greatest resource—their people.

Managing People

Management training is an important priority. As the bridges between the executive office and the staff, middle managers can make the difference between a well-

Figure 19-1. TRAINING IS A WISE INVESTMENT

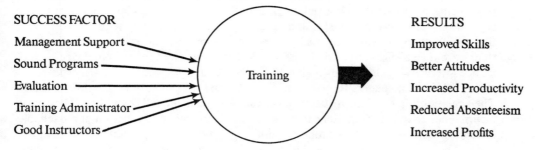

SUCCESS FACTOR

Management Support

Sound Programs

Evaluation

Training Administrator

Good Instructors

Training

RESULTS

Improved Skills

Better Attitudes

Increased Productivity

Reduced Absenteeism

Increased Profits

run company and a chaotic one. Managing people is a most important task in a business with as long a chain of command as a retail company. While the technical expertise of managers must differ along the line, the basic people skills apply universally.

The manager's prime responsibility to the company is the successful accomplishment of company goals through the faithful commitment to standards and policies. A manager's most potent influence in getting subordinates to reach standards and achieve goals is his or her own display of commitment. Through their own work habits, conversation, even appearance, managers communicate to others their sense of personal standards and commitment to the corporate mission. When managers show determination in solving knotty problems and in carrying out routine duties, subordinates are more likely to make a strong commitment themselves.

Part of that commitment requires an understanding of performance goals and standards, and the good manager explains these clearly to the staff, and reviews them periodically. It helps to put the primary goals of an individual on paper so the employee can look at them occasionally and be reminded of them. The good manager also specifies how these goals can be achieved, and what the employee should be doing to achieve them. Standards of performance should also be explained so the employee knows what he will be measured on. These standards should be explicit, observable, and measurable. It is of little help to tell employees "we want quality here." The manager must demonstrate what he means by quality. Show the employee examples of quality reports or files, or have the employee observe a model handling of transactions. Point out what makes that handling exemplary. Do not leave the interpretation of words like "quality," "courteous," "imaginative," up to the individual employee.

A few extra minutes spent instructing a new employee in the fundamentals of the job, or in directing an experienced employee through a new procedure, is a wise investment. There will be fewer problems and surprises to undo later on. If the manager can anticipate some of the problems the employee might face, he should raise these. Let the employees know what to expect so they can be prepared for and deal with problems.

The good manager helps subordinates see how their roles fit into the overall company goals and operation. This kind of explanation often enables employees to see the reason for certain tasks which otherwise might seem to be without purpose. Knowing the reason, employees are less likely to ignore seemingly insignificant tasks like cross referencing orders or stacking tickets in a uniform manner. Asking subordinates for suggestions on procedures, tasks, and efficiency can increase their sense of worth and their commitment to company goals. It might also generate improvement in the ways things are done. This kind of dialogue should not be reserved for the employee performance interview. It should be conducted frequently in a non-evaluative atmosphere.

Middle managers therefore must be able to lead and at the same time to listen. Their relationship is a delicate balance between enforcement and counseling. They must be firm enough to get things done in the appropriate manner and time, yet approachable enough to have subordinates propose useful suggestions and highlight problems in the work. The manager must know the staff well enough to make the best use of their individual skills, to guide and train people as they need it. Good middle managers speak up for their people when they need a spokesman, and are not afraid to make the tough decisions, even when these might be unpopular.

In appraising performance, for instance, the good manager is honest and direct. Supported by relevant, objective data he gives praise and criticism as needed in a tactful, professional manner. Praise should not be seen as a sign of "softness" in a manager. Most people work better when their contribution is recognized and acknowledged.

Praise is most effective when it is specific. That is, praise a particular action. For example: "You handled that customer very well, Helena. She was wrong but you remained courteous and followed the store's policy." Mentioning the specific behavior or actions tells the employee that the manager knows what is going on and is alert to what the employee is doing. It also indicates that the praise is genuine, not a means of manipulation.

The employee should not have to do anything extraordinary to warrant a pat on the back. People are doing their jobs when they handle their routine chores well. Good managers acknowledge that solid though routine performance, and generally find they receive that kind of performance consistently.

Praise should come as soon after the successful completion of a task as possible. When the employee is praised today for what he did yesterday, he is more likely to be enthusiastic and effective again today. This point means that managers must be ready to give that praise when it is called for, not just when they happen to be in the mood. Managers must be able to rise above their own troubles and frustrations to compliment an employee when the compliment is called for.

The same principles apply for corrections. That is, when an employee makes a mistake the manager should be quick to point it out. Do not pounce on it, but let the employee know as soon as tactfully possible that a mistake was made. Be specific in explaining the action that was wrong. Try to focus on the action or behavior, and not to criticize the person. Criticism of behavior is more likely to be accepted as instructive. "Frank, this report is incomplete," focuses on the behavior. "Frank, can't you ever finish anything?" may be perceived as character assassination. The effect—and managers must always be concerned with the ultimate effect—will probably be more positive when focused on the behavior or action.

Good managers get each subordinate to work to capacity in a spirit of cooperation rather than competitiveness with co-workers. Short, open-exchange group meetings are held to improve the teamwork in the department and to foster mutual respect. When conflicts arise the manager tries to help the individuals involved resolve them. This often takes patience, an ability to listen. A good approach in resolving disputes is to sit down with both parties and have them explain the problem as they see it. Often by asking questions rather than giving answers the manager can lead the two to their own resolution of the conflict.

Important to this notion of teamwork is the manager's treatment of individuals. The manager lets people know that success is achieved by doing one's job, not by outdoing someone else. Knowing the interrelationships of jobs, employees should see that all will have greater success if all succeed. That kind of success depends on teamwork.

The manager must be aware of peer pressures and attitudes. A good rule of thumb is to praise in public and correct in private.

Managing Time

"There just are not enough hours in the day." Conscientious people often bemoan the fact they have too much to do and not enough time to do it in. Sometimes the work load is the problem. But often the real issue is how we manage, or mismanage, our time.

Figure 19-2. TIME-SAVING THOUGHTS

- The primary objective of time management is to work smarter, not harder. It should allow you to accomplish more without necessarily working harder.

- Recognize that not everything can get done. Don't waste time feeling guilty about what you cannot do. Rather, concentrate on accomplishing what there is time to do.

- Recognize as soon as possible when an activity is unproductive, and cut that activity off.

- Enjoy what you are doing as much as possible. It is always easier to be effective if you enjoy what you are doing.

- Whenever feasible, delegate those tasks that can be performed by an assistant. Reserve your time for A-Priorities.

- Time management is not accomplished by an automatic formula. It is a result of internal self-discipline. Increased effectiveness will never occur unless you make it happen.

A lack of time can result in serious consequences—poor job performance, clashes with co-workers, and infringement on one's personal and family life. You may find yourself sleeping less, eating on the run, and just "squeezing in" people and activities that deserve more time and attention.

If you find yourself caught in any of these conflicts regularly, you are a candidate for a time management review.

Planning Priorities

The foundation of time management is planning. To be in control of our time—and our lives—we cannot simply complete tasks as they become crises. Instead, we must understand the larger picture, and plan from top down.

Specifically, time experts agree that the most useful approach is an A-B-C priority system. Draw up a list of tasks to be accomplished and assign a value of A, B, or C to each. For each A task (or top-priority item), develop an activities list of things that must be done to complete the task. This is your workplan. For example, if preparing the merchandise assortment plan is your current A task, activities such as reviewing last year's records, assembling new vendor items, analyzing item profitability, comprise your workplan. To complete the A task, you must complete each part of your workplan.

Scheduling

By determining your priorities you are doing some long-range planning. To increase your chances of accomplishing long-term goals, however, you must also plan each week's and day's activities. That is, specify a day, and a time in each day, for work on each A task. This assumes you can estimate accurately how long each task will take. It also requires that you consider deadlines, lead times, and other factors in your planning.

An important element in scheduling is the difference between *internal* and *external* prime time. Internal prime time is the time you work best. For some people this is early morning. For others it is after lunch or later in the day. The point is to schedule your A tasks, especially the most difficult or challenging of these, for your internal prime time.

Ironically, many people waste their prime time reading the newspaper, answering routine mail, chatting with co-workers, or doing other B- or C-priority tasks. This leads to the frustration of always dealing with A tasks while "under the gun" or when they are tired or less alert.

External prime time is the best time to attend to other people. That may be when your boss is most accessible, when you can reach the branch stores, or meet with vendors. Determine what that external prime time is and plan your schedule accordingly.

Unfortunately, in some instances, your internal and external prime times conflict. For example, you may work best in the morning, but this is also the time you have to give subordinates their assignments and handle their problems. If so, you will have to develop another internal prime time. That takes discipline, but it can be done.

The key point in scheduling, then, is to allocate time to accomplish your objectives in the most efficient and effective manner.

Time Management Tools

You can develop schedules and stick to them by keeping the following points in mind:

1. *Use a to-do list.* This helps in organizing and tracking daily activities. For the list to be most helpful:

- Revise and use it every day.
- Use a long sheet of paper, not scraps, so you keep to one long-range schedule.
- Do not skip over difficult items.
- Keep the list visible.
- Make the list slightly optimistic for what you expect to accomplish.

2. *Handle each piece of paper only once.* Most items that cross your desk can be dealt with the first time you see them. Do not look at the paper once and put it aside for later. That is just paper shuffling.

3. *Avoid Parkinson's Law.* This law says that work expands to fill the time allowed for its completion. Instead, work ahead and give any time saved as a reward to yourself.

4. *Apply the 80-20 rule.* Generally, 80% of the value of our work comes from 20% of the tasks we perform. Do not waste time on items that produce little or no value. Concentrate on those that yield the greatest benefits.

5. *Master the art of accommodating others.* A C-priority for you may be an A-priority for someone else. Compromise can reduce potential conflicts. By giving someone the key item of a request, you may satisfy his A-priority without infringing too much on your own, especially if you do this during your non-prime time.

6. *Learn to say no.* If you agree to do more than you possibly have time for, or at a time that is most inconvenient for you, you will adversely affect the quality of your work and life.

7. *Be selective in your reading.* Scan periodicals for items of relevance, rather than reading cover to cover.

8. *Monitor your use of time.* Throughout the day ask yourself, "Am I making the best use of my time right now?" If the answer is no, get yourself back on task.

Overcoming Procrastination

One of the greatest and most common blocks to effective time management is the inability to get started on a new task or overcoming roadblocks on current activities. There are many ways to short-circuit procrastination. Several widely used techniques are listed below.

1. *Break down an overwhelming A-priority task.* Use "instant tasks" to poke holes in an unpleasant or overwhelming A-priority task. By breaking an A-priority task into smaller tasks, it is easier to get started and get tasks accomplished.

2. *Make a commitment to someone.* By promising someone else that you will accomplish a certain task, you increase your incentive to perform the activity.

3. *Set up a meeting as a special deadline.* A meeting provides an extra incentive to begin and complete activities by forcing you to prepare for the meeting.

4. *Plan the next step of the task.* By defining remaining tasks clearly, you can avoid getting bogged down in detail.

5. *Don't let fear slow you down.* The fear of making a mistake or a bad decision can lead to inaction. Tell yourself you will make a start even if you have to change it later.

6. *Recognize the real price of delay.* An unpleasant task only gets worse if put off—it never goes away. Delaying a task means that there may not be sufficient time available to do a quality job. "Working well under pressure" frequently means that quality suffers.

7. *Set up a self-reward system.* Set rewards for yourself contingent on completing tasks on time. Dispense or withhold these rewards based on your performance.

8. *Shock therapy.* As a last resort, sit at your desk for 15 to 20 minutes doing absolutely nothing. You should soon become very uneasy that time is slipping by while major tasks go undone.

Managing Language

When Henry Ford II was asked to name the qualities one needs for success in business, he answered: "For starters I'd list honesty, candor, good judgment, intelligence, imagination, and the ability to write clear, concise memos."

The ability to write clearly is sometimes overlooked in management development programs. Yet the higher one rises on the organizational chart, the more critical writing becomes.

Writing crosses all divisional lines in a retail organization. The finance people write plans and control procedures. Systems specialists document information flows with written narratives. Merchandisers write evaluations of lines, stores, vendors, and promotions. Operations spells out everything from dress code to loss-prevention guidelines. The personnel office develops training manuals, explains benefits, and writes a hundred and one different kinds of letters.

Clarity and Brevity

Common to all of this writing is the need for clarity and brevity. Ironically, a lot of business writing is unclear and wordy. Overblown language, complicated sentences, and disjointed thoughts camouflage rather than convey ideas.

Certainly every writer begins with the intention of being clear and to the point. But something happens along the way. While the writer concentrates on *what* to say, he often ignores *how* he's saying it. This is natural. At the moment the writer is searching for words to express one idea, the mind is racing ahead to the next thought, or backtracking with an afterthought. New insights spring up, changing the direction or complexion of the argument.

Review and Revise

After recognizing these dynamics in the writing process, the next step is to deal with them. That is, let the mind create as imaginatively as it can. Then review and revise every document. Revision is the key to clear, concise writing. Revision involves two major aspects: (1) organization of ideas and (2) construction of sentences.

Organizing Ideas. In reviewing a draft, whether a one-page memo or a fifty-page report, look for the pattern of its ideas. For the reader to follow your train of thought easily, ideas must flow logically. You can achieve this logical flow by working with paragraphs. Like rungs on a ladder, paragraphs carry the reader through an explanation one idea at a time. Though the paragraphs are linked, each presents a different topic, or a different aspect of a continuing thought. For example, in a memo recommending a new procedure on the loading platform, one paragraph might describe the new procedure, a second might outline its benefits, a third could list the costs, and a fourth might cite the flaws of the current method.

By devoting a paragraph to each idea you are more sure of giving each a full treatment, with all of the details, examples, and particulars needed to make the idea clear to the reader. In reviewing the document, check to see that you follow this "one paragraph—one idea" format.

Then question the order. Does your draft present ideas in the most logical sequence for your reader? In the case of our example, would it be more effective to begin with the flaws of the current procedure, then present the new one?

Once you know the ideas (paragraphs) are in the best order, see if they flow smoothly from one to the other. You can help the reader see the connection by placing expressions such as "therefore," "in addition," "on the other hand," "then," at the beginning of paragraphs.

Or you can begin a paragraph by repeating a key word or phrase from the end of the previous paragraph. For example, assume one paragraph ends: "For these reasons the current procedure is highly inefficient." Begin the next paragraph like this: "We can achieve greater efficiency by converting to the XYZ procedure. . . ." The two paragraphs are linked by the repetition of the idea "efficiency".

In reviewing your draft for the organization of ideas, check for:

- One paragraph—one idea
- The most logical order of ideas (paragraphs)
- Connectives linking paragraphs

Of course, the more planning you do before the writing, the less you have to do in revision. But even with detailed planning, the dynamics of the writing process make this kind of revision necessary.

Revising Sentences. With your ideas or content properly organized, you are ready to review your expression. That is, examine each sentence to be sure you have expressed your ideas in the clearest, briefest manner. To do this, apply the following eight principles of sentence construction to each sentence.

1. *Limit sentences to one or two ideas.* Readers can better digest new ideas when they are fed one at a time rather than in bunches. Determine the number of ideas by counting the verbs. For instance, here is a simple sentence:

Management *expects* that sales *will increase* in the second quarter.

At times you may include three ideas:

Management *was* pleased with the first quarter figures but now *expects* that sales *will increase* in the second quarter.

But be careful. You may end up with this:

Because the interest in video games *continued* into January and *generated* unanticipated volume, management *was* pleased with the first quarter figures but now *expects* that sales *will increase* in the second quarter.

To reduce such sentences to digestible units, parcel ideas into separate sentences:

The interest in video games *continued* into January and *generated* unanticipated volume. Management *was* pleased with the first quarter figures and *expects* that sales *will increase* in the second quarter.

2. *Keep the average sentence length at 18 to 20 words.* Brevity is the essence of wit and a tremendous aid to clear, effective writing. The Gettysburg Address has only 268 words; The Lord's Prayer, 69. In revising your sentences, keep them short.

Step One in our approach to merchandise planning *is* a review of recent history of department performance based on unit control records and department contribution reports which *provide* the necessary basis for sales predictions and purchase requirements for a period of time. (42 words)

Though this sentence contains only two verbs, it is more than a mouthful. Break this kind of sentence into a number of shorter ones.

Step One in our approach to merchandise planning *is* a review of recent history of department performance. (17 words) The review *includes* unit control records and department contribution reports. (10 words) This information *provides* the necessary basis for sales predictions and purchase requirements for a period of time. (17 words)

Twenty words is not an absolute maximum. Too many very short sentences in succession make the writing choppy. But strive to keep the average length at 20 words.

Keep in mind Mark Twain's concern for brevity: "Forgive me for writing such a long letter. I didn't have time to write a short one."

3. *Avoid expressions that lead to wordiness.* For example: "The changes led to the enhancement of our accounts receivable procedure" can be put more simply: "The changes improved our accounts receivable procedure."

Many length-builders are nouns made from verbs, often ending in *-ment* and *-tion.* Instead of these, use the verb itself to write a shorter, more powerful sentence. Write "we discussed," not "we had a discussion about," "they evaluated," not "they conducted an evaluation of;" "she assessed," not "she made an assessment of."

Another type of length-builder is the phrase that is longer than it needs to be. "In light of the fact that" really means "because"; "affords me the opportunity to" can be replaced by "lets me"; "for the purpose of" is the same as "to".

4. *Omit unnecessary words.* In reviewing each sentence in your draft, look for unnecessary words that add length and cloud meaning. For example, here is a wordy sentence:

> Morale has reached a serious low point and employees are not happy in their work.

Cut the unnecessary repetition, and it becomes:

> Employee morale has reached a serious low point.

5. *Avoid false starters like "there are" and "it is."* Expressions like "there are" and "it is" often increase length unnecessarily. By restructuring the sentence you can write a shorter, better sentence. Compare the following two statements:

> There were occasional signs of life in the market, but generally it remained quiet.
> The market showed occasional signs of life, but generally it remained quiet.

6. *Keep the verb close to the subject.* With too many words between the subject and the verb, the reader can lose the train of thought. For example:

> Information on how vendors adhere to company requests and how their products fare in terms of receptivity, sell-through and markdown percentage, as well as profitability, must be considered in preparing buying plans.

The subject, "information," is dangerously far from its verb, "must be considered." Rewrite the sentence, placing these ideas closer together. This might mean restructuring the sentence:

> In preparing buying plans, the buyer should consider information on how vendors adhere to company requests and how their products fare . . .

7. *Make references clear.* Careless use of pronouns such as *he, it, they* can cause a reader to misread or reread a sentence. For example, in the following sentence it is impossible to know who "he" is. But in the rephrased sentence below, the reader knows definitely and immediately who was leaving town.

> Jackson sent Oliver the unedited draft because he was leaving town that afternoon.

> Because Oliver was leaving town that afternoon, Jackson sent him the unedited draft.

> When modifiers are misplaced, confusing and sometimes ridiculous sentences

result:

> We have just hired a buyer who worked for a major retailer named Jennifer Stapleton.

Put the name where it belongs:

> We have just hired a buyer named Jennifer Stapleton, who worked for a major retailer.

> Writers often misplace the word "only": "We only received two shipments on

this order." The writer really means: "We received only two shipments on this order."

8. *Use conversational language.* Conversational language makes reading easier and clearer. Yet, despite the efforts of people like Edwin Newman *(Strictly Speaking)* and William Safire *(On Language)*, insurance policies, legal documents, government publications, and a lot of business writing are filled with grandiloquent expressions or overblown language. For example:

> We will conduct an ongoing review of performance for the purpose of instituting remedial action as the situation warrants.

> Put in more conversational language:

> We will review performance continually so we can make changes when necessary.

> Common examples of grandiloquent expressions, with their conversational substitutes in parentheses, include:

> a multitude of (many)
>
> obviate (prevent)
>
> rectify (correct)
>
> inception (beginning)
>
> deem it advisable (suggest)
>
> establish (set up)

Some people feel that with every promotion they must move one step further away from conversational language. They wear out the thesaurus looking for more elaborate words. They feel they must write about their business the way Howard Cosell talks about football. But if they are interested in being understood, they stand a better chance using conversational language.

Other elements of writing, such as punctuation, grammar, and mechanics, also affect clarity. In addition, writers can learn to slant their material to the particular audience and purpose, and to make it forceful and persuasive.

But the place to begin is with clarity and brevity. The revision checklist given here may take time, but with practice these techniques become habitual. And clarity and brevity are two habits you won't want to kick.

Revision Checklist
After writing your first draft, revise it by applying these principles:

I. Organization of Ideas.
   A. Devote one paragraph to one idea.
   B. Put ideas (paragraphs) in the most logical order.
   C. Link paragraphs with connectives.

II. Construction of Sentences
   A. Limit sentences to one or two ideas.
   B. Keep the average sentence length at 18 to 20 words.
   C. Avoid expressions that lead to wordiness.
   D. Omit unnecessary words.
   E. Avoid false starters like "there are" and "it is".
   F. Keep the verb close to the subject.
   G. Make references clear.
   H. Use conversational language.

To test your skill, you might want to try the following exercise. Each of the sentences below could be improved by applying one of the sentence construction techniques to it. To designate which technique should be used, write the letter of the technique as it appears in the revision checklist. Then rewrite the sentences yourself, following the principles of brevity and clarity.

_____ 1. Ms. Tracy made recommendations for the implementation of a new procedure.

_____ 2. The annual contribution is $1,000.00 a year.

_____ 3. Because projections are based on assumptions about circumstances that have not occurred, they are subject to variations that may arise as future modifications are made.

_____ 4. Merchandise plans are used for the purpose of improving inventory control.

_____ 5. In the approach to systems implementation, an assessment of user requirements is the first step because without it we would have no solid basis for the purchase of new equipment or for the design of new systems.

_____ 6. Your solution to increase productivity in each of the departments identified as being below industry levels simply restates the problem.

_____ 7. Revise the introduction to the report and add some graphics to it.

_____ 8. To rectify the erroneous transaction, we deem it advisable that modifications be applied to the aforesaid methodology.

_____ 9. Indicate by letter the most logical order for three paragraphs on these ideas.
   a) Suggestions for dealing with pilferage are welcome.
   b) Pilferage is at an all-time high.
   c) A new security system has been created.

_____ 10. Which would be a good connective between paragraphs b & c in question #9? a) In addition b) Therefore c) On the other hand

20

Theory Z:
People, Productivity, and Profit

OVERVIEW: Japanese success in business and industry in the last 20 years demands that we study their system of management. Working deliberately toward employee loyalty and long-term goals, Japanese management has developed a managerial structure that improves productivity at every level.

When business executives talk seriously about people management, the discussion almost always includes Japanese management practices. The facts show that the Japanese have been outpacing the United States in productivity for a number of years. Since World War II, productivity in Japan has increased at 400% the rate in the U.S. The annual turnover rate in American companies is 26%, while the rate in Japan is 6%. Absenteeism is lower in Japan. According to a report in *Time*, Japan lost 1.4 million work days due to strikes in 1978, while the U.S. lost about 39 million during the same year.

In a book entitled *Theory Z: How American Business Can Meet the Japanese Challenge*, Dr. William G. Ouchi analyzed the reasons for Japan's great success. In brief, Ouchi believes that success results from better management of people. "The problem of productivity in the United States will not be solved with monetary policy nor through more investment in research and development," Ouchi says. "It will only be remedied when we can learn how to manage people in such a way that they can work together more effectively."

Ouchi contends that productivity is high in Japan because workers feel a sense of commitment toward their companies and see a personal gain in being productive.

Working in a culture based on trust and intimacy, the Japanese worker, at every level, feels he is an important element in his company's success, and corporate success adds to his own sense of self-esteem. His opinion is asked for, and he shares responsibility for both good and bad decisions.

The underlying principles of people management in Japan are not new, nor are they exclusive to Japanese firms. Ouchi says the same principles are also found in a number of American companies—IBM, Eastman Kodak, Hewlett-Packard, Dayton-Hudson, and others. Ouchi calls American companies that embody the traits of successful Japanese firms "Z Companies." (The use of "Z" is an intentional reference to Douglas McGregor's Theory X and Theory Y. A Theory X manager assumes that people are fundamentally lazy, irresponsible, and need constantly to be watched. A Theory Y manager assumes that people are fundamentally hard-working, responsible, and need only to be supported and encouraged.)

Theory Z poses a major challenge to American management, and retailers owe it to their organizations to at least examine the points in that challenge.

Basic Principles of Theory Z

According to Ouchi, a Theory Z company is characterized by three basic principles: lifetime employment, slow evaluation and promotion, and nonspecialized career paths. These principles support a structure that encourages and elicits loyalty, teamwork, and a long-range view of individual and corporate goals.

Lifetime Employment
Japanese management trains and retains its employees. Major firms hire graduates who stay with the company until age 55. At that time, they retire with five to six years salary and a part-time job at a minor or subsidiary company. Promotions are almost always from within, and very rarely is an employee fired. About one-third of Japanese workers enjoy lifetime employment with one firm.

All workers get bonuses during profitable years, and no one gets a bonus during a bad year, regardless of individual performance. Firms even cut salaries during slumps, but rarely resort to layoffs. The reasoning is that when things pick up again, the company has an experienced staff on hand and wastes no time in reaching its peak efficiency. (A by-product of this approach is the incentive to save during "good times." Japan's rate of savings is four times that of the United States.)

Though "slouching" may seem to be a characteristic of lifetime employment, this is not the case in Japan. The reason, perhaps, lies in other basic principles of organization.

Evaluation and Promotion
By American standards, the Japanese promote their workers at a snail's pace. All workers are paid and promoted at the same rate as their peers hired at the same

time. Only after a long time, about ten years, will a major evaluation be given, and only at that time—after one has proven himself—will distinction in performance be stressed and will "irreversible" titles be bestowed. The Japanese feel this slow progression fosters cooperation and a team spirit, and eliminates the corporate "games" that characterize the fast-trackers and "up or out" philosophies in American companies.

The incentive to do a good job comes not from the possibility of a quick promotion but from the healthy pressure exerted by other team members. Short-term successes and ambitions are replaced by the long-term view, both in terms of one's personal career as well as the corporate mission. As the two intertwine, productivity increases.

But with rapid promotion common to American companies, if one does not move up qickly he moves out, thus creating a slot to fill with another new, inexperienced person. The time spent training that original person is wasted, and his potential use to the company is lost.

Nonspecialized Career Paths
The career path of a Japanese manager is more like a winding road than a straight line. Each person works on varied assignments in different departments, and so gets to know many people and functions in the organization. This leads to better coordination.

In companies with a high degree of specialization, it is more difficult to integrate functions. Specialists may have difficulty in modifying their goals and in developing new skills when company objectives change. Yet as the United States faces a slow-growth economy, Ouchi feels we may need to adapt the concept of the "generalist" to keep people interested in their work without offering promotions.

Turnover at professional and managerial levels in America is greater than 25% each year. People in American businesses desire a high degree of specialization so they can move to a similar slot in another company. They often keep posted on such openings in other companies, and even establish contacts there, in case they are not satisfied or things change at the current company.

To counteract the effects of this revolving door syndrome, American management pushes standardization even further, so replacements for functions can be made more easily. But this simply keeps the revolving door spinning faster and faster.

Z Characteristics

Flowing from the three basic principles of lifetime employment, slow promotion, and nonspecialized career paths are a number of important features of the Theory Z Company.

Mechanism of Control
The American system of management calls for specific target objectives (management by objectives) for each manager or function, set down by upper management.

In Japan, sharing in a common set of values enables each manager to set his own objectives, to function in a way he knows the company as a whole would want.

"Egalitarianism," Ouchi says, "is a central feature of Type Z organizations. Egalitarianism implies that each person can apply discretion and can work autonomously without close supervision, because they are to be trusted. Again, trust underscores the belief that goals correspond, that neither person is out to harm the other. This feature, perhaps more than any other, accounts for the high levels of commitment and of productivity in Japanese firms and in Type Z organizations."

Collective Decision Making

Common experience and common understanding facilitate collective decision making, a critical element in the Japanese theory of management. By "collective" the Japanese do not mean five or six people making a decision, but rather 50 or 60. A small team of three is responsible to talk to all 50 or 60 and write a proposal on an issue. With each significant modification, the team goes back to those previously consulted.

This kind of process is very slow, but it does ensure full commitment to the decision. Implementation then comes faster and with more enthusiasm.

Inherent in collective decision making is "the intentional ambiguity over who is responsible." Again the team, rather than any single individual, shares the blame for a bad decision or the credit for a good one.

An article in *Business Week* ("Teamwork Pays off at Penney's," April 12, 1982) attributes much of J.C. Penney's success to this kind of management thinking:

> For years, Penney followed personnel policies usually associated with the Japanese. The Company adheres strongly to employment security and to nonadversarial relations with customers and employees. Now, with those practices firmly ensconced, Penney seems to be successful in adopting another quintessentially Japanese business concept: consensus management.

Collectivism

A large organization with many people must depend on coordination and cooperation rather than individualism. By instilling a spirit of collectivism in its workers, Japanese management can achieve coordination less through its own urgings than through the natural inclination of the people.

"Japanese firms almost never make use of individual work incentives, such as piecework or even individual performance appraisal tied to salary increases," Ouchi says. To the Japanese, "everything important in life happens as a result of teamwork or collective effort."

Holistic Concern for People

What management does to stimulate that cooperation is to treat its workers as whole people, with lives and interests that go beyond the job. Many experiences outside of work are shared, helping to form a personal bond between workers. The social and

**Figure 20-1. DIFFERENCES BETWEEN JAPANESE
AND AMERICAN COMPANIES**

Japanese	American
Lifetime employment	Short-term employment
Slow evaluation and promotion	Rapid evaluation and promotion
Nonspecialized career paths	Specialized career paths
Implicit control mechanisms	Explicit control mechanisms
Collective decision making	Individual decision making
Collective responsibility	Individual responsibility
Holistic concern for workers	Segmented concern for workers
Characterized by:	Characterized by:
homogeneity	heterogeneity
stability	mobility
collectivism	individualism

economic lives are integrated so that an intimacy among workers develops, their values become compatible, and trust and understanding grow.

Philosophy, Policy, Procedures

In analyzing the Z companies in America, Ouchi has found that a clearly defined statement of philosophy underlies all of the companies' policies, procedures, and operations. These philosophies are found not just on the books but in actual practice. Efforts are made to ensure that all employees know, and live, the corporation's philosophy.

One company that allows corporate philosophy to direct its operations is Hewlett-Packard. In its philosophical commitment to employees, Hewlett-Packard decided that it would not become a "hire and fire company." At times the company has to turn down lucrative government contracts of relatively short duration rather than hire people for a year or two, knowing those people would have to be let go when the contract expired.

At a time when retailers are caught in the pincers of high interest rates and inflation, when competition is at its keenest, productivity has taken on greater importance. Many retailers have sought productivity gains only through technology. They ignore the fact that retailing is a people-oriented business, and overlook the impact on profits of people-productivity. A serious look at *Theory Z* can help refocus attention on people.

Epilogue:
The Technological Evolution
in Retailing

The technological advancements of the past decades have introduced dramatic changes in the retail environment, and present innovations indicate that these changes will be more than matched in the next decade alone. We have already discussed in Part II the role in retailing of MIS, POS, POM, and electronic marking and reading technologies. Elsewhere we have discussed the use of computers in merchandise planning and store and warehouse operations. These computer-based technologies are not the wave of the future—they dominate the present, especially in the large retail operation.

With the declining cost of computer power, today even the small retailer can afford to computerize many retail functions. In fact, considering the benefits computerization offers and the competitive nature of retailing, many retailers can't afford *not* to computerize.

Technological innovation will help the retailer face a number of perennial challenges:

- A changing consumer
- Changing forms of retail operations
- Increasing number of new products
- Economic uncertainty

- Rising costs and decreasing productivity
- Increasing competition

The location and buying habits of consumers have undergone almost continual change. As the consumer moved to the suburbs, the retailer followed. As the postwar generation gained more buying power and greater leisure time, retailers adapted to meet their demands. Economic conditions, the proliferation of special interests, the diversity of ethnic groups, and the shifting predominance of age groups have resulted in an increasing fragmentation of the consumer population, a fragmentation strongly felt in the retail industry.

The retailer needs more than ever to know who the customers are and what their needs are. Data captured at the point of sale, through credit systems, and through data banks can be analyzed and monitored to ensure the retailer has current customer information. If this information is computerized, it can be used to develop specialized mailing, targeted advertising, and the salesperson's customer records.

New forms of retail operations have developed to service consumers and their needs. The old dry goods store has gone through several transitions: downtown, department store, suburban department store, and boutiques within the department store. Likewise, the local grocery store has gone through similar transformations as the supermarket, the superstore, and the combo store. Mass merchants, specialty stores, home centers, catalog showrooms, and, most recently, off-price retailers have sprung up. The electronic retailer is the latest form to emerge. It is discussed in more detail later in this chapter. The time between the appearance of each new form has decreased, and existing retailers are hard pressed to keep up. Their challenge is to keep abreast of the new forms as they develop and respond appropriately in the marketplace.

New products are being introduced at an ever faster pace. A walk through a small electrics department will reveal a multitude of products not there even a year ago. A walk through domestics will show an increasing number of styles and colors. Selecting products is a growing challenge that is matched by the challenge of managing them once they are in the store. Again, technology offers the retailer assistance in managing products by making more data available in more usable forms. The same techniques that have enabled the personal computer to be used by nontechnical people can be employed in the retail company. Buyers and executives with limited computer experience can begin to access information efficiently and use it effectively.

Economic uncertainty has been a hallmark of the 70s and 80s and it is unlikely that relatively stable or predictable cycles will resume. It seems more likely that the economy will continue to change frequently and be difficult to predict. The retailer must therefore be aware of changing conditions on a very timely basis and be prepared to respond appropriately. Again, the retailer must have the information available to determine what the economic conditions are and what actions can be taken to produce desired results. Technology can assist in that process.

In the past two decades, nearly every retailer has experienced dramatic cost increases as well as productivity declines. The retailer has responded by tightening costs and reducing payroll, especially on the selling floor. It is unlikely that further cuts can be made without jeopardizing service and the flow of goods. New and creative ways must be found to control or reduce costs. The store information system discussed later presents some ideas on how technology can assist in this area.

A related problem is getting qualified people to work in the various facets of retailing. To deal with the lack of skilled personnel, management has broken tasks down, simplifying them, and leaving less to the judgment of individuals. Technology can enhance the productivity of employees at all levels of the retail operation. These changes can improve management's control of operations and its collection and use of information.

All of the challenges listed above have made retailing an even more competitive industry than it was before. To remain competetive, management must be prepared to address these challenges. Managing and using technology effectively may well be the key to meeting these challenges successfully.

Management has already moved slowly out of finance to the selling floor and buying area. The 70s saw POS consume major amounts of capital and human resources. POS was followed quickly by purchase order management and merchandise processing systems. Retailers who can harness the power of the computer to process information and streamline operations will be best able to compete.

Three special areas of the technological evolution warrant the attention of forward-looking retailers: the store information system, electronic shopping, and electronic funds transfer.

The Store Information System

Initially retailers made do with whatever computer technology and programs were available. The trend today, however, is toward greater customization. Retailers are more aware of the possibilities of tailoring computer power and various modular systems to suit their own needs and situation. This trend toward total customization is likely to reach its peak in the late 1980s. The decade of the 1970s was the decade of POS. The 1980s will be the decade of the store information system.

The retail store of 1990 will probably make use of a variety of types of computer terminals. The store computer system will be the source for a number of information tributaries throughout the organization. Sales clerks on the selling floor will have their own POS terminals hooked into the network, enabling them to get up-to-the-minute information on stock, shipments, and price changes. The cashier's office will use a terminal for check verification and cashing, for placing deposits, and making payments. The customer, too, will make use of a store terminal in gaining information on products, prices, colors, availability, and related items. The store manager will use a store terminal to do analyses similar to those done at the central office regarding sales, profitability, and stock. Salesperson scheduling will become a computerized function, reducing the manager's time on this activity, while improving the use of store personnel.

The store computer will increase efficiency in the use of energy, regulating the flow of fuel in lighting, cooling, and heating the store. Security measures will be a part of the store's information system so that surveillance and display reflect traffic, susceptibility, and profitability of departments.

The biggest benefit to the retailer of the store information system is improved customer service. Service is improved on the selling floor through salesperson use of POS and customer activated terminals. As retailers grow more sophisticated in their use of POS on terminals used by salespeople, customer questions on the availability of merchandise will be answered quickly and efficiently. Use of POS for authorization both of the retailer's own card as well as checks and third-party cards will speed up service at the register. Customer-activated terminals are in use today in a variety of ways, and more will evolve in the future. Many retailers have automated the traditional bridal registry and made it available to the customer via a touch-screen. The customer, unaided, can determine what items the bride wants that have not yet been purchased. Some retailers have looked at similar systems for gifts or baby registry.

Another interesting application involves use of a computer terminal to assist in car stereo selection. In this system the customer can enter information such as type of car, tape or not, type of music, price range, etc. to narrow the selection to two or three products. Another application uses a chemical process to analyze the colors to be mixed to match paint chips. With the match determined, the customer enters the quantity and type of paint desired. These systems provide good service and provide information salespeople typically do not.

The store information system, therefore, will be a unified network through which data are cross-referenced and transferred for optimum use. To acquire and use this state-of-the-art technology, management must reconcile itself to the technological evolution. Developing new attitudes and training people will take more effort than installing the equipment. How rapidly an organization's people can adapt can affect its competitiveness in the next decade.

An important factor in this move toward the total store information system is cost. Though the price of technology is declining, costs are still significant and must be assessed carefully in the planning stages. Technical expertise is another important factor. A company must have knowledgeable people to plan, lead, direct, and train. The wrong people, or too few people, can result in significant waste of time and money and even in the failure of the project.

Buying and selling the right goods at the right price will still be the object of retailers, but how they go about that practice will change greatly in the next ten years. Two phenomena in particular are likely to have a dramatic effect on the way consumers make purchases—electronic shopping and electronic transfer of funds.

Electronic Shopping

At conferences across the country today, retail executives have raised three basic questions on the issue of electronic shopping: Is it too far down the road to worry about? Is it a threat to our way of doing business? Is it a new opportunity?

Although it is still viewed as a thing of the future, rather than the immediate present, electronic shopping has undergone enough experimentation to be taken seriously. Electronic shopping offers consumers the opportunity to shop from home via telephone or computer hookup. Warehouse, catalog, and mail-order businesses have been around for years, and electronic shopping is the next step because it provides greater speed, convenience, and accessibility than these earlier modes.

Electronic shopping enables consumers to see information about products on their TV or computer screens, to key in their needs, and to receive immediate responses about costs, availability, alternatives, and other factors. They receive suggestions for companion purchases as well. A further refinement displays a picture of the item on the screen.

Telephone lines, cable, or satellites are used to send information to the TV set and to retrieve information from the consumer. Decoders and keypads make direct two-way communication possible. For some systems, the consumer must use the telephone to order.

Warner Communications' QUBE was one of the first experiments in two-way communication through television. This was not used for retailing but for collecting and analyzing consumers' responses to television programs.

Comp-U-Card of America, however, has put into operation a computerized shopping service. Cardholding members learn what product they want, including the brand, model number, and price. Comp-U-Card's operations scan electronic listings that are updated daily. To buy, the member supplies his membership and credit card numbers to the operator.

Consumers Distributing in Canada is even more advanced, sending a 500-page "electronic catalog" to about 250 homes in the Toronto area. Part of the experiment is designed to determine how best to organize the information for consumers to find what they want quickly and easily. Presently all merchandise is broken down into eight categories. Through a branching technique and a series of prompting questions, the consumer in his home can call up a number of lists from each category. He then orders directly through TV terminals rather than via the telephone.

The technology for electronic shopping is available and rapidly improving. As advances are made, the cost is dropping, making computer equipment and services more accessible. Since the mid-1960s, the cost of data processing equipment has dropped between four and ten times. The home computer of today has the capability of many of the large computers of 20 years ago at a fraction of the cost.

Home computers, a critical element in the electronic shopping network, are fast becoming a hot item. Used for personal business, for entertainment, and for educational purposes, the home computer must be seen as an important medium for communication with the private consumer.

There are more uses being found for the home telephone, and consumers are learning about them and adopting them. Telephone lines provide links to banks to pay bills and to track key dates. Telephones are used by more and more people to order merchandise and for comparative shopping. The phone also provides a link between home terminals and mainframe computer systems for work, school study, stock market quotes, and many other uses.

There is an increasing variety of terminal-type products that are relatively inexpensive, simple to use, and geared to the individual consumer with little sophistication in computer products. Evidence of this is seen in the tremendous popularity of the home Apple, TRS-80, IBM Personal Computer adaptors to turn the television into a terminal.

Cable television is a growing medium, not only for entertainment but also for information, advertising, and shopping.

Paralleling these advancements in technology is the change in consumer attitudes. More than ever before, consumers are interested in convenience and in their leisure time. With more than half the women in the country holding jobs outside the home, the traditional shopper has less time to make purchases for herself and her family. She also has less energy and desire for traveling and bucking crowds in stores.

Today's consumers are better-educated than before and are smart shoppers. They look for quality, price, and service, and will go back to the retailers and the brands that satisfy. This reliance on individual stores—and more particularly on brand names—is another factor that makes electronic shopping a very real possibility.

Five Scenarios

Assuming that these indicators herald the birth of electronic shopping, what will happen? There are a number of alternative scenarios that are likely to unfold independently of each other and perhaps simultaneously.

The first of these is the establishment of "electronic-only retailers." These will be companies new to retailing, formed expressly to serve consumers through electronic means. They will offer lower prices because of their lower overhead. Since their building, inventory, and staff needs are less than those of the traditional retailer, these electronic upstarts can come into operation very quickly. Where will their customers come from? From existing retailers.

Contending with these new retailers will be those who have for some time been trying to lure customers away from the traditional retail store. These are catalog and direct-mail retailers who will make the logical extension of their operations into electronic shopping. They already have the link to customers through the mail as well as the facilities and the operation to service them. By adding electronic capabilities they can enhance their product offerings, particularly if they tie into cable television, giving customers a better look at products.

A third scenario shows the manufacturer bypassing the existing retail distribution channels and going directly to the consumer. Cutting out the middleman, these manufacturers can offer lower prices and possibly expand their market share.

A fourth potential competitor for retail customers is found in the media offerings. This can come in the form of newspapers branching out into electronics-in-the-home services, or cable television companies, or computer service companies. Each of these media industries can advertise, offer easy price-comparison for shoppers, and provide the customer with a link to a retailer or a manufacturer. This kind of service will make traditional retailing more price-competitive than ever. Traditional retailers will have to offer other things besides price to gain a competitive edge.

But the traditional retailer is by no means out of the electronic shopping picture. A fifth and very viable possibility calls for the traditional retailer to expand his services to include this new alternative. Over the last few years many retailers have expanded their offerings through circulars and catalogs; so the electronic mode would only be another service to customers.

At a time when capital for new stores is difficult to come by, electronic shopping may be a less expensive way of increasing market share. If nothing else, electronic shopping may be the means by which retailers retain customers.

Implications

This review of the possible scenarios might suggest that traditional retailers will have to get into electronic shopping whether they want to or not. That may or may not be true, but certainly retailers have time to weigh their decision.

Traditional stores will not disappear. There is still an element of social benefit, even some entertainment value, for people in traditional shopping that will continue to bring them to the stores. People will still want to see, touch, and try on many items before buying.

In addition, electronic shopping is an evolution, not a revolution. It will take time to develop fully, giving retailers the chance to learn more about it, to assess its impact, and to absorb it into their operation.

This, therefore, is not the time to panic. Electronic shopping at the moment can only be a threat if it is ignored, and if customer needs and wants are ignored. But now is the time to study and to plan. Now is the time to seize this innovation as an opportunity for retaining old customers and adding new ones. Electronic shopping can be the opportunity to enter new markets with new products.

Specifically, retailers can use the time wisely to do the following:

- Review local and national experiments.
- Review their customer base—who are they, what do they buy?.
- Conduct a customer survey on attitudes toward electronic shopping.
- Review trends in their mail order and telephone business.

- Review their merchandise for its appropriateness to electronic shopping.
- Conduct a limited experiment of their own.

Electronic shopping can, no doubt, change the way retailers operate. But basically, the name of the game will remain the same: do what has to be done to satisfy the customer.

The Economics of Electronic Shopping

Let us now take a look at the economics of electronic shopping, specifically in a supermarket. Let us take a quick rundown from the top to the bottom line of a hypothetical $100 million-a-year chain of 20 conventional supermarkets grossing $5 million a year each. From a margin of 22.32%, we can allocate the following costs:

Labor	
Stores	12.00%
Warehouse	2.16
Delivery	.64
Energy	
Stores	1.50
Warehouse	.18
Rent	
Stores	1.20
Warehouse	.45
Delivery, exc. labor	.49
Other, incl. depreciation	2.26

This leaves a pretax net operating profit of $1,437,000 (1.44%). Can the electronic supermarket compete?

It's important to remember that the electronic supermarket is not a direct replacement for the conventional supermarket. Its customers will be dispersed differently; there will be fewer customers; the average customer order will be larger; and the merchandise mix will be narrower.

As always, each retailer who enters this new retailing arena will bring a different set of marketing and merchandising luggage. Here, for example, is an outline of one possible approach:

1. The retailer offers a free home delivery service of 2,000 grocery and produce items with a minimum average order of $30. There is a guarantee that the retail price will be competitive on a market basket comparison basis with other food retailers.

2. The customer completes a preauthorized draft agreement allowing the retailer to direct-debit the customer's bank account for each order.

3. The retailer provides a descriptive list of the 2,000 items with check-digited order numbers. From this a customer can prepare a shopping list.

4. The customer calls an order-entry telephone number at any time between 8 a.m. and midnight. A computer terminal operator takes the customer's name, personal identification number, and required delivery date, and then enters the item numbers and the quantities required. Customers are advised of out-of-stock items. At the end of the call the operator confirms the order and informs the customer of the total.

5. The retailer's computer, starting at midnight, sorts down the orders into item sequence and instructs the warehouse to move bulk quantities into the repack facility sufficient to fulfill the day's orders.

6. Next, the computer prints picking tickets for each order in the sequence in which they will be loaded onto the delivery truck for optimum routing. These picking tickets will go with the order to form the customer's itemized bill. At the same time the computer will direct-debit the customer's bank account.

7. The computer will print a truck routing list and accommodate the various adjustments and corrections. Finally, it will maintain warehouse inventory and suggest reorders based on historical rates of sale.

8. The order is picked in the repack facility and is placed in a disposable cardboard tote. Styrofoam beads insulate frozen and chilled items.

9. The truck delivers the order to the customer's home according to predefined instructions. If the customer does not want the order to be left while no one is home, it will be dropped off at a regional pickup center. The customer owns the merchandise once an order is placed.

Eliminate the Operator

One aspect of this scenario undercuts the "electronic" aspect. That, of course, is the use of live operators. Their eventual obsoleteness is taken for granted. Low-cost intelligent terminals will eventually become as common as clock radios. But there is no economic need to wait for that. An electronic ordering business that grosses $100 million (the same as our hypothetical chain of conventional supers) should get by on an annual budget for operators of about $715,000. (That's assuming that about 50% of the calls will occur in a four-hour peak period in the evening, requiring about 70 operators. During the day about 24 operators would be required.)

Computers continue to gain in usefulness in the traditional warehouse-supermarket system of distribution. Their capabilities will be even more important in the electronic supermarket. The timeliness of their work will increase as unit inventory reports are updated daily.

The computers in electronic shopping applications will not have to account for as many stockkeeping units as they do today in a conventional supermarket. There will be an absence of impulse items. With the use of daily updates of unit sales data, buyers will be in a position to maximize total warehouse inventory turns.

In the electronic supermarket, orders will be assembled in boxes for delivery to

THE ELECTRONIC SUPERMARKET COMPANY
INCOME STATEMENT

	$ Amount	% Of Sales
Sales	$100,000,000	100.00
Cost of Goods Sold	77,680,000	77.68
Gross Margin	22,320,000	22.32
Labor		
Warehouse	2,163,000	2.16
Repack	2,100,000	2.10
Telephone	715,000	.72
Delivery	7,263,000	7.26
Energy	200,000	.20
Rental	500,000	.50
Other delivery	3,026,000	3.03
Other expenses	2,000,000	2.00
Total Expenses	**17,967,000**	**17.97**
Net Operating Income, Pretax	$4,353,000	4.35

the consumer. The average $30 order would contain about 20 items and be picked in a sequence designed to facilitate special handling of frozens and efficient handling of the 500 or so core items. For the sales volume we have assumed ($100 million), a staff of about 90 people will be needed at an annual cost of $2.1 million. The repack facility itself will probably occupy an area about 10% of the size of the warehouse.

The principal selling point of this retail form is, of course, home delivery. If the service can be provided free of charge—and the consumer feels that the item prices are competitive—then it doesn't seem the retailer will have a tough marketing problem.

United Parcel Service, by way of comparison, will pick up, consolidate and deliver a 25-pound package across town for $3.15. So it's reasonable to assume that delivery of a presorted standard carton in the projected system could be accomplished for considerably less than $3.00. By making some simple assumptions concerning productivity, labor rates, and truck operating costs, it is possible to arrive at an average of $3.09 per order for a total of $10,289,000 per year ($7,263,000 for labor and $3,026,000 for trucking costs).

Given these assumptions on costs, it is possible to project an overall operating statement (see accompanying table). Labor and energy costs shrink to 56% of company gross margin, compared to 74% in the conventional operation discussed above. Most significant, the bottom line has tripled to 4.35%.

Too easy, you say. Perhaps. But even recognizing the many simplifying assumptions made along the way—and that building a $100 million business is no easy task—it can be argued that there is a real investment opportunity.

Public acceptance of computer terminals and the demand for convenience shopping is a matter of record. (Whether their demand would support a delivery fee hasn't been proved out, so none is included in this model.) The establishment of a network of conversational computers in homes is an inevitability. Once it exists a flick of a switch will summon up a bank, a department store or—a supermarket.

As electronic retailing evolves from dream to reality, one great question will be answered: Will existing supermarket operators fight or join the revolution?

Electronic Funds Transfer

Another innovation just over the horizon for retailers is electronic funds transfers. It has been more than ten years since the financial community started talking about the checkless-cashless society, or electronic funds transfer. At the time, people predicted a rapid expansion of EFTS-type services because the banking community was being overwhelmed by the cost and burden of processing commercial checks. And it was assumed that business, including retailers, as well as consumers, would readily accept these electronic means of exchange.

Like many new ideas and concepts, however, the EFTS revolution turned into a slow evolution. People approached EFTS with caution, experimenting and piloting before giving a final endorsement. Some of the experiments failed, or did not show that EFTS could be viable for all parties involved or that it did much to satisfy the needs of consumers. In addition, the banking industry has *not* been totally overwhelmed, inundated, or unable to process the volume of commercial checks, despite continued growth.

Though the EFTS movement was slowed, it did not fizzle and die. Services were changed to be economically viable and profitable to both business and the banking industry. At the same time, greater attention was paid to meeting specific consumer needs. These changes, coupled with the public's increasing familiarity with things electronic, have brought EFTS to a point where it is having a significant impact on American business. Paper processing has been reduced or eliminated, cash flows have been improved, and faster handling of transactions at the POS terminal have given customers better service.

Because some EFTS services are already entrenched in retailing operations, and because further extensions of these are available or on the horizon, retailers would do well to review the EFTS options in light of their current needs and future plans.

History of EFT

From an historical perspective, we can see that initially there was a flurry of EFTS activity. Many of the early efforts met with varying degrees of success, some even achieved their objectives. By and large, however, these experiments went beyond most customer needs and business capabilities. Many of these, for example, dealt with the debit card. The customer, using a debit card, would make a purchase and his bank account would be debited immediately and the retailer's credited. The problem with such transactions was that it was costly for the banks, did little to increase sales for retailers, and had a low acceptance among consumers.

In the latter half of the 70s, many of these experiments had proved to be unsuccessful or extremely costly, the push to EFTS slowed, and the industry reevaluated the products and services required. In addition, Congress commissioned a study group to look into the need for legislation to regulate EFTS services, and this further cooled industry fervor for implementation. Much of the continuing discussion on reorganization within the financial industry was another braking force on the EFTS movement.

But while many took a "look-see" approach to EFTS, other parties, who felt they could benefit from EFTS, continued to pursue the issue. Retailers and financial institutions studied further one another's needs and began to develop products and services that could benefit all parties. Banks changed some of the services they were offering and made them more attractive to retailers and consumers. At the same time, the novelty of such transactions was wearing off and both consumer and retailer were more willing to accept them. Today, many of these services seem to be a way of life in America and are perceived to be of significant value.

A Quick Review of Services

Let us look at some of the specific services being used by retailers and consumers and discuss what each service provides.

Bank cards. The majority of retailers today accept bank cards and/or travel and entertainment cards. For example, more than 55 million MasterCards have been issued and more than 1,800,000 merchants accept them. This is a dramatic change from a few years ago when major retailers, as well as industry consultants, were vehemently stating that the major chains in the industry would not accept those cards in the foreseeable future. But acceptance has occurred for a variety of reasons. For one, retailers became painfully aware of the cost of their own private cards. For another, they saw a growing number of consumers who were making purchases while out of town. Similarly, as foreign tourism in America increased, retailers saw the bank card as a means by which to capture these additional sales. In addition, card issuers became more competitive in their discounts, and developed new and creative ways to make the cards attractive to retailers.

As a result, all three parties in the transaction benefit. The retail customer has added convenience in terms of choice of payment mechanisms within the store, even when traveling or moving to a new area. The financial institution has added income through the discount rate charged to the merchant and financial charges levied on the customer. And the retailer benefits from incremental sales achieved by accepting the bank cards.

Typically, the card issuer will either reduce the discount fee for the retailer providing electronic media, or pay a per transaction amount to the retailer. The benefit to the issuer is elimination of a data entry function. The obvious benefit to the retailer is additional cash through payment of the lower discount rate or the cash received from the issuer for providing the electronic media.

Bank branches or automated teller machines. Initially retailers were reluctant to have bank branches or automated teller machines set up on store premises. The prime reason was that banks were not willing to pay retailers for the space, and yet banks were insisting on prime selling-floor locations. In the increased understanding that has developed over the years, however, banks have been able to identify less valuable selling space that is still very useful for their purposes. And they are more willing to pay for the space.

Consumers appreciate the convenience of having their "bank" right in the store. It means one less stop, a time and energy savings, and the opportunity to make unanticipated purchases.

Retailers are finding that the branch or automated teller machine in the store brings in additional traffic and reduces clerical costs because customers are handling all of their banking transactions directly. The retailer does not have to serve as middleman.

By having branches or automated teller machines in retail stores, the banks can offer customers an additional service and greater convenience. They can gain new customers while keeping new building costs down.

Debit cards. The debit card can be seen as the equivalent of a check because it authorizes the withdrawal of money from a bank account for payment to a particular individual or company. MasterCard and Visa, as well as many market funds, are now offering debit cards. The retailer probably cannot tell whether the card given him by a customer is a debit or credit card. In all likelihood, however, it is a credit card since consumers have not widely accepted the notion of having money withdrawn from their accounts in this manner.

The debit card is just reemerging on the EFTS front; retailers should be aware of its presence and follow its movement.

EFTS Experiments

A number of EFT trials have been conducted over the last ten years, but only recently have they shown great acceptance and promise. A program in Des Moines, Iowa, is being conducted jointly by NCR, Iowa Transfer System, Inc., and Dahl's Foods and Hy Vee, two supermarket chains. A number of banks, including Chemical of New York, are conducting tests to offer bank-at-home services. OAI, Inc. is testing in supermarkets the use of the same plastic cards used in automatic teller machines for EFT.

Texaco and Mobil are among oil companies experimenting with card-activated gasoline pumps to transfer funds electronically after a purchase.

Kroger Supermarkets is trying out a direct debit system in Cincinnati that is tied into the Instant automatic teller machine. Within the Kroger system, a customer accesses Concord computer terminals, located at courtesy counters, with a bank-issued debit card. The customer punches in the desired transaction and the request is routed electronically to the card-issuing bank. The terminal issues a receipt which the customer hands to the check-out clerk. Transaction data is then sent to the Instant central switch for daily processing and settlement.

Many retailers have already found that EFTS-type services can help increase sales, and they are keeping abreast of new developments. Others who have not yet entered into the checkless-cashless society would do well to consider doing so. As credit cards became popular in our society, comedians would tell jokes with the punch line "Do you take cash?" We may soon get to the point where consumers no longer carry cash, or checks, but will buy everything from the morning paper to a grand piano with a plastic card.

Index

role in warehouse replenishment, 54
use of assortment plan, 32
use of computer for plan revision, 64
use of OTB, 45
use of sales plan, 13
buying plan, 5, 32–35
buying staff, and interactive approach, 5

cable television, 275
capital expenditures, 165
capital investments, 149, 150, 151
career paths, nonspecialized in Theory Z, 267
cash budget, 160
cash concentration, 164
cash control, 164
cash cycle, 159
cash disbursement, 162–163
cash discounts, 162
  advantages of, 38–39
  excluded from purchase markup, 25
cash flow, 151, 200
cash management, 158–169
cash register
  electronic, 98–99
  POS terminal as, 96
cash sales, POS effect on, 97
cash savings identification, 164
Census of Business Reports on Retail Trade, 227
center of gravity analysis, for warehouse location
  planning, 237
central site applications analysis, 101
Chambers of Commerce, as source of information,
  227
change, lack of. *See* stagnation
Chapter XI of Bankruptcy Act, 184, 197
chargeback, for MIS, 87, 89–90
check, preauthorized, 161
check clearing, 161
checklist method, of employee evaluation, 247–248
chief executive officer, information needs, 83–84
claims processing, automated, 76
classifications
  assortment planning, 31–32
  comparison in qualitative merchandise
    plan , 7
  merchandise arranged in store by, 229
  sales forecasts, 16
clearing house, for electronic transmission, 124–125
clerical errors, as cause of shortage, 171
collection float, in cash cycle, 159, 160

collection of receipts, 161
collectivism, in Theory Z organization, 268
collectors, component of POS, 98
color, as factor in merchandise assortment, 30–31
communication, 208
  capabilities of on-line inquiry system, 99
  developments, 128
  network provided by MIS, 82
  systems and growth, 205
  weaknesses and retail failure, 183, 185
communications ability, of job applicant, 244
community characteristics, consideration in site
    selection, 225
Comp-U-Card of America, 274
companies
  changes in structure as cause of retail failure,
    198
  electronic transmission between, 124
  image. *See* image, company
  impact of profile on store location, 222
  merchandise policy, 5
  mission, 213
  needs and priorities of MIS, 95
  objectives, 210, 213–214
  plans and cash budget, 160
  strategic plan, 213–215
  vendor compliance with policies, 33
compatibility
  employee to job environment, 244
  POS and existing hardware, 99–100
compensation incentives, as means of reducing
    shortage, 174
competition
  analysis, 226
  changes reflected in sales forecasts, 13
  discount, 195
  and retail failure, 196
  and store location, 223
computer-aided merchandise planning system
    (MPS), 61–65
computer job accounting packages, 90
computers, 60–76, 270, 274–275
  component of POS, 98
  customization for retailers, 272–273
  interactive purchase order development, 73
  and performance analyses, 67
  use for reordering, 57
  use in MIS, 80
  use with planogram, 234
  use with purchase orders, 72

costs, 54
depth, 30
effect of POS on, 110
formula for season average, 23
growth as threat of failure, 202
inconsistency and retail failure, 195–196
reconciliation, 172
reduction, 197
replenishment, 50–57
shortage, 16, 17, 139, 170–177
turnover, 28, 86, 151
inventory control
effect of warehousing on, 55
as MIS use, 82–83
potential for savings, 164–165
and retail failure, 183
inventory investment, 4, 234
costs, 54
inventory levels, 16, 165
average, 28
minimum, 75
monthly, planning methods, 20–24
planning and market constraints, 24
projected, 19
Inventory Shortage Reduction Study [Touche Ross & Co.], 173
investment portfolio, for cash investment, 163
invoices, 73, 76, 123, 124
item analysis, 86, 119
item profitability analysis, 33

Japanese management practices, 265–268
job applicant, interviewing, 244–245

LIFO [last in-first out] inventory methods, 140–143
language management, 258–264
layout of store, 229–230
lead time, 51, 52, 54
effect on display quantity, 231
factoring as MPS refinement, 66
reduction through use of electronic transmission, 129
and stock level planning, 21
and warehouse stock, 55
leadership. See Top management
leases, 126, 130, 195
leverage, 150
liability for merchandise in transit, 40
lifetime employment, component of Theory Z, 266
lighting, in warehouses, 239–240

liquidity, and threat of failure, 200–201
liquidity drain cycle, 203
load factor, added to cost of foreign goods, 42
location, component of distribution facilities planning, 237–238
lockbox service, 161
long-range planning, 213, 256

MIS. See Management information systems
MPS [merchandise planning system], computer-aided, 61–65
magnetic marking of merchandise, 117
magnetic tape, 124
mainframe computers, 67, 110
maintained markup, 25–26
maintenance
as part of RFP, 108
of POS system, 112
management
control by, 183, 205
control of purchasing, 72
information needs of, 83
limitations of resources leading to failure, 204
reaction to inflation and disinflation, 150–152
reports created with POS, 97
role in controlling shortage, 173
selection criteria, 204
stagnation as cause of failure, 207–208
supervision of subordinates, 253–254
support of employee training, 250
training, 252–255
management by objective, 248
management consultant, 169
management information systems, 79–96
chargeback, 90
complaints about, 90
expense allocation, 87–90
steering committee, 93
uses, 81
management profile studies, 210
manufacturers, 42, 115
markdowns, 33, 45, 58–59, 193, 202
allowance, 40, 41, 59
cost reduction from MIS, 82
effect of POS on, 110
effect on softgoods average price, 16
net, 139
planned, 16, 17–19, 28, 45
policy, 191
variance report for, 71
market conditions, buyer reaction to, 45

market research, 218
market trends, and sales forecasts, 13
market trip, itinerary, 35
marketplace review, 214
marking merchandise, 113–121
markups, 33, 38, 135
    formula for cumulative, 138
    formula for percentage, 25, 26, 27
    planned, 25–27
mass merchandising, ticket reading process, 117
mass transportation, as factor in store location, 225
material requirements planning (MRP) system, 238
maximum on-hand level, formula, 52
merchandise mix, and retail failure, 183, 191, 198
merchandise performance analysis, 67–71
merchandise processing, 73
merchandise reporting, 86
maximum on-hand level, formula, 52
McGregor, Douglas, 266
measurement errors, as cause of shortage, 171
memo writing, 258–264
merchandise
    chart for assortment buying plan, 34
    classifications, 4, 5, 11
    control, 44–59
    effect of MIS on decisions, 80
    flow affected by purchase order management, 72
    management using computer systems, 60–76
    movement decisions, 57–59
    OTB as budget for, 45
    planning, 3–35
    processing, 73, 74
    in qualitative merchandise plan, 11
    quality, 5, 33
    reporting, 86
    return, 7, 40–41
    warehousing of, 55–56
merchandise manager, 6, 35
merchandise mix, 28, 183, 191, 198
merchandise performance analysis, 67–71
merchandise planning system, computer-aided, 61–65
merchandising division, 3–4
merchandising vice-president, information needs, 84
microcomputers, 66–67, 160
middle management, 252–253
mini-computers, use in warehousing, 238
minimum stock, requirements of display, 51

mission, corporate, 213
model stock method, 230
model stock replenishment method, 52
modified gravity model, 224
monitoring process, for strategic plan, 215
monthly action plan, in qualitative merchandise plan, 11
monthly open-to-buy form, 48, 49

narrative review, in employee evaluation, 247
National Retail Merchants Association (NRMA), 110, 114, 173
    Financial Executives Division, 142
    Information System Division Board of Directors, 125
natural disasters, and retail failure, 196
negotiation of purchase, 36–43
Neisner Brothers [discount store], failure of, 193–198
net period, for cash discounts, 38
net price, after trade discount, 37
net sales, 138, 147–148
new business ventures, planning for, 214
new markets, 13
new products, 7, 13, 33, 35, 128, 271
nonperishable and nonprecious merchandise, 56

OCR-A [Optical Character Recognition—Type A], 114, 115–116
objectives
    corporate, 213–214
    measurable, 217
    of employee training programs, 251
    strategic, 216
obsolescence, technological, 126–130
office communication developments, 129
on-line inquiry system (POS type), 99
on-line interactive system (POS type), 99
open-to-buy [OTB], 13, 25, 44–50, 76
    and need for base plan revision, 64
    and purchase order management, 72
    computer updating, 57, 62
    included in buying plan, 35
    variance report for, 71
open-to-buy form, 47, 48, 49
operating budget, 4, 209
operating expenses, 4, 149, 151, 235
operating strategies, 214
opportunity market, 224
order approval, 72
order processing costs, of inventory, 54

organization structure, 185, 191, 204
Ouchi, William G., 265
out-of-stock conditions, 24, 55, 76
out-of-stock policy, 51
outgoing shipments, export houses expediting of, 42
overage, 170
overhead, 89, 202, 209
overstocking, 20, 24, 151
ownership, of goods in transit, 40

POM. *See* Purchase order management
POS. *See* Point-of-sale system, electronic
POS Trends in the 80s, 110
pack size, effect on display quantity, 231
pack space, 234
paperwork, 72, 174–175, 206
past sales information, review of, 5–6
payback areas, for cash management improvement, 168
payment for goods, and cash discounts, 38
payment period, net, 162
payroll, as MIS use, 81
payroll reductions, 197
performance, planned vs actual, affect on OTB, 46
performance assessment, 67–71
performance criteria, for ranking of stores, 67
performance measurement, 144–152, 210, 211
performance objectives, 212
performance standards
  for employees, 248
  from POS, 176
performance statistics, 6
performance tracking, 154–157
periodic studies, to reduce chance of failure, 210
perishable merchandise, 56
perpetual inventory system, 52
personal computer, 66–67, 110
personnel, 83, 204
personnel profile studies, 210
physical inventories, 135, 139, 172
picking mode, in warehouse, 238–239
pitfalls, of systems planning, 94–95
planned . . . *See* remainder of phrase (e.g., Markups, planned; Purchases, planned; Stock, planned; etc.)
planning conference, 215
planning cycle length, 94
planogram, 231–235
point-of-sale (POS) system, electronic, 52, 82, 96–112, 176–177

pooled stocks, 55
population studies, 205, 214, 223–224
praise, role of in employee supervision, 254
preauthorized check, 161
preauthorized debiting, 161
precious merchandise, 56
preliminary tactical plans, by department, 214
presentation stock, 51
price changes. *See* Markdowns
price line analysis, 11, 31, 86
price lines, 5, 31
price look-up function, on POS equipment, 99
pricing policies, 17
primary opportunity market, 224
prime time, 256
print-only marking of merchandise, 117
print/punch marking of merchandise, 117
priorities planning, 95, 102, 256
private labels, 183
procrastination, overcoming, 257–258
product exclusivity, and use of vendor, 33
product life cycles, 7
productivity, 72, 97, 243–264, 265
profit and loss sheet, 200–202
profit margins, 5
profit measures, to reduce chance of failure, 210
profit per square foot, as performance measure, 152–154
profit performance measurement, 144–152
profit to square feet ratio, 230
profitability, 11, 51, 209, 230
profitability of department, 86
profits, 145, 172
  gross, 86
  maximization, 4
  net, 235
project team for POS, 100
projected stock levels, 19
promotion effectiveness, testing, 218–220
promotion of employees, 266–267
promotion of merchandise, 13, 17, 28, 218–220
purchase/lease analysis, 127
purchase markup, 25
purchase negotiation, 36–43
purchase order management (POM), 72–76
purchase orders, 72, 73, 75, 82, 122–123
  automatic preparation, 82
  electronic transmission of, 75, 122–123
  entry, 72, 73
purchases, planned, 24–25, 35

stock-out conditions, 123
stock planning methods, comparison, 21
stock status reports for warehouse, 54
stock-to-sales method, 20
stock-to-sales ratio, 20, 21, 62, 82
stock turnover method, 21
stock turnover rate, 23, 28
store activities analysis, 101
store-and-forward terminal, 99
store-by-store performance, tracking, 154
store location, 187, 193, 205. *See also* Site
    selection
store managers, 185
store openings, reflected in sales forecasts, 13
store operations, potential for shortages, 171–
    172
store performance analysis, 67–71
store planning, use of computers, 66
stores
    limitations to comparing, 67, 69
    merchandise performance by type, 69, 70
    replenishment, 51
    transferring merchandise between, 57–58
    variance reports for, 69, 71
strategic planning, 212–220
strengths, company, assessment of, 214
styles of goods, effect on reordering, 56
suggested retail price, 37
supervisor, role in employee evaluation, 248
Survey of Buying Power, 227
systems development, 92, 129
systems planning, 90–95, 100

tactical plans, preliminary, by department,
    214
target customer, 7
task identification, 174
taxes, impact of FIFO or LIFO on, 140–143
technological change, 270–283
technological obsolescence, 126–130
technology acquisition, 129–130
telecommunication developments, internal, 129
telephones, 275
terminals, 98, 99
theft, 171, 172
Theory X and Theory Y, 266
Theory Z, 265–268
ticket, merchandise, 113, 118–119
time management, 255–258
timesheet reporting systems, 90

top management
    and cash management improvements, 168–169
    and interactive approach, 5
    and retail failure, 184
    of Robert Hall, 190, 193
    role in systems planning, 91
    and strategic plan, 215, 216
    support of employee training, 250
top-down approach, to merchandise planning, 4
total sales, 18, 86
    by classification, 7
Touche Ross & Co., study of POS, 110
trade discounts, 7, 37
trade journals, as source for new product
    information, 35
traffic flow studies, 205
training, 108, 112, 185, 249–252
    administrator for, 251–252
    development of programs, 250–251
    role in reducing shortage, 175
transfers of merchandise, between stores, 57–58
transportation costs, and warehouse location, 237
trend forecasts, 7

Uniform Communication System [USC], 125
unit and dollar classification plan. See Six-month
    merchandise plan
unit control data, by price lines, 31
unit control records, 5–6, 32
unit control reports, 7
unit information, 11
unit plan, 61
unit sales, 14, 82
unit sales estimates, 4–5
United Merchants and Manufacturers, 186
U.S. Census Reports, 226
Universal Product Code [UPC], 114, 116
updating of plans, 94

variable costs, of MIS division, 89
variety store failure, 181–186
vendor requirement section, component of request
    for proposal, 108
vendors, 199, 200
    analysis, 7, 32–33
    correspondence and performance quality, 210
    electronic transmission benefits for, 124
    evaluation criteria, 109
    lead times, 54
    pack size, 56